TEACHING

FOR

SOCIAL

JUSTICE

TEACHING FOR SOCIAL JUSTICE

A *Democracy and Education* Reader

EDITED BY
WILLIAM AYERS,
JEAN ANN HUNT,
AND THERESE QUINN

THE NEW PRESS NEW YORK
TEACHERS COLLEGE PRESS NEW YORK

The publisher is grateful to reprint the following copyrighted material: From *Black Teachers on Teaching* by Michele Foster. Copyright © 1997. Used by permission of The New Press. From *Fires In The Mirror* by Anna Deavere Smith. Copyright © 1993 by Anna Deavere Smith. Used by permission of Doubleday, a division of Bantam Doubleday Dell Publishing Group, Inc. "Writing the Word and the World" by Linda Christensen. Reprinted with permission from *Rethinking Schools* Vol. 3, No. 1, Rethinking Schools, 1001 E. Keefe Ave., Milwaukee, WI 53212, http://www.rethinkingschools.org; 800-669-4192. Reddy, Maureen T., *Crossing the Color Line: Race, Parenting, and Culture.* Copyright 1994 by Maureen T. Reddy. Reprinted by permission of Rutgers University Press. Bill Bigelow. Reprinted with permission from *Rethinking Schools*, Vol. 11, No. 4, Rethinking Schools, 1001 E. Keefe Ave., Milwaukee, WI 53212; http://www.rethinkingschools. org; 800-669-4192.

ISBN 1-56584-420-3

Published in the United States by The New Press, New York,
and Teachers College Press, New York
Distributed by W.W. Norton & Company, Inc., New York

The New Press was established in 1990 as a not-for-profit alternative to the large, commercial publishing houses currently dominating the book publishing industry. The New Press operates in the public interest rather than for private gain, and is committed to publishing, in innovative ways, works of educational, cultural, and community value that might not be considered sufficiently profitable. The New Press's editorial offices are located at the City University of New York.

Printed in the United States of America

9 8 7 6 5 4 3 2 1

To the fighting poet spirits of Paulo Freire,
Haywood Burns, and Allen Ginsberg—
fallen teachers who combined fire with grace
as they danced into battle—we dedicate this book.

—Acknowledgments

With awe and gratitude, Therese thanks her children, Mearah and Aza, and her sweetheart, Patricia Guizzetti, for love and lessons.

Jean Ann wishes to thank her children, Ryann, Keenan, and Ian for their extraordinary teachings, and her husband David for his love and support.

Bill thanks Zayd, Malik, and Chesa for their love and inspiration, and his partner-in-crime for three decades, Bernardine Dohrn.

This book would never have been completed without the good humor and spark manifested daily by Lorraine Scott.

—Contents

—Preface: Of Stories, Seeds and the Promises
of Social Justice
Jean Ann Hunt   *xiii*

—Foreword: Popular Education—
Teaching for Social Justice
William Ayers   *xvii*

—Introduction: Teaching for Social Justice
Maxine Greene   *xxvii*

1—Education for Action—Preparing Youth
for Participatory Democracy
Joel Westheimer and Joseph Kahne   *1*

2—The Human Lives Behind the Labels—
The Global Sweatshop, Nike, and
the Race to the Bottom
Bill Bigelow   *21*

3—Writing the Word and the World
Linda Christensen   *39*

—An Activist Forum I: Awakening Justice
Haywood Burns
Caroline Heller
Lisa Delpit
Mike Rose
Barbara T. Bowman   *48*

—Portraits: In the Raindrop   *55*

4—School Days
Nelson Peery   *59*

5—"We'd All Be Holding Hands"—A Reentry
Women's Learning Community
Diane Horwitz   *68*

6—A Grassroots Think Tank—Linking Writing   *81*
and Community Building
Hal Adams

7—Roses and Daggers   *98*
Patrick McMahon

8—No Little I's and No Little You's—Language   *102*
and Equality in an Adult Literacy Community
Kate Power

—An Activist Forum II: Fault Lines   *124*
Anna Deavere Smith
Therese Quinn
Jonathan Silin
Kim Murray
Elizabeth Alexander

9—On a Mission—Hazel Johnson and Marvin Garcia   *135*
Therese Quinn

10—A Dream That Keeps on Growing—   *150*
Myles Horton and Highlander
William Ayers

11—The Good Fight—Bill Gandall   *157*
Susan Huddleston Edgerton

12—History of My Subversive Teaching   *161*
Rachel Koch

13—The Fourth R   *169*
Maureen Reddy

—An Activist Forum III: Counter Tales   *186*
Rashid Khalidi
William Watkins
Jennifer Dohrn
Noel Ignatiev
Luis J. Rodriguez

—Possibilities: Joining Hands   *197*

14—"Do You Know Where You Are?"—A Memoir   200
of Becoming a South Sider
Jamie Kalven

15—The Cheney, Goodman, and Schwerner Academy   211

16—Women of Hope   215

17—Chaos Theory—A Journal Entry   228
Rick Ayers

—An Activist Forum IV: Pledging to the World   237
Jay Rehak
Chris Carger
Jim Carnes
Mark Perry
George Wood

18—School Projects Investing in Community   249
Development

19—A Story for Justice   254
Jaylynne N. Hutchinson and Rosalie M. Romano

20—Welfare Workbook   270

21—Teaching for Change   277
Deborah Stern

—Afterword: Some Reflections on Teaching   285
for Social Justice
Herbert Kohl

—An Activist Forum V: Racing Justice   288
Michele Foster
Henry Giroux
Gloria Ladson-Billings
Jonathan Kozol
Michael Apple

—Resources   295

—Books   316

—Classroom Resources   *297*

—Organizations   *297*

—Periodicals   *303*

—Popular Education Institutes   *308*

—Websites   *309*

ABOUT THE AUTHORS   *311*

—Preface
Of Stories, Seeds and the Promises of Social Justice

Jean Ann Hunt

When I was a fourth grader I discovered a set of books housed on the homemade pine shelves in the back of our classroom. These blue-denim-bound volumes had worn gold embossed spines and frayed covers—so obviously used, they called to me. I remember dozens of these short biographies—stories of activists, heroes, suffragettes, abolitionists, and teachers. I took the books home and hid in my bedroom for hours reading and rereading, escaping from a world in which I felt powerless and oftentimes alone. Even after I had to give them up, the voices of these ordinary people making extraordinary differences sung in my head. For me they held a promise that anyone living in this world could take risks, turn despair into hope, and change the world.

Teaching for Social Justice is at the core of democratic education. It serves as a reminder not only of the inequities and biases that continue to wear away at the foundation of democratic values, but of the powerful stories which inspire us to work toward change, to make the world a better place. When issues of social justice are at the heart of our classroom teaching, our students benefit from the rich history of people who didn't settle for the way things are: Fannie Lou Hamer, Jane Addams, Myles Horton, Chico Mendes, and numerous others—as well as lesser-known heroes such as the Tuskegee Airmen; the Navajo Code Talkers; suffragettes; and countless union workers, teachers, and good neighbors. A focus on Teaching for Social Justice reminds us that our children need not only a firm grounding in academics but also practice in how to use those academics to promote a democratic society in which all get to participate fully.

Democracy & Education, the journal of the Institute for Democracy and Education at Ohio University, devoted a special issue to Teaching for Social Justice on which this book is based. In these pages, you'll find stories of teachers and others whose work inspires us with ideas and hope. These vignettes demonstrate the connection between school and community, learner and activist, courage and change. As you read the portraits of teachers and community leaders you will see risk takers, visionaries, hard workers, learners, seekers—everyday heroes who recognize that tomorrow's history is created from today's actions. The legacy of social justice continues because of those who embrace education and its vital connection to social change.

In light of this vital connection, we also share with you some possibilities: schools and programs developed by groups of educators and others, implemented to provide a structure which supports teaching for social justice. We've also included a variety of resources for personal and classroom use.

As a teacher and mother, I have to believe that within each one of us there are the seeds of change. I teach; I parent—each an audacious act of faith that the way things are is neither inevitable nor immutable. I live in the actual world, I participate, I act—but one eye gazes toward a world that could be but is not yet. I am armed with an imagination, a hope, a passion, a willingness to choose. Look for me in the whirlwind. We are alerted to that possibility by our stories, as I was as a ten-year-old girl. Each day brings more stories that hold both promise and pain: stories of children blooming and also stunted, of families cohering and also rent, of lives propelled into clarity and into chaos.

But for the seeds borne in these tales to bear fruit, we must take time to listen to one another. Stories can create community, they can let us know that we are not alone. Stories reveal the possibilities within ourselves, within others. Stories provide, as well, the impetus for action. The world bumps along—uneventful, unchallenged—until a different way of living, a new way of being enters our consciousness. We see our troubles suddenly in a whole new light. Life as it is becomes excruciating, unbearable. We are moved to act. It is no surprise, then, that *Uncle Tom's Cabin* became the greatest recruitment tool to the union cause, or that *Invisible Man* fired the imaginations of a generation of civil rights activists. We need to create, to seize, public space where people can come together in their urgency and pain, with passion, anger, and dreams, to speak to each other in authentic voices— unfiltered, unconstrained, uncensored.

The lack of public space and focus would have us think that others' stories are not part of our lives, but they are. We may think we can ignore them—we cannot. We may think those struggles belong to others—they are ours. We must listen, we must teach, we must find ways to nurture the seeds in each of us, to get it done. In this book you will find people who have created spaces for stories, tended seeds sown, and made a difference. Turn the page. The garden beckons.

Popular Education—Teaching for Social Justice

William Ayers

The fundamental message of the teacher is this: You can change your life. Whoever you are, wherever you've been, whatever you've done, the teacher invites you to a second chance, another round, perhaps a different conclusion. The teacher posits possibility, openness, and alternative; the teacher points to what could be, but is not yet. The teacher beckons you to change your path, and so the teacher's basic rule is to teach.

To teach consciously for social justice, to teach for social change, adds a complicating element to that fundamental message, making it more layered, more dense, more excruciatingly difficult to enact, and at the same time sturdier, more engaging, more powerful and joyful much of the time. Teaching for social justice demands a dialectical stance: one eye firmly fixed on the students—Who are they? What are their hopes, dreams, and aspirations? Their passions and commitments? What skills, abilities, and capacities does each one bring to the classroom?—and the other eye looking unblinkingly at the concentric circles of context—historical flow, cultural surround, economic reality. Teaching for social justice is teaching that arouses students, engages them in a quest to identify obstacles to their full humanity, to their freedom, and then to drive, to move against those obstacles. And so the fundamental message of the teacher for social justice is: You can change the world.

Education, of course, is an arena of hope and struggle—hope for a better life, and struggle over how to understand and enact and achieve that better life. We find ourselves living in the midst of cruelty and oppression; we uncover a long story of domination, oppression, and catastrophe; we come to believe that we can become makers of history—not merely the passive objects of the great human drama, but actors and catalysts and full subjects in the action. At that moment we realize that no teaching is or ever can be innocent—it must be situated in a cultural context, an historical flow, an economic condition. Teaching must be toward something; it must take a stand; it is either for or against; it must account for the specific within the universal.

In the heroic upheaval of the civil rights movement, a group of activists wrote the *Mississippi Freedom School Curriculum—1964* (forthcoming from The New Press) as part of the effort to create an educational experience that could transform individual victims of racism and, at the same time, change the world:

> One of the purposes of the Freedom Schools is to train people to be active agents in bringing about social change. We have attempted to design a developmental curriculum that begins on the level of the students' everyday lives and those things in their environment that they have either already experienced or can readily perceive, and builds up to a more realistic perception of American society, themselves, the conditions of their oppression, and alternatives offered by the Freedom Movement . . .

The BASIC SET OF QUESTIONS is:

1. Why are we (teachers and students) in Freedom Schools?
2. What is the Freedom Movement?
3. What alternatives does the Freedom Movement offer us?

The SECONDARY SET OF QUESTIONS is:

1. What does the majority culture have that we want?
2. What does the majority culture have that we don't want?
3. What do we have that we want to keep?

There are other, perhaps smaller stories of teachers struggling in a world of woe and waste. In *A Lesson Before Dying*, Ernest Gaines creates a riveting fictional portrait of a teacher locked in struggle with a resistant student, wrestling as well with his own doubts and fears about himself as a teacher and a person, and straining against the outrages of the segregated South. Grant Wiggins has returned with considerable ambivalence to teach in the plantation school of his childhood. He feels trapped and longs to escape with his love, a teacher named Vivian, to another place—a place where he might breathe more freely, grow more fully, achieve something special. He has told his elderly Tante Lou, with whom he lives, "how much I hated this place and all I wanted to do was get away. I had told her I was no teacher, I hated teaching, and I

was just running in place here. But she had not heard me . . ."
(14–15).

The story begins in a courtroom with Tante Lou and her lifelong friend, Miss Emma, sitting stoic and still near the front. Emma's godson, Jefferson, had been an unwitting participant in a failed liquor store stickup—his two companions and the store owner are dead—and as the sole survivor he is convicted of murder. The public defender, pleading for Jefferson's life, plays to the all-white jury with zeal:

> "Gentlemen of the jury, look at this—this—this boy. I almost said man, but I can't say man . . . I would call it a boy and a fool. A fool is not aware of right and wrong . . .
>
> "Do you see a man sitting here? . . . Look at the shape of the skull, this face as flat as the palm of my hand—look deeply into those eyes. Do you see a modicum of intelligence? . . . A cornered animal to strike quickly out of fear, a trait inherited from his ancestors in the deepest jungle of blackest Africa— yes, yes, that he can do—but to plan? . . . No, gentlemen, this skull here holds no plans . . . A thing to hold the handle of a plow, a thing to load your bales of cotton . . . That is what you see here, but you do not see anything capable of planning a robbery or a murder. He does not even know the size of his clothes or his shoes . . . Mention the names of Keats, Byron, Scott, and see whether the eyes will show one moment of recognition. Ask him to describe a rose . . . Gentlemen of the jury, this man planned a robbery? Oh, pardon me, pardon me, I surely did not mean to insult your intelligence by saying 'man' . . .
>
> "What justice would there be to take this life? Justice, gentlemen? Why I would just as soon put a hog in the electric chair as this." (7–8)

But it's no good. Jefferson is sentenced to death. He has only a few weeks, perhaps a couple of months, to live. As devastating as the sentence is, it is that last plea from the public defender—that comparison of Jefferson to a hog—that cuts most deeply. "Called him a hog," says Miss Emma (12). And she turns to Grant Wiggins: "I don't want them to kill no hog" (13). She wants Grant to visit Jefferson, to teach him.

Wiggins resists: "'Yes, I'm the teacher,' I said. 'And I teach what the white folks around here tell me to teach . . . They never told me how to keep a black boy out of a liquor store'" (13). More than this, Wiggins is shaken by the challenge and the context. He explains to Vivian:

> "The public defender, trying to get him off, called him a dumb animal," I told her. "He said it would be like tying a hog down into that chair and executing him—an animal that didn't know what any of it was all about . . . Now his god-mother wants me to visit him and make him know—prove to these white men—that he's not a hog, that he's a man. I'm supposed to make him a man. Who am I? God? . . .
>
> "What do I say to him? Do I know how a man is supposed to die? I'm still trying to find out how a man should live. Am I supposed to tell someone how to die who has never lived? . . .
>
> "Suppose . . . I reached him and made him realize that he was as much a man as any other man, then what? He's still going to die . . . So what will I have accomplished? What will I have done? Why not let the hog die without knowing anything?" (31)

Miss Emma and Tante Lou, along with their preacher, insist that Grant join them in their visits to Jefferson. It is an alliance filled with pain and tension—Grant has refused to go to church for years and, outspoken in his agnosticism, is looked on by the elderly trio as, in turn, the devil himself and Jefferson's best hope. The sheriff doesn't want Grant visiting, "Because I think the only thing you can do is just aggravate him, trying to put something in his head against his will. And I'd rather see a contented hog go to that chair than an aggravated hog" (49). Grant is haunted by the memory of his own former teacher, a bitter man: "You'll see that it'll take more than five and a half months to wipe away—peel—scrape away the blanket of ignorance that has been plastered and replastered over those brains in the past three hundred years. You'll see" (64). The former mentor's message is that nothing a teacher in these circumstances does can matter, can make a difference. Worse than that, Jefferson himself is wracked with hopelessness; he is uncooperative, resistant: "It don't matter . . . Nothing don't matter" (73), he says, as he refuses to eat unless his food is put on the floor, like slops for a hog.

Vivian alone pushes Grant to go to Jefferson, to teach him. She reminds him that a teacher's life is one of commitment and struggle. He begins by simply visiting Jefferson, being there, speaking sometimes, but mostly just sitting in silence. Witnessing. He brings Jefferson some small things: peanuts and pecans from his students, a small radio, a little notebook and a pencil. He encourages Jefferson to think of questions and write down his thoughts. And sometimes he accompanies Miss Emma, Tante Lou, and the reverend to the day room for visits. There he walks with Jefferson and talks to him. This monologue begins with Grant encouraging Jefferson to be kind to his grandmother, to eat some of the gumbo she has brought:

"I could never be a hero. I teach, but I don't like teaching. I teach because it is the only thing that an educated black man can do in the South today. I don't like it; I hate it . . . I want to live for myself and for my woman and for nobody else.

"That is not a hero. A hero does for others . . . I am not that kind of person, but I want you to be. You could give something to her, to me, to those children in the quarter . . . The white people out there are saying that you don't have it—that you're a hog, not a man. But I know they are wrong. You have the potentials. We all have, no matter who we are . . .

"I want you to show them the difference between what they think you are and what you can be. To them, you're nothing but another nigger—no dignity, no heart, no love for your people. You can prove them wrong. You can do more than I can ever do. I have always done what they wanted me to do, teach reading, writing, and arithmetic. Nothing else— nothing about loving and caring. They never thought we were capable of learning these things. 'Teach these niggers how to print their names and how to figure on their fingers.' And I went along, but hating myself all the time for doing so. . . .

"White people believe that they're better than anyone else on earth—and that's a myth. The last thing they want is to see a black man stand, and think, and show that common human- ity that is in us all. It would destroy their myth . . .

"I need you much more than you could ever need me. I need you to know what to do with my life. I want to run away, but go where and do what? I need someone to tell me what to do. I need you to tell me, to show me . . .

". . . all we are, Jefferson, all of us on this earth, [is just] a piece of drifting wood, until we—each of us, individually—

decide to be something else. I am still that piece of drifting wood . . . but you can be better. Because we need you to be and want you to be . . ."

He looked at me in great pain. He may not have understood, but something was touched, something deep down in him—because he was still crying . . . (191–93)

After Jefferson is electrocuted, a white deputy sheriff drives out to bring the news to Grant:

"He was the strongest man in that crowded room, Grant Wiggins," Paul said, staring at me and speaking louder than was necessary. "He was, he was . . . he looked at the preacher and said, 'Tell Nannan I walked.' And straight he walked, Grant Wiggins. Straight he walked." . . .

"You're one great teacher, Grant Wiggins," he said.
"I'm not great. I'm not even a teacher."
"Why do you say that?"
"You have to believe to be a teacher."
"I saw the transformation, Grant Wiggins," Paul said.
"I didn't do it."
"Who, then?"
"Maybe he did it himself."
"He never could have done that. I saw the transformation. I'm a witness to that." (253–54)

A Lesson Before Dying is a teacher's tale. While the circumstances here are extreme, the interaction is familiar, recognizable. Every teacher appreciates the irony of teaching what we neither fully know nor understand. Each of us can remember other teachers who counseled us not to teach, and each of us recognizes the resistant student, the student who refuses to learn. And we can each uncover moments of intense self-reflection, consciousness shifts, and personal growth brought on by our attempts to teach.

Many teachers also know what it means to teach against the grain; against oppression, opposition, and obstinacy; against a history of evil; against glib, common-sense assumptions. When the sheriff compares education to agitation, and the teacher to an organizer "trying to put something in his head against his will," one is reminded of Frederick Douglass's master exploding in anger when he discovers that his wife has taught the young Douglass to read: "It will unfit him to be a slave." One is reminded as well of the charge "outside agitator," hurled by the bosses at union organizers, or by the college trustees at student radicals. When the sheriff grins at Wiggins for giving Jefferson a journal, because a hog can't write authentic thoughts or experience real human feelings, we are in a familiar space. And when Jefferson writes in the journal, "I cry cause you been so good to me Mr. Wiggins and nobody aint never been that good to me an make me think I'm somebody" (232), we recognize something close-in about teaching, and we cry too.

Education, of course, lives an excruciating paradox precisely because of its association with and location in schools. Education is about opening doors, opening minds, opening possibilities. School is too often about sorting and punishing, grading and ranking and certifying. Education is unconditional—it asks nothing in return. School routinely demands obedience and conformity as a precondition to attendance. Education is surprising and unruly and disorderly, while the first and fundamental law of school is to follow orders. Education frees the mind, while schooling bureaucratizes the brain. An educator unleashes the unpredictable, while a schoolteacher sometimes starts with an unhealthy obsession with a commitment to classroom management and linear lesson plans.

Working in schools—where the fundamental truths and demands and possibilities of teaching are obscure and diminished and opaque, and where the powerful ethical core of our efforts is systematically defaced and erased—requires a reengagement with the large purposes of teaching. When the drumbeat of our daily lives is all about controlling the crowd, managing and moving the mob, conveying disembodied bits of information to inert things propped at desks before us, the need to fight for ourselves and our students becomes an imperative. Central to that fight is the understanding that there is no basis for education in a democracy except for a belief in the enduring capacity for growth in ordinary people. For me it is a faith that requires no proof and no corroboration—it is an activist's conviction: the people with the problems are also the people with solutions.

As people are increasingly thingified, manipulated, alienated, and abused, I am drawn to a poem by Wislawa Szymborska, the Polish Nobel laureate,

Out of every hundred people,
those who always know better:
fifty-two.

Unsure of every step:
almost all the rest.

Ready to help,
if it doesn't take long:
forty-nine.

Always good,
because they cannot be otherwise:
four—well, maybe five.

Able to admire without envy:
eighteen.

Led to error
by youth (which passes):
sixty, plus minus

Living in constant fear
of someone or something:
seventy-seven.

Capable of happiness
twenty-some-odd at most.

Harmless alone;
turning savage in crowds:
more than half, for sure.

Cruel
when forced by circumstances:
it's better not to know,
not even approximately.

Wise in hindsight:
not many more than wise in foresight.

Getting nothing out of life except
things: thirty
(though I would like to be wrong).

Balled up in pain
and without a flashlight in the dark:
eighty-three, sooner or later.

Those who are just:
quite a few, thirty-five.

But if it takes effort to understand:
three . . .

Worthy of empathy:
ninety-nine

Mortal:
one hundred out of one hundred—
a figure that has never varied yet.

The complexity of the teacher's task is based on its idiosyn-
cratic and improvisational character—as inexact as a person's
mind or a human heart, as unique and inventive as a friendship
or a love affair, as explosive and unpredictable as a revolution.
The teacher's work is about background, environment, setting,
surround, position, situation, connection. And, importantly,
teaching is at its center about relationship—with this or that
person, in this specific world, at a particular moment. As Martin

Heidegger said, teaching is tougher than learning in one respect: teaching requires the teacher to *let learn*. Learning requires action, choice, and assent from the student. Teaching, then, is an invitation offered and an act of faith. It is filled with hope and undertaken without guarantees.

Seeing the student, seeing the world—this is the beginning—to assume a deep capacity in students, an intelligence (sometimes obscure, sometimes buried) as well as a wide range of hopes, dreams, and aspirations; to acknowledge, as well, obstacles to understand and overcome, deficiencies to repair, injustices to correct. With this as a base, the teacher creates an environment for learning that has multiple entry points for learning and multiple pathways to success. That environment must be abundant with opportunities to practice social justice; to display, foster, embody, expect, demand, nurture, allow, model, and enact inquiry toward change. A classroom organized in this way follows a particular rhythm: a first set of questions focuses on issues or problems (What do we need or want to know? Why is it important? How will we find out?); a second set focuses on action (Given what we know now, what are we going to do?).

This collection focuses on teaching for social justice. Several early chapters provide portraits of popular educators, snapshots of teachers who teach for justice, whether in classrooms or communities. There are lessons here for any teacher who cares to inquire, adapt, and adjust. Several later chapters focus on possibilities—practical advice for teachers from teacher-activists. Throughout the collection a group of educational activists comments on our teaching for justice under the rubric "An Activist Forum." We are profoundly aware that we offer these thoughts, sketches, dreams in a time of crisis and silence. This book is intended as a light in a long night and a forthright invitation to teachers and to students—change your lives, change the world.

—Introduction
Teaching for Social Justice

Maxine Greene

T he voices of indignation and protest have resounded through the years in response to injustices and human suffering. Think of William Blake, finding his metaphor in the image of a naked child thrust down a chimney:

> When my mother died I was very young,
> and my father sold me while yet my tongue
> Could scarcely cry "weep!" "weep!" "weep!"
> So your chimneys I sweep, and soot I sleep.
> (1967, 21)

Think of Karl Marx, in the midst of a theoretical discussion of capitalist production, describing a nine-year-old boy who was seven when he began working in a pottery, "running moulds." "He came to work every day in the week at 6 A.M. and left off about 9 P.M. 'I work till 9 o'clock at night six nights in the week . . .' Fifteen hours of labor for a child of seven years old!" (1906, 269). Then Marx goes on to talk about the high death rate from pulmonary disease among the potters, and how each generation is more dwarfed than the preceding. After a piling up of details about suffering and degeneration, he calls for setting up a social barrier that "shall prevent the very workers from selling, by voluntary contract with capital, themselves and their families into slavery and death" (330). The concreteness of his examples communicates his outrage, as it enables us to "see." And there is Frederick Douglass writing about the ways slaveholders used holidays to keep down "the spirit of insurrection." Giving enslaved people some free time, slaveholders forced alcohol on them "to disgust slaves with freedom by plunging them into the lowest depths of dissipation. For instance, the slaveholders not only like to see the slave drunk of his own accord . . . but make bets on their slaves, as to who can drink the most whisky without getting drunk; and, in this way, they succeed in getting whole multitudes to drink to excess . . . So when the holidays ended, we staggered up from the filth of our wallowing, took a long breath, and marched to the field—feeling, on the whole, rather glad to go, from what our master had deceived us into a belief was freedom, back to the arms of slavery" (Gates and McKay 1997, 345). And there is Langston Hughes's "Harlem":

> What happens to a dream deferred?
>
> Does it dry up
> like a raisin in the sun?
> And then run?
> Does it stink like rotten meat?
> Or crust and sugar over—
> like a syrupy sweet?
> Maybe it just sags
> like a heavy load
> *Or does it explode?*
> (Gates and McKay 1997, 1267)

And there is (among countless women) Marge Piercy:

> The weight of the Tower is in me. Can I ever straighten?
> You trained me in passivity to lay for you like a doped hen.
> You bounce your gabble off the sky to pierce our brains.
> Your loudspeakers from every television and classroom
> and your transistors grafted onto my nerves at birth
> out you are impregnable and righteous forever.
> But any structure can be overthrown.
> (1994, 123)

I could go on; my readers could go on—attesting to the persistence of injustice, unfairness, particular experiences of violation and manipulation and lack of care. To teach for social justice, however, is not only to assemble the particulars, significant though they are. Yes, they may awaken certain somnolent ones; they may penetrate indifference here and there; they may even stimulate "the sense of injustice" (Cahn 1949): But they do not, in and of themselves, help people understand what social justice means for everyday collective life. Justice, after all, is thought to be the primary value of political life if it is incarnated in human action in spaces where people live together. Thinking of it as a normative ideal, a notion of how persons *ought* to live together, most of us would agree that there should be an equitable, a fair distribution of goods and services. Select groups of men and women ought not to have extra space at the cost of others' suffering; and, surely, people ought not be used for others' benefit, certainly not without being consulted. Indeed, one of the requirements in a just society ought to be that everyone affected by a decision ought to have a part in making the decision.

One of the horrors of the chimney-sweeping practice was that the children sold by their poverty-stricken fathers were neither told nor consulted about what was happening to them. The "voluntary contract" that infuriated Marx was the single option offered laborers in situations over which they had no control. The only part they could play (under the pretense of "voluntary contract") was to sell "themselves and their families into slavery and death." So it was when the slaves were deceptively offered a "free" choice of spending a holiday steeped in alcohol. So it was with the rotting dream Langston Hughes describes. So it was with the imposed passivity, the media indoctrination suffered by the woman poet, only first becoming aware. It is not only that these people were being cruelly treated; they were being unfairly treated. In most instances such treatment served the interest of others—ordinarily the white, the privileged, the male. Accounts of such predicaments usually suggest that some few people in the period described were riding a high tide of relative wealth and entitlement, while most others (in the same place, and at the same time) were deprived. As significantly, the privileged few were the ones with the opportunities to map and dominate the linguistic universe. The imbalance, the undeserved advantages in that domain as well as in the socioeconomic and political worlds are evidences of the most glaring social injustice. In a just society, at the very least, every person should have an opportunity to "develop and exercise her or his intellectual, social, emotional, and expressive capacities" (Young 1993, 123). This points directly at a potential role for democratic education in enabling people to pursue social justice. But it also raises questions, nagging questions, about the connection between the satisfaction of basic needs and the free use of opportunities to develop the capacities described.

Teaching for social justice, we must remember, is teaching what we believe ought to be—not merely where moral frameworks are concerned, but in material arrangements for people in all spheres of society. Moreover, teaching for social justice is teaching for the sake of arousing the kinds of vivid, reflective, experiential responses that might move students to come together in serious efforts to understand what social justice actually means and what it might demand. That means teaching to the end of arousing a consciousness of membership, active and participant membership in a society of unfulfilled promises—teaching for what Paulo Freire used to call "conscientization" (1970), heightened social consciousness, a wide-awakeness that might make injustice unendurable. We speak often of generating a sense of agency in young people; and it seems evident that this mode of teaching is at least likely to communicate a sense of agency, if the young can feel themselves engaged with those around. Once awakened (as a group, a small community) to concrete examples of injustice (the humiliation of immigrant children, the refusal of decent housing to single mothers or the aged, the deterioration of certain classrooms and not others, the closing of playgrounds in ghetto neighborhoods) they might, together, invent a project of remediation, palliation, repair.

To invent is to move from an imagined state of things to a mode of action by which, as John Dewey said, "ideas and aspirations can be used to reorganize the environment" (1916, 405). An aversion to existing conditions, he wrote, may well stimulate imagination; but there is always a danger of imagination running loose. "When we find the successful display of our energies checked by uncongenial surrounding, natural and social, the easiest way out is to build castles in the air and let them be a substitute for an actual achievement which involves the pains of thought" (404). This can happen, not only within an individual but within a group or a class. Even as they come together, young people may find themselves focusing on their own thoughts and desires, rather than on projects that might bring about change. Obviously, more is required than indignant or empathetic responses to what may be discovered in the world around, once people's eyes are opened, once they begin (often in incredulity) to "see."

It cannot be taken for granted that everyone will notice instances of injustice nor recognize it for what it is. It certainly cannot be assumed, given the pressures and seductions of the media, that young people will resist the temptations of consumerism, competitiveness, fashion, and conventionality. There is the matter of knowing enough (and feeling enough) to argue the cause of justice and persuade others of the importance of moving beyond self-interest to a consideration of their responsibility as members, as citizens, or (sometimes in the extreme) as a contemporary version of resistance fighters. What can teachers do to empower young people to criticize the emphasis on efficiency and efficacy as primary values—instead of justice and equality? How can teachers open students to the possibility that there may be more fulfillment to be discovered in living in a just society than in an arrantly inequitable one? What can be done to help people perceive (and take action against) the cruelty and aggressiveness in current challenges to "dependency"? How can they be helped to recognize the violations in the continuing objectification of women and children? What situations can be created that might motivate students to combat the endless process of silencing found in so many schools, what Michelle Fine calls "the muting of students and their communities" (1991, 32)?

The point that the silencing that goes on not only prevents numbers of young people from saying how it is with them, from "naming" and describing the world from their own vantage points; it makes them subject to official languages presumably representing a social reality in which discrimination and oppression are "natural," resistant to both questioning and change. When we consider the opportunities opened to the articulate and well-to-do, not merely to speak for themselves but in the name of those they consider "other," we can recognize the degree to which silencing plays a part in freezing unjust relationships. This too takes a high degree of critical insight and commitment to action. Not only do spaces have to be opened for dialogue among those whose voices have been marginalized. The young have to be released somehow to move imaginatively between what is called the center and what is called the margin or the border. What conception of social justice holds meaning for the one who situates herself or himself at the center? What can be done to counteract what Edward Said describes as the role of centrality, "the television commentator, the corporate official, celebrity . . . what is powerful, important, and *ours*" (1993, 324). And then: ". . . centrality gives rise to semi-official narratives that authorize and provoke certain sequences of cause and effect, while at the same time preventing counter-narratives from emerging" (324). Teaching for social justice ought to support the emergence of counter-narratives, even as it calls attention to the views of social justice embodied in our normative ideas.

Americans are taught to take pride, after all, in being the nation founded in a commitment to "life, liberty, and the pursuit of happiness" (no longer, presumably, for white, male property owners alone), a belief in human rights and in conceptions of equity variously articulated by our presidents and Supreme Court justices. Most are, on some level, aware that the ideals that are intended to govern our being together have seldom been realized, and that they are sometimes used as masks for what is actually happening in the social domain. Nevertheless, when we are being defensive or when we are engaged in protest, we point to them, appeal to them as if they were fixed stars in the sky. When, for instance, Jonathan Kozol speaks of "savage inequalities," he seems to be taking it for granted that most of his readers join him in judging inequality to be "savage" and an offense against our most cherished ideals. It is startling to many of his readers to find him saying, near the end of this book: "There is a deep-seated reverence for fair play in the United States, and in many areas of life we see the consequences in a genuine distaste for loaded dice; but this is not the case in education, health care, or inheritance of wealth. In these elemental areas we want the game to be unfair and we have made it so; and it will likely so remain" (1991, 223). Whether everyone will agree this is the case or not, those who do will turn to the sacred writs, the traditional norms, and declare (as they are likely to do) that this is immoral, unjust, wrong.

In an introduction to the winter 1996 issue of *Daedalus*, entitled "Social Suffering," Stephen Graubard speaks of "human problems that have their origins and consequences in the devastating injuries that social force inflicts on human experience." He goes on to say that "Social suffering results from what political, economic, and institutional power does to people, and, reciprocally, from how these forces of power themselves influence response to social problems" (1996, xi). This may be another way of saying that "we want the game to be unfair and we have made it so." It is another way of drawing attention to what is so wrong about injustice: it not only offends against the values we are supposed to hold most dear; it causes human suffering. Pointing to the interweaving of health, welfare, moral, religious, cultural, and political factors where such suffering is concerned, Graubard talks about how frequently we see individuals across the bureaucratic landscapes of institutions and agencies, and how this covers up the suffering our policies are intended to cure. As Michael Ignatieff has said, even when professionals feel themselves to be responding in the most benevolent and understanding fashion to people in need they too often relate to those they are helping as "moral strangers" impervious to anything but survival needs (1984, 17).

Schools also find it difficult to register the meanings of lived oppression or exclusion or pain. Focusing on curriculum frameworks, on critical questioning, on new approaches to the teaching of reading and science (as surely they must), those who feel themselves responsible for enabling the young to become literate, to understand their worlds, to cope with the complexities of work and citizenship, find themselves retreating from signs of real suffering. It is hard and unbearably frustrating much of the time to attend to the desolation in some children's faces, the panic inflicted by experiences of homelessness, the uncomprehending horror at a parent's death from AIDS, the terror in the face of "drive-by" killings, the fearful absence when a youngster has taken refuge in drugs. Faced with the spectre of social injustice, the ravages of injustice, that battle may seem to ask too much. It is enough, educators reassure themselves (if they care at all) to work for such humane changes as those Theodore Sizer lists in *Horace's School*, "a site where the resources to help young people use their minds well are deliberately and generously concentrated" (1992, 198). There is no question but the use of exhibitions instead of multiple-choice tests, an effective and creative use of technology, a willingness to accept an "educational coat of many colors" (200) may do a great deal to aid the young, at least those fortunate enough to go to schools with sufficient resources, sufficient care and good will. Understandably, this may appear enough to those involved and authentically devoted to the becoming of young people and children in all their promise and diversity. Why, then, teach for social justice? Will not a concern for fairness develop naturally as young people become adult and ethically mature? Most, in any case, would agree that they play fair with their family, their friends, their coworkers. Others may speak of gang loyalties, concrete local obligations and ties. They may agree that individuals should play by "the rules," although they may not agree on what the rules signify or to whom and what situations they apply. Most feel themselves to be capable of care and concern for those around and, abstractly, for those who suffer cruelties and humiliations. But the idea of principled action to achieve social justice, not only for those around but for strangers, may seem alien to them.

Those who teach the young today probably have to ask

themselves what they believe about human beings (their own students, specifically) that makes them so sure that the young *can* become principled enough, committed enough to reach beyond their self-interest and take responsibility for what happens in the space between themselves and others, what has been called the public space. Thinking back to the issues that set all kinds of people marching and, at times, struggling for civil rights, we look with a kind of wonder at those who surmounted their own self-interest and rode Freedom Buses or worked to bring out voters on dusty roads in the South. Thinking back to those who actually sacrificed by protesting the Vietnam War, engaging in antinuclear activity or in campaigns for human rights, we may ask ourselves what moved them to find the connection they seemed to find between their private concerns and the public space. What led to their choosing themselves as the kinds of human beings whose life projects had to do with fairness, equality, freedom, peace, and respect of each human being's dignity? What is it that permits some people to resist the mystifications of the media, the hegemonic pressures that bear down so much of the time? We are constantly told that few people today are particularly troubled by the suffering of strangers (whether they are victims of the war in Bosnia or molested children in the neighborhood). We are told that feelings of altruism have been eroded by the continual reminders that people are responsible for their own failures in the not very sympathetic world. Partially in consequence of what seems to have become conventional wisdom, there is less and less said of teaching for social justice in the schools.

There is, of course, a tradition of concern for justice reaching from Immanuel Kant to John Rawls and Jurgen Habermas, and being extended these days by a number of women philosophers. Many teachers recall the work of the psychologist Lawrence Kohlberg in the context of what he called the "formalist" tradition. His was a staged theory of moral development, at the height of which people were viewed as capable of autonomy and self-direction. They became capable, he said, of "making judgments in terms of universal principles, applicable to all mankind" (1986, 207). Particularly concerned for moral reasoning (or the forms of it), he said that at Stage 6 in moral development, "personally chosen moral principles are also principles of justice, the principles any member of a society would choose for the society if he did not know what his position was to be in that society . . ." (208). He encouraged dialogue and the formation of "just" communities in schools, where youngsters were asked to resolve a series of moral problems or dilemmas to advance the course of their moral development.

The origin of this mode of thinking is to be found in the philosophy of Immanuel Kant (1959), especially in his *Foundations of the Metaphysics of Morals*. He viewed each human being as free and equal. The moral individual was responsive to the moral law; and, in his autonomy, could not but choose to act according to internalized principle—principle that was universalizable. To be principled in that manner meant that all acts that were performed were to be considered morally incumbent and obligatory, not only for the single rational individual making the choice, but for all humankind. When rational individuals come together, he believed, and apply their principles to the structure of society, those principles become principles of justice. They are what Kant called categorical imperatives, meaning principles of conduct that apply to every living person in view of his nature as a free and rational being. On the face of it, those who teach for social justice may find this linkage of freedom, rationality, and belief in justice to be not only appealing but inspiring. It may take a while before they realize that Kant emphasizes what is logical and rational to the exclusion of emotion, compassion, and even a sense of consequence of what is undertaken.

When, in 1971, John Rawls published *A Theory of Justice*, it was as if the issue of justice had taken on a new life. Still in the formalist, rationalist tradition, Rawls's theory did not relate the concept or the principle of justice to the moral law. For him (as for Kohlberg, who borrowed the point of view) a group of mutually disinterested individuals, no one of them acquainted with his place in society, would inevitably arrive at a notion of justice after a process of deliberation involving each as a free-standing rational person. Inequalities in any given society, they would agree, would be so arranged as to benefit the least advantaged. Everyone would be treated equally and guaranteed equal rights of citizenship; and each would be encouraged in the development of a life plan and the pursuit of his or her self-development. For Rawls, the view of justice he describes is not necessarily universal, nor does it reflect some higher order. In his Dewey Lectures in 1980, he wrote: "The task is to articulate a public conception of justice that all can live with who regard their persons and their relations to society in a certain way . . ." (518). Justice must, he added, regulate not only social relations but each person's self-esteem, since it is principle that defines our nature—the very principle that governs the conditions under which we define our purposes. There is no way, he said, "we can get beyond delibera-tive rationality."

Stirring though it may be to think in terms of justice providing a regulative framework for what individuals think and do in a free society, we need to realize that Rawls is writing with a focus on the self-determining citizen as an individual, not necessarily as a par-ticipant member of a community. Moreover, in this tradition, little attention is given to the economic circumstances that prevent so many from even entering the discussion about principle or from designing "life plans" they believe they can realize. In teaching for justice, we have to consider a diversity even modern Kantians do not acknowledge. We have to create situations that allow for many modes of meaning-making, many modes of "seeing" and "saying," moving outward from the self-interest and individualism that still define liberalism into a wide moral, political, and social domain.

At once, we cannot thrust aside the place of reason and/or intelligence in our efforts to teach for social justice and to per-suade others of its necessity, certainly where democracy is con-cerned. As we do so, we have to hold in mind the importance of new explorations and revelations when it comes to the life of principle and the very meanings of morality. There is the work of philosophers such as Amelie Rorty (1988), Martha Nussbaum (1986), Seyla Benhabib (1987), and many others who have by now drawn eloquent attention to the emotional and affective foundations of ethics and, by implications, political and social theory as well. They have challenged the ideal of autonomy and self-sufficiency as an ideal developed after the model of successful men in a public space or in the spaces opened by a free-market economy. Those teaching for social justice today, even when con-cerned for principled pursuit of a fairer social world, cannot but pay heed to the importance of embodied relationships, mutuality, care, and concern. Of course what Deborah Meier calls "the power of ideas" (1995) remains important, but not to the exclu-sion of relationality among those who seek such power in a less combative world. If we are not made indignant by the shoddiness and filth in certain neighborhood schools, would we make judg-ments of unfairness? If we are not moved half to tears by watching a ten year old bring his tiny, half-dressed sister to school in time for breakfast in the morning, would we begin mustering help for the establishment of a day care center? If we were not outraged by the sight of idle youngsters in homeless shelters, would we begin making phone calls to find tutors, social workers, poets, those who might offer spiritual and social support? And yet Kant (and, to an extent, John Rawls) wanted to separate principled action and sympathetic identification, rational judgment and emotion, logical projection and care.

Jurgen Habermas, who belongs in many respects to the Kantian tradition, offers a possible solution for teaching for justice in what he describes as a theory of "communicative democracy" (1979). The idea is for people to come together without coercion and of their own free will to discuss issues of significance for them. He speaks about participants taking their lived situations and their cultural vantage points into account, and committing themselves to the kind of communication aimed at some mutually binding outcome. He stresses that all proposals made in the context of such discussion should be held open to question, and participants are to be influenced by arguments, explanations, different modes of persuasion, and (on occasion) varied ways of expression deriving from lived social experience. Iris Marion Young makes the point that one function of discussion is to transform people's preferences, and this may be extremely relevant to the speech situations that can be created in classrooms. The discussions Habermas has in mind may indeed alter people's preferences, as they may (to turn to Young again) "refine . . . their perception of the needs and interests of others, their relations to those others, and their perception of collective problems, goals and solutions. Communicative democracy aims to arrive at decisions through persuasion, not merely through the identification and aggregation of preexisting preferences. By having to speak and justify his or her preferences to others who may be skeptical, a person becomes more reflective about these preferences, accommodates them to the preferences of others, or sometimes becomes more convinced of the legitimacy of his or her claims. By listening to others and trying to understand their experience and claims, persons or groups gain broader knowledge of the social relations in which they are embedded and of the implications of their proposals. These circumstances of a mutual requirement of openness to persuasion often transform the motives, opinions, and preferences of the participants. The transformation often takes the form of moving from being motivated by self-interest to being concerned with justice" (1993, 129–230).

Even as we grant that the model of such discussion may still be academic, oriented to a wholly rational atmosphere, the connection between conversation or discussion or dialogue must be taken seriously. Teaching for social justice demands, as we have said, openings to all sides: to that of persons desirous of telling their stories or picturing them in some fashion; to that of newcomers striving to make sense of the very notion of consensus or mutuality; to that of children and young people, familiar with the languages used at home (oftentimes, not standard English) or with the languages of the street.

Pondering these alternative ways of thinking about justice and teaching for social justice, we need to take a passing glance at the differing contemporary approaches to what is called "reform" of the public schools. The official reform stems from the "center," lately from the federal government itself. It is involved deeply with the struggle for "world-class achievement," with testing programs, with the need for standards of performance, and (always) with "goals 2000." All of these are phrased in such a fashion as to suggest to parents that a kind of insurance is being proffered to each individual child. The fee must be paid in good behavior, hard work, mastery of the English language, abstinence with regard to sexual relations and to drugs, a resounding no in the face of what is thought officially to be temptation.

What is increasingly overlooked is the first requirement of justice: that distinctions should be made among the young whenever there are relevant differences among them. Equitable or fair treatment, it must be remembered, does not mean equal treatment—certainly when that means treating people with widely disparate needs in the same way. Those who once identified equality with sameness overlooked the damage done to children by poverty or discrimination or disruption of a family. In the education legislation of the 1960s, compensatory or remedial measures were provided for in order to counteract the most painful inequities. Today's large, resounding proclamations about bringing the young together by means of the Internet, about the ways in which inequality is overcome in cyberspace, drown out the voices of millions of young ones, as they curtain over the scars and deprivations due to the workings of power. Meanwhile, there is the drumbeat of free market, of individual responsibility, of the uses of efficiency, of character education and training in the "virtues." And now and then there are glimpses of a mythic past, a golden age of harmony and grandeur. It is an age, we are told, in which educated and practical Americans will work for globalization, for pluralization, for free markets everywhere, and (always) a burgeoning technology. As for injustices and social suffering at home: the millions being made by private interests will find their own needs served (we are informed) by—justly or unjustly—redistributing wealth around the world.

There are, of course, other movements of educational reform: charter school movements; privatized school systems, "small schools" of an endless variety; afro-centric schools, schools centered on adolescent girls or pregnant teens or the hopelessly delinquent. The tension among the various movements is evocative of some of the oldest divergences in American life: the road leading to material success; the road leading to enhanced insights, imaginative play, the naming of an incomplete world. The schools most likely to be hospitable to the conversation relating to social justice (and perhaps to small advances to actual transformations) are some of the latter-day "progressive" schools, which now and then are geared to open possibility (Rose 1995). They are most often geared to "active learning," to young people's authentic questioning and journal keeping. They are constructivist, in the sense of encouraging the young to find or construct meanings rather than to go in search of meanings already predefined.

The teachers involved ordinarily reject the old objectivist approach with their assumption of an objective domain of values "out there." They utilize one or another version of the hermeneutic, or an interpretive approach to past and present histories. Relying on a transactional approach to inquiry, they encourage perspectival knowing, situated approaches to learning—to what is being analyzed and reflected on and gradually understood. Learners are asked consciously to impose differing orders on their experience, orders that defamiliarize (as literary works may do), that clarify, highlight, render problematic. Certain modes of ordering or structuring derive from the disciplines as viewed from the diverse vantage points captured by a given class. There is an acknowledgment of what are called multiple realities, on occasion an affirmation of cultural pluralism.

The education offered in many of the small schools may be argued for in the light of fairness, as well as in the light of efficacy and generosity. At the very least, there are opportunities for the long-silenced to be heard, for the invisible to become visible. In contrast to many of the mainstream schools, they are open to multiplicity and difference. They can afford provocations to individuals to choose themselves. Some explicitly teach for a kind of awakening, for critical consciousness. Now and then, we can find a school committed enough to transform its neighborhood to speak explicitly about social justice. Now and then we can find one working to enable students to overcome what Paulo Freire described as "internalized oppression" (1970). That means, of course, to learn to reflect on experience in the culture and the social world, to discover how much of the stuff of actually lived experience has been shaped by an oppressor somewhere—a landlord, an inspector, a principal, a physician—and how much has been freely chosen by the individual empowered to create her- or himself as she or he lives a life. There is then the question of finding out how many others recognize and share the same mode of oppression of dehumanization. At that point, there may be a coming together to invent the kind of dialogue that will explore the meanings of social justice and, at once, lead to transformation of a particular corner of the world.

That may become a beginning of teaching for social justice. We need to ask whether justice is a matter of individuals, one by one, arousing themselves to shake off what holds them in place. We need to wonder whether it demands the creation of situations in which young people, now aware of suffering and unfairness, can gather together in the name of justice to heal somehow, to remedy, to repair. It is difficult not to think of Albert Camus's novel, *The Plague* (1948), for all its colonial treatment of the Arab characters. What is important now is the decision of a group of citizens in Oran, now badly plague-stricken, to form sanitary squads to fight the pestilence:

> Those who enrolled in the "sanitary squads", as they were called, had, indeed, no such great merit in doing as they did, since they knew it was the only thing to do, and the unthinkable thing would then have been not to have brought themselves to do it. These groups enabled our townsfolk to come to grips with the disease and convinced them that, now that the

plague was among us, it was up to them to do whatever could
be done to fight it. Since the plague became in this way some
men's duty, it revealed itself as what it really was, that is, the
concern of all (121).

Here, too, the standard appears to be one of rationality, which the
narrator calls "clear-sightedness," and we are reminded again of
the themes of the Kantian tradition. The plague, the writer says,
was "some men's duty." They felt a categorical imperative; they
were obliged to fight. The narrator (who turns out to be Dr.
Rieux) believes that the justness of battling the plague is as obvious as two and two make four. He believes that, as a doctor without a sign of a cure, fighting the plague is "only logical." Again, he
can only explain his own commitment and that of the sanitary
squads as motivated by some rational demand or imperative. For
a while, it seems to him to have nothing to do with the compassion he feels and the isolation and the helplessness.

Only later, when the plague begins to relent, does he allow
what seems to have been repressed to surface. There had been a
voice calling the forlorn people "back to the land of their desire,
a homeland . . . under free skies and in the custody of love"
(270). He is beginning to think that the citizens joined the squads
in the name of love; his own insistence that it was only "logical"
becomes tempered. It is as if he discovers that principled action
need not be devoid of passion, an almost wordless upsurge of
emotion; and in some strange fashion Dr. Rieux is reborn. He
resolves to tell the story and bear witness, so that some memorial
"of the injustice and outrage done to them might endure; and to
state quite simply that what we learn in a time of pestilence: that
there are more things to admire in men than to despise" (278).
We have to assume that his mother and his dying wife, in their
fidelity and concern, would be included somehow in "men."
Rieux knows there is no final victory, and his record would only
be one account of what had to be done, "and what assuredly
would have to be done again in the never-ending fight against
terror and its relentless onslaughts, despite their personal afflic-
tions, by all who, while unable to be saints, but refusing to bow
down to pestilence, strive their utmost to be healers" (278).

This image of citizens coming together in what turns out to be
a struggle against injustice summons up Richard Rorty's idea of
solidarity and, at once, his rejection of the claim that solidarity

refers to something essential, some thing at the core of all human beings. He knows that our sense of solidarity is strongest with relation to those who are close to us; and, refusing a notion of a "core self," defines solidarity as "the ability to see more and more traditional differences (of tribe, religion, race, custom, and the like) as unimportant when compared with similarities with respect to pain and humiliation . . . the ability to think of people wildly different from ourselves as included in the range of 'us'" (1989, 192). As we reach out for shared commitments and obligations that will make it more likely for some persons' duty to become "the concern of all," we have to admit that social justice is a concept contingent on particular historical circumstances. It does not exist in some supersensible realm, anymore than in the minds and souls of individual human beings. That is why (following Habermas and Rorty and the fictive Dr. Rieux) our teaching must stress the importance of speaking clearly and persuasively enough in situations where everyone is uncoerced in her or his freely chosen participation. Again, we realize that not everyone who enters our classrooms recognizes that social justice is a primary value in the polity (or that women have the right to be treated equally, or that freedom of speech must be defended, or that torture must be categorically condemned). The best we can do is to keep referring to a "we," which can be enlarged and rendered more inclusive over time.

"In this classroom," we can say, "in this school, we listen with respect to everyone's opinion. When we are against that opinion, this does not mean we look at the person holding the opinion with scorn or dislike. And we do not exclude that person from our dialogues. That is the way we work together in this school, and we hope you will want to be part of our community." We may try to create something approximating Habermas's speech situations, opening them to a variety of voices and points of view, and oriented (as Habermas's are not) to action on the part of the community. We need to open multiple spaces where such talking can take place, spaces like the kitchens and back rooms Michelle Fine describes, spaces like the one Hannah Arendt had in mind, in which an "in-between" can develop among those willing to articulate their own perspectives as they speak in terms of "who" and not "what" they are (1958, 184). They might well become the kinds of spaces in which persons might choose (free of domination and critically conscious of the seductions of power) what participant roles they hope to play, what their projects are in the world.

Returning to Stephen Graubard's point about the way articulations of suffering are so often met by institutions that do not register what they mean, I think it important to find a language that breaks through the surfaces of formula and cant. I am reminded of John Dewey writing in *The Public and Its Problems* about how difficult it is to "create adequate opinion on public matters." He went on to say that people's conscious life of opinion and judgment often proceeds on a "superficial and trivial plane." But their lives, he said, reach a deeper level. And then:

> The function of art has always been to break through the crust of conventionalized and routine consciousness. Common things—a flower, a gleam of moonlight, the song of a bird, not things rare and remote, are means with which deeper levels of life are touched so that they spring up as desire and thought. This process is art . . . Artists have always been the real purveyors of the news, for it is not the outward happening in itself which is new, but the kindling by it of emotion, perception, appreciation (183–84).

The mention of a "deeper level" does not mean that communication should take place below the level of reflective consciousness. It does suggest that the capacity to be in touch with images, memories, funded meanings, is to render accessible ordinarily repressed desires and self-reflective explorations on the multiple levels of wonder and of thought.

In *Democracy and Education*, Dewey singled out "the area of shared concerns, and the liberation of greater diversity of personal capacity" as hallmarks of democracy (101–2). These can only be sustained by voluntary action and interest, which must be made possible by means of education. He saw connections, as others have, between the personal voice and the public space. It seems likely that, when personal voices are released among a few persons in a small space, a registering of others suffering may emerge in the very sharing of inquiry and exploration, when unexpected and deeply shared concerns arise as desire and thought.

Adrienne Rich, who believes that writing poetry depends on the belief that an 'I' can become a 'we' without extinguishing others and that "a partly common language exists to which strangers can bring their own heartbeat, memories, images" (1993, 85), helps to clarify what we mean when we speak of moving from the private to the public, from the particular to the general, in the teaching for social justice that is our main concern. We may ask ourselves, still pondering what is involved, how much that "partly common language" can do when it comes to responding, registering, trying to do something about the suffering of others. We recall the sounds and look of children's poetry, or the words in young people's journals and the conversations that sometimes arise in answer. We think of the marvel of personal presentness, not in offering charity, nor in efforts merely to "do good." What is important are the efforts to mobilize equivalents of Camus's invented sanitary squads, to make the cause of social justice a concern of all. It requires the realization of classroom-schoolyard communities in which children and young men and women discover what it means to incarnate commitments to fairness, decency, and authentic concern—and to act on them in what they conceive to be their world.

Teaching for social justice, teachers can learn how to communicate that a commitment to it as significant norm brings people into the deepest kind of contact with others, diverse though some of the values they bring with them may be. In a novel by Dennis MacFarland, *The Music Room* (1990), there is an adaptation of an actual sermon given by a black woman preacher. Here, she talks about joy, and about how the ability to rejoice is related to what people desire. And then:

> But can we learn to rejoice over the coming of justice, over the large and small transformations in our own lives that signal such a triumph? Can we learn to rejoice over the healing of the brokenhearted, the liberation of the captives, over women and men putting on the mantle of justice? Can we learn to rejoice over such things? Can we learn to proclaim our joy when the lowly have been raised up, when the hungry have been given every good thing (188)?

Yes, these claims are contingent on some of the ways in which human beings have learned to live together; but they are also suggestive of the "partly common language" through which the young may be moved to choose.

Finally, there is the importance of arousing the "sense of injustice" and of keeping it alive. When, Edmond Cahn writes, justice is thought of as an ideal condition, the response is likely to be only contemplative. "But the response to a real or imagined instance of injustice is something quite different; it's alive with movement and warmth in the human organism." What he is proposing involves a view of justice as an "active process of remedying or preventing what would arouse the sense of injustice" (1949, 13). The sense of injustice does not arise mainly because of some cognitive recognition. The reasons lie much deeper, below the threshold of feeling. Moreover, the experience of the sense of injustice is fundamentally social, involving a recognition that what may or may not affect the individual human being in her or his immediate situation will inevitably touch someone somewhere.

Opened, by means of the arts or an "almost common language" to what the suffering of others may mean, brought through active and collaborative learning to name the cause of it and the expanding consequences, students may come to see that each one's status really depends on a just order. It must be an order that extends further and further, from small group to small group, from classroom to kitchen, from kitchen to a back room in a church or a hospital. Extending as it might, more and more persons in their engagements with others may be caught up in the currents of such extension, of the river overflowing its banks and nourishing the land. To teach for social justice is to teach for enhanced perception and imaginative explorations, for the recognition of social wrongs, of sufferings, of pestilences wherever and whenever they arise. It is to find models in literature and in history of the indignant ones, the ones forever ill at ease, and the loving ones who have taken the side of the victims of pestilences, whatever their names or places of origin. It is to teach so that the young may be awakened to the joy of working for transformation in the smallest places, so that they may become healers and change their worlds.

REFERENCES

Arendt, H. 1958. *The Human Condition.* Chicago: University of Chicago Press.

Benhabib, S. (1990). Communicative ethics and contemporary controversies in practical philosophy. In *The Communicative Ethics Controversy*, edited by S. Benhabib and F. Dallmayr. Cambridge: MIT Press.

———. 1987. The generalized and the concrete other: the Kohlberg Gilligan controversy and moral theory. In *Feminism as Critique*, edited by Benhabib and Cornell. Minneapolis: University of Minnesota Press.

Blake, W. 1967. *Selected Poems.* New York: Appleton Century Crofts.

Cahn, E. 1949. *The Sense of Injustice.* New York: New York University Press.

Camus, A. 1948. *The Plague.* New York: Alfred A. Knopf.

Dewey, J. 1954. *The Public and Its Problems.* Athens, Ohio: Swallow Press.

——. 1916. *Democracy and Education.* New York: The Macmillan Co.

Fine, M. 1991. *Framing Dropouts.* Albany: State University of New York Press.

Freire, P. 1970. *Pedagogy of the Oppressed.* New York: Herder and Herder.

Gates, H.L. and McKay, N.Y. eds. 1997. *Norton Anthology of African American Literature.* New York: Norton.

Graubard, S. 1996. Preface to the issue 'social suffering'." *Daedalus, Social Suffering,* winter, v–x.

Habermas, J. 1979. *Communication and the Evolution of Society.* Boston: Beacon Press.

Ignatieff, M. 1984. *The Needs of Strangers.* London: Chatto and Windus.

Kant, I. 1959. *Foundations of the Metaphysics of Morals,* translated by Lewis Beck. New York: Bobbs-Merrill.

Kohlberg, L. 1972. Moral education in the schools: A developmental view. In *Curriculum and the Cultural Revolution,* edited by Purpel and Berlanger. Berkeley: McCutchan Publishing Company.

Kozol, J. 1991. *Savage Inequalities.* New York: Crown Publishing.

MacFarland, D. 1990. *The Music Room.* Boston: Houghton, Mifflin.

Marx, K. 1906. *Capital: A Critique of Political Economy.* New York: The Modern Library.

Meier, D. 1995. *The Power of Their Ideas.* Boston: Beacon Press.

Nussbaum, M. 1986. *The Fragility of Goodness.* Cambridge: Cambridge University Press.

Piercy, M. 1994. The tower struck by lightning reversed; the overturning of the tower. In *Circles on the Water.* New York: Knopf.

Rawls, J. 1971. *A Theory of Justice.* Cambridge: Harvard University Press.

Rich, A. 1993. *What Is Found There: Notebooks on Poetry and Politics.* New York: W.W. Norton and Co.

——. 1988. Communication as the context of character. Part 4 in *Mind in Action: Essays in the Philosophy of Mind.* Boston: Beacon Press.

Rorty, R. 1989. Contingency, Iron, and Solidarity. New York: Cambridge University Press.

Rose, M. 1995. *Possible Lives.* Boston: Houghton, Mifflin.

Said, E. 1993. *Culture and Imperialism.* New York: Knopf.

Sizer, T. 1992. *Horace's School.* Boston: Houghton, Mifflin.

Young, I.M. 1993. Justice and communicative democracy. In *Radical Philosophy: Tradition, Counter-Tradition, Politics,* edited by R. Gottlieb. Philadelphia: Temple University Press.

1—Education for Action: Preparing Youth for Participatory Democracy[1]

Joel Westheimer
Joseph Kahne

The purpose of education is not just for kids to have choices, but for kids to act on their knowledge, to create structures and to change and transform structures so that the world is a better place for everybody.
A teacher at C. Wright Mills Middle School[2]

It is often said that today's youth will be called on to solve tomorrow's problems. Schools provide essential preparation for this task. Despite this rhetoric, curriculum that considers the nature of social problems and ways youth might respond as citizens rarely gets center stage. Rather than focusing on ways youth might participate through democratic institutions to foster a better society, curricular discussions focus on the acquisition of academic and vocational skills. To the extent that the democratic purposes of education are raised, educators emphasize conveying knowledge regarding U.S. history and government structures, on opportunities for community service, and on exercises where students simulate the operations of various public institutions such as courts and legislatures. Occasionally, reformers focus on eliciting student input on the design and implementation of a curriculum or on better aligning curriculum materials with students' lived experiences (Wigginton 1986; Wood 1992). When students conduct oral histories of community members, for example, they fulfill an ideal of democratic education by showing that academic disciplines such as history and English have relevance to issues in their own lives and the lives of their community.

These matters are all worthy of attention, but they differ in fundamental ways from efforts to prepare students to improve

1. The authors would like to thank Bill Ayers, Melinda Fine, Ellen Lagemann, Barbara Leckie, Gordon Pradl, and Therese Quinn for their helpful comments on drafts of this chapter.
2. All names that appear in this chapter are pseudonyms.

society. In this chapter, we consider what it might mean to move preparation for membership in a participatory democracy to the center of a school's educational agenda. *Participatory* democracy stands in contrast to *procedural* democracy. In the latter, citizens maintain the right to vote and take part, while in the former, they actually do take part. In framing our discussion of education for participatory democracy—that is, education that fosters youth's ability to work collectively toward a better society—we examine a school designed to promote participatory democracy—a school unabashed in its commitment to fostering the attitudes, skills, and knowledge required to engage and act on important social issues. C. Wright Mills Middle School seemed to us to offer such a model, doubtless one among many alternatives.[3]

We recognize that some find this orientation romantic and that other goals are also of great importance. Given the fundamental significance of these democratic goals, however, we believe this alternative agenda warrants careful attention in order to understand its potential, its risks, and the complexities associated with its pursuit.

VOICES FROM THE PAST: PROMOTING CRITICAL ANALYSIS, CIVIC PARTICIPATION, AND ACTION

In the second and third decades of the twentieth century, conceptions of democratic education rooted in commitments to improving society through collective action achieved a wide hearing among educators. Known as "social reconstructionists," these reformers emphasized teaching students to be active participants in a democratic civic community, able to envision, articulate, and act on conceptions of a better world.

Some, such as Harold Rugg, focused on critical analysis of major social issues and institutions. He wanted students to examine "Problems of the 'market' and its historical development," "How the press developed its influence at various times in our

---

3. This portrait is based on a one-and-a-half-year ethnographic study conducted by one of the authors which included extensive observations, interviews with the entire staff and two dozen students, analysis of lesson plans and of school documents (for details, see Westheimer 1998).

growth," and "The history of labor problems; movements for the increase of cooperation between capital and labor; problems of wages, hours, living conditions" (1996:1921, 47). Rugg developed a series of textbooks and learning materials which sold more than one million copies during the 1930s. The goal of this series and of the social reconstructionists more generally, was to engage students in the analysis of major institutions and social issues so that social problems, causes, and ways to respond could be identified. The series of textbooks sold well until the start of World War II, when nationalist sentiments made critiques of American society unpopular. Rugg's texts became a lightning rod for the rising anti-Communist power in politics (Fine 1995; Kliebard 1995).

A second group of curriculum theorists and educational reformers were attracted to experience-based approaches that emphasized projects tied to social needs. "As the purposeful act is thus the typical unit of the worthy life in a democratic society," wrote William Kilpatrick in 1918, "so also should it be made the typical unit of school procedure" (323). These educators believed that experiential activities could transform students' political and social orientation toward fighting injustice. Their focus bridged their concern for the coarse individualism of the 1920s and the social dislocation of the 1930s with their desire to create "miniature communities" through which students learned the value of working together to identify and respond to problems they confronted (Dewey 1900). This focus on communal undertakings tied to social needs led many progressive-era educators to promote what they called the "core curriculum" (see Faunce and Bossing 1951; Alberty 1953). The "core" was designed to place multidisciplinary analysis and action regarding social problems and themes from social life at the heart of students' school experience. It was a common feature of many schools participating in the Progressive Education Association's Eight-Year Study, for example. Students in the thirty schools that took part in this study commonly spent between two and three hours a day in core classes initiating projects where they examined and responded to major issues facing both individuals and their community. For instance, they studied and initiated programs of environmental improvement, did work with the elderly, orphans, and infants, and examined safety issues in the home and community (Giles, McCutchan, and Zechiel 1942).

Then as now, many of those who endorsed "progressive," experience-based curriculum downplayed the importance of analysis, critique, and action related to social institutions and the pursuit of social justice. Then as now, many progressive educators, particularly those who emphasized a child-centered approach, attended to students' individual interests and needs without engaging students in critical analysis of social issues. What made this period unique was its critical mass of leading educators who believed that "by manipulating the school curriculum they could ultimately change the world" (Cremin 1988, 187).

Those focused on reconstructing society to make it more democratic found a leader in George S. Counts who, at the 1932 meeting of the Progressive Education Association (PEA), delivered a speech ("Dare Progressive Education be Progressive?") which became the book *Dare the School Build a New Social Order?* He argued that Progressive Education had "elaborated no theory of social welfare" (1932, 258), that "it must emancipate itself from the influence of class" (259), and that "it cannot place its trust in a child-centered school" (259). In short, he argued that if progress was the goal of progressive education, then progressive educators needed to be explicit about what progress required. Writing during the Great Depression, he was highly critical of our economic and social norms of competition, selfishness, individualism, and inattention to human suffering. He wanted educators to do more than engage students in analysis of these issues. He wanted them to "engage in the positive task of creating a new tradition in American life" (262). As he put it, "the word [indoctrination] does not frighten me" (263).

The speech had enormous impact. Discussions scheduled for the rest of the convention were replaced by informal discussions of Counts's challenge, and the PEA leaders and members continued to discuss these matters in detail in committee meetings and through their publications (see Graham 1967, 66–67). Counts's argument and reactions to it provide a helpful frame for discussing the educational implications of concern for participatory democracy, particularly in relation to the creation of democratic communities which focus explicitly on matters of social betterment.

For some, Counts's writing was a much appreciated wake-up call. It led educators like Paul Hanna (1932) to recommend redesigned teacher education programs that could address this agenda. Indeed, even educators like Dewey and Bode who did not endorse Counts's call for indoctrination, fearing that it mistakenly implied that there were fixed truths that could be transmitted to students, often did support Counts's critique of the educational system. Dewey praised Counts for "arousing teachers to think more about existing conditions, and in exposing the kind and amount of indoctrination for a reactionary social order that goes on in the schools" (Dewey cited in Graham 1967, 14).

Writing in a similar vein, Boyd Bode supported Counts's general critique that progressive educators needed a direction, but not his program of indoctrination. In *Progressive Education at the Crossroads*, he wrote, "If progressive education is to fulfill its promise, it must become consciously representative of a distinctive [democratic] way of life" (1938, 5). He argued, as we do in this article, that educators must aim at creating a communal mode of life which reflects democratic sensibilities and social analysis— collective undertakings and the creation of common bonds are not sufficient. This democratic orientation could, he argued, provide direction and norms for school communities without requiring indoctrination.

If those committed to democratic communitarian goals had strong allies, however, they also had fierce critics. "The school is not an agency of social reform," wrote Franklin Bobbit, a leader of the social efficiency movement, "Its responsibility is to help the growing individual. [This may improve society.] But this improvement is not a thing directly aimed at" (1937, 75). Moreover, as noted earlier, many educators who were attracted to experiential project-based activities rejected Counts's proposal. They preferred child-centered goals such as creativity and individual freedom. Elizabeth Moos (1932) reflected the mood of many members of the PEA when she argued that the focus on the child rather than on society was most appropriate for elementary schools: "During these years, foundation for emotional and spiritual growth is laid, and this work must not be subordinated to any particular social situation" (264). Many educators also worried that the emphasis on radical politics might marginalize the PEA by limiting the support of teachers and administrators (Cremin 1961, 262). Carlton Washburne (President of the PEA in 1940–42), for example, argued against disseminating the report of Counts's Committee on Economic and Social Problems in 1933, believing that the report might stir "up a feeling on the part of many people who are at the present time overly sensitive that the association has gone radical" (in Graham 1967, 69). These tensions both in the PEA and among progressive educators generally were never resolved. To the extent that a working consensus was achieved, it came through invoking the goal of "democracy as a way of life," something the different factions within progressive education could support. This support, however, seemed as much a function of the goal's vague nature as of a meaningful consensus (Graham 1967).

C. WRIGHT MILLS ACADEMIC MIDDLE SCHOOL

On a crowded, bustling side street in a Latino community sits C. Wright Mills Academic Middle School. In 1984, the school, located in the heart of a major North American city, closed and reopened under a court-ordered consent decree with an almost entirely new staff and the goal of attracting a diverse student population. Currently, Mills enrolls a student body that is 38 percent Spanish surnamed, 20 percent "other" white, 14 percent Chinese, 9 percent African American, and 6 percent Filipino. Once counted among the poorest performing schools in the district, Mills now boasts high attendance rates, high performance on standardized tests, and numerous awards.

Following the consent decree restructuring, the new Mills faculty created a series of mission statements and learning objectives. In many ways their mission is progressive, but not unique. The school "seeks to develop the whole child academically, socially, and emotionally." The faculty uses a "student-centered approach" that develops "self-esteem." They maintain "high academic expectations," recognizing that students "bring a rich diversity of cultures, experiences, languages, and learning styles that can be developed and shared in [the] school setting."

The Mills tenets, however, also include less typical commitments to improving society. The faculty wants students to "think critically about what they are learning, draw appropriate conclusions, and discover what is relevant to their lives." Students will "carry out complex projects involving predictions, research, analysis, and evaluation" and they will do so in "contexts relevant to their education and to their lives." They will learn to "work individually and cooperatively," taking responsibility for "their own lives and actions and for the well being of both the local and global community." (For an in-depth discussion of Mills, how its teachers work collectively, professional development activities at the school, and its governance structure, see Westheimer 1998, chapter 3).

The teachers at C. Wright Mills aim to instill in students hope for a more just society and equip them with the tools to pursue that hope. As one teacher explained,

> I'd like to see them have an awareness of what makes the world, in their eyes, a good place and a set of skills that allows them to act on their vision. I'd like [students to understand] the need for individuals and groups to act collectively to make the world a good place.

SOCIAL STUDIES AND PROJECT-BASED CURRICULAR GOALS

The curricular approach taken at Mills, similar to that taken by pioneering progressive schools, is to emphasize what the Mills staff call transdisciplinary projects aimed at social needs, and to couple these with academic analyses of the social and institutional context. These projects and related analyses comprise a substantial portion of students' work at the school. Indeed, an introducing group of four subject-area teachers designing the year's curriculum are more likely to begin with learning objectives linked to their goal of preparing responsive citizens and then think of ways to make links to academic material than the other way around. The challenge for this school and others with a democratic mission is to structure curriculum activities that advance these goals while simultaneously supporting systematic and sequential development of disciplinary knowledge.

In an effort to link the curriculum to the school's mission, teachers decided early on to base their transdisciplinary curriculum in the social studies. To make clear the import of their discussions, teachers provided links to students' present-day realities. Mills's "Learning Challenges," for example, reflect the faculty's belief in the power of interdisciplinary experiences and hands-on, purposeful activities to achieve these ends. Developed in conjunction with Project 2061, a national effort to promote science in schools,[4] these learning challenges bring students and faculty at Mills together in interdisciplinary groups to study problems of social consequence.

In many schools, interdisciplinary curriculum revolves around themes. Elementary school students might study dinosaurs through stories, art, and science. Middle school students might carry the theme of "cities" through each of the subject areas. The learning challenge is structured differently. It begins with a prompting challenge that requires investigation and response— how to respond to hunger or homelessness in the community, for example. The subject areas are then employed in answering the prompting challenge. As Bernard Farges, a Project 2061 director explains, the educational purpose shifts from the learning objective to *learning from the objective.* Students work in groups on pieces of a larger project, make presentations on their findings, and take actions with respect to their ongoing commitments to the community. At Mills, the commitment to democratic education means that each challenge that is selected (between six and ten each year) revolves around an issue of social significance.

"Addressing Violence in Our Everyday Lives" was a challenge for an eighth-grade group that began with the question: How can you empower yourself and your peers to address the violence in your life and in society in a positive way? The two-week challenge began with five days of regular core academic classes that provided students with the background knowledge and skills they would need for week two. Students then broke into groups focused on one of five "subchallenges." The first, led by the social studies teacher, assessed violence in the media. Students watched television and movies, chronicling observations and statistics about what they saw. They interviewed experts in an effort to analyze media portrayals of violence critically. They asked questions such as "When you sit down in front of the television, you're doing the watching—but who's really in control, you or the show?" and "Does the media show violence as it really is?" Based on their analysis, students formulated, wrote, and revised action recommendations for their peers.

---

4. Though Project 2061 is devoted to science curriculum reform, in Mills's school district, it serves a broader curriculum reform role across the subject areas; at Mills, in particular, the "learning challenges" inform efforts in democratic education by linking academic learning to social issues.

A second group dealt with the problem of gang violence. The language arts teachers engaged students in readings, discussion, and written exercises that examined the causes and impact of gang membership. A group led by a physical-education teacher who voluntarily joined this particular family's challenge activities examined violence in sports. They asked how society has condoned and encouraged violence in sports. The math teacher explored the economic costs of violence in their city. After researching the statistics on the costs of different violent activities, students were required to develop solutions to urban violence. Finally, the science teacher led a group that explored violence in families. They talked about the myths and realities of rape, sexual abuse, and domestic violence. They assembled a survival guide with tips and community resources for other teenagers and created a public service announcement which they distributed on video.

For each "subchallenge" project, students were required to complete learning logs, oral and visual presentations, a substantive written product, and an evaluation of their group's cooperative work process. As would be expected, the curriculum appears to have affected youth in different ways. For one student, the two weeks spoke to personal issues: "I had never dared to talk about all of these things [how violence affects me] before this week. It made me realize how much violence is in my life." Another student was more focused on the imperative of action: "I hope that by talking about some of these things in the classroom, we'll be more able to speak out in the streets about these problems." Though these sentiments were commonly expressed, they were not universal. Many were drawn more to the excitement generated by the experiential nature of the projects than by the emphasis on critical politics:

> It was fun. Like well, it was a lot of hard work because you had to do a lot of research, calling up people . . . We did all the things on our own. And you know, it wasn't like sitting in class and listening to the teachers talk. It was just like doing things on our own.

Moreover, students did not select this school because of its focus on social issues; they were attracted because of the "high (academic) standards," "the teachers really want you to learn," and "the school is safe and teachers are nice." Not all students were ready or interested in engaging in sustained analysis of social issues.

On the other hand, many were. When asked about the learning challenge on violence in their community, for example, one student responded: "We did a poster on violence that had a slogan: If you don't like a gun in your face, look back to your roots and your race." He went on to explain that learning about the Aztecs can help Latin gang members understand their condition, namely that "they're all killing each other for a color . . . we're trying to say just look back to your roots and it shows that you guys are all the same [all descendents] from Latins and also we're all just people."

A PROJECT-BASED CURRICULUM

If the desire and capacity to respond to social needs are prerequisites for participatory democracy, young people need to have experiences which develop this orientation and foster these abilities. In addition to traditional academic discipline-based goals, preparation for participatory democracy requires that youth develop both a "spirit of service" and the civic skills needed for effective civic action. Making speeches, writing memos, facilitating and participating in group discussions, organizing community events, and mobilizing fellow community members are examples of skills required for effective participation in civic democracies. Such opportunities are rare in traditional classrooms, which focus primarily on the academic performance of individual students. Indeed, an extensive review of the literature (Berman 1997) reveals that social studies texts rarely emphasize the importance of or skills connected with civic participation, that teachers rarely engage students in such activities, and that students tend to view participation in their community and school as unrelated to their status as a "good" citizen (also see Dynneson and Gross 1991). In contrast, both teachers at Mills and social reconstructionists during the progressive era pursued this democratic agenda by making projects connected with social needs a central component of their curriculum.

For example, in one learning challenge we observed at Mills, "The Garden Against Hunger," students produced a brochure showing sites of soup kitchens in their neighborhood, wrote to parents and leaders of city agencies inviting them to attend a fund-raiser, and published a newsletter. They created computer data bases to share information with other groups, parents, and members of city agencies, and chose sites for brochure distribution. Finally, they made presentations to parents and representatives from city agencies, homeless organizations, local media, and members of the local community.

These learning challenges modeled for students the importance of civic participation and required that students employ the skills needed to engage such tasks. This emphasis is reminiscent of early reforms that engaged youth in projects of social significance to make schools "a genuine form of active community life, instead of a place set apart to learn lessons" (Dewey 1900, 1956, 14).

A SOCIAL STUDIES-BASED CURRICULUM

Mills orients both its overall curriculum and its transdisciplinary projects around social studies. Nationally, the trend is in the opposite direction. Increasingly, mandated tests and other school policies emphasize math, science, and literacy skills rather than social studies. New York State public schools' new curriculum standards, for example, specify achievement standards across three areas—math, language arts, and science—omitting social studies entirely. For the New York State Board of Education and others, social studies provide topics, as needed, in the service of acquiring skills in these other three disciplines, but is not viewed as a primary concern. At Mills, in contrast, disciplinary learning is used in the service of social studies—that is, in the service of projects, themes, and objectives of social interest and consequence. Thus, interdisciplinary learning challenges focused on the environment, political elections, food production and distribution, and violence in the community.

In an effort to make students aware that the social issues being studied were not simply matters for abstract speculation, the curriculum consistently linked topics to contemporary issues and their personal experiences. In a literature class, for example, students read a biography of a Native American woman and discussed historical oppression—the treatment of native peoples by the U.S. government. Teachers used this as a springboard to examine contemporary and controversial examples of oppression and injustice in their city. A science class studied the environmental impact of European colonization of the Americas and also explored recent environmental damage from an underreported oil spill off a nearby coast.

EDUCATION FOR PARTICIPATORY DEMOCRACY: TWO CHALLENGES

1. *Development of Academic Skills.* Although we argue for emphasizing links between academic work and civic priorities, we also recognize that many educators' hesitation to endorse civic education stems from the concern that this focus distracts them from their most fundamental task—development of academic skills. We believe such concerns are warranted. Some experiential activities and projects which aim primarily at social development may neglect academic priorities. A math teacher at Mills, for example, described his frustration with trying to tie sophisticated understandings of math concepts to project-based activities:

> Some interdisciplinary projects are great and can be a good way to learn. But it's not the best way for all curriculum. Math always ends up accomodating the other subjects, statistics one day, land area the next . . . A student like Tom ends up doing algebra on the side. It's fine, but are they learning? They're learning math in a way . . . but mainly social skills, how to keep on task, issues of tolerance, research skills. That's fine, but pressure's on me to get the math through; I won't get through all I have planned this year because of Challenge Week, Ocean Week, Awareness Month . . . All these things take away, [and] how it takes away bothers me.

Similarly, Dewey (1931) worried that the projects undertaken as part of the "project method" were often "too trivial to be educative" (86) and that the learning that results is often of "a merely technical sort, not a genuine carrying forward of theoretical knowledge" (87).

Designing curriculum similar to Mills's learning challenges that enable sequential development of disciplinary knowledge is enormously difficult. Often, teachers may not have the time, commitment, or insight necessary to implement this kind of curriculum. This concern parallels contemporary discussions of "hands-on" math and science education where educators worry that the focus on experience may undermine attention to the formal and theoretical aspects of the disciplines (Driver et al. 1994; Varelas 1996).

To note this risk, however, is not to concede the case. The same math teacher quoted earlier went on to say:

> I like [the interdisciplinary projects] because it gives me a chance to see how students do all around, like Lisa [a science teacher] and I were just talking, you get a broader range on each student . . . So I can't *not* do challenge week. Instead, I have to say, how else can I do it? Maybe I'll do probability.

This parallels Dewey's (1931) perspective on the project method:

> The defect is not inherent. It is possible to find problems and projects that come within the scope and capacities of the experience of the learner and which have a sufficiently long span so that they raise new questions, introduce new and related undertakings, and create a demand for fresh knowledge (86).

Similarly, Deborah Meier (1995), George Wood (1992), and reformers who advocate whole language approaches and constructivism have demonstrated that curriculum that promotes the development of disciplinary knowledge through methods consistent with democratic priorities can be successfully implemented in contemporary schools (see also Fine 1995 for discussion on the unnecessary division between teaching the "basics" and teaching democratic values). Indeed, Mills was a popular school primarily because of its reputation for high academic standards, and students consistently performed in the top 20 percent of the district on standardized tests.

2. *Education or Indoctrination.* If a group of visitors walked down the hall at Mills prior to the recent California election, they would have seen walls covered with a variety of posters. Some of these posters simply communicated information:

PROPOSITION 204—THE CLEAN WATER ACT
Pro: More water in residential and agricultural areas.
Con: Increase in water costs and taxes.

WHAT IS PROPOSITION 210, THE MINIMUM WAGE?

Currently the minimum wage is $4.25/hour. Proposition 210 would raise the minimum wage to $5.00/hour as of March 1, 1997 and to $5.75/hour as of March 1, 1998.

Other posters, however, presented clear positions on issues of social and political significance:

YES TO PROPOSITION 204: Safe, Clean, Reliable Water Act. Encourage safe drinking water.

NO ON PROPOSITION 209: 209 Will take away affirmative action and with it the chance for everyone to go to school.

DANA MARTIN FOR THE HOUSE OF REPRESENTATIVES: She is Pro-Choice! She Supports Affirmative Action!

Although most educators and parents agree that the ability to analyze and form opinions on issues is an important part of students' education, the specifics of curriculum and pedagogy that aim to accomplish this goal are far more controversial. When a social studies teacher in a school in Oregon taught a unit on the history of environmentalism, some parents and schoolboard members objected, asserting that the unit was indoctrinating children to be antilogging and pro-environment. Similar concerns led Oregon board members, along with officials of several other districts and states, to ban the Dr. Seuss book *The Lorax*, which depicts a factory rapidly chopping down all the trees to make a popular but useless product. Similarly, opponents of New York City's proposed "Rainbow Curriculum" argued that the section on prejudice was not to be part of the school curriculum because it contained a passage encouraging tolerance for homosexuals. The conflict ended with not only the exclusion of the passage, but also the resignation of the chancellor of the New York City schools.

When does teaching become indoctrination? How can schools teach students to be critical thinkers when it comes to matters of social policy while maintaining a judicious balance of alternative perspectives? What happens when students examine current issues and explore paths to improving society that conflict with mainstream or parental values? At Mills, for example, some parents and administrators had misgivings about the signs in the hallways described earlier that advocate particular candidates or positions. Before addressing these questions, it is worth noting that the Mills faculty and educators of the progressive era share two approaches to meaningful explorations of important social issues, and that these approaches are themselves the subject of serious debate.

First, both linked their discussion and analysis of important issues to action. Both groups believed in challenging the prevailing culture of inaction and passivity with respect to issues of social significance and saw action as essential to the workings of a participatory democracy. The primary value of this action lies not in the service it provides, these educators argue, but in the opportunity it offers students to develop skills related to participatory democracy and in the social, participatory orientation it models. This perspective was well articulated by a Mills student who, when asked about the learning challenges, told us: "It teaches us how important it is to have social responsibility, like telling people about what's happening in the world, like the teachers are doing for us, and we're going to do it for the community."

Second, both the Mills faculty and the progressives worked to ensure that students were exposed to—and could understand—a range of alternative perspectives. A democracy cannot function meaningfully without informed and critical analysis of issues and social problems. Although it is common for social studies teachers and others to engage students in exercises where they must differentiate between "facts" and "opinions," rarely are these discussions linked to participation and action. At Mills, for example, information and perspectives on the legislative issues described earlier are not simply learned, but are communicated to the school community.

Moreover, the ability to discern fact from opinion is developed through explicit challenges to widespread cultural assumptions rather than through reexamination of historical issues which, by virtue of time, have become unassailable. Whereas many teachers demonstrate to students the potential tyranny of opinion over facts in landmark historical controversies (ill-informed legislative decisions based on the idea that black Americans could not be as intelligent as their white counterparts, for example), both Mills teachers and the progressives understood that to develop the capacity for critical analysis, students need to examine issues for which their own perspectives and positions could be challenged. That there are not, as of yet, clear "answers" (widespread cultural agreement) to the questions raised specifically makes those issues useful. Whether gay men should be allowed to serve in the U.S. military becomes a more useful issue for discussion and critique than whether African American men should be allowed to serve. The former forces difficult analysis and consideration of a variety of viewpoints, while the latter, piggybacking on already-established widespread agreement, fails to do so.

Progressive educators may correctly recognize that students must have experiences engaging controversial issues, but this does not mean that they have worked out strategies for doing so that are consistent with both democratic sensibilities and parental concerns. The tensions raised by the approaches to teaching critical analysis and linking learning to action described above are many; educators' pursuit of such goals through curriculum is fraught with complications. At their base, these "complications" arise because the rhetoric of participatory democracy is being taken seriously and enacted. The prevailing culture of inaction and passivity with respect to issues of social significance is being explicitly and overtly challenged. The hesitancy of many educators to engage critically and then act on controversial issues, however, has a rational basis.

First, although the actions students take in conjunction with the Mills learning challenges may be beneficial, others may be inappropriate. In a well-functioning democracy, citizens act when they find issues compelling and after gathering sufficient information. Frequently, students will not find all issues worthy of civic action or will not achieve the level of clarity regarding an issue which would make actions appropriate. Moreover, teachers must have a certain degree of control over their curriculum. Many kinds of actions that would be appropriate for citizens, such as attending a protest or working with a community organization, may not be structured in ways that enable a teacher to be sure a given action will be safe or educationally valuable. Thus, while experiences at Mills demonstrate the substantial educational potential of civic action as part of students' curriculum, there are reasons to temper blanket support of this practice.

Second, the broad consensus that teachers should help students think critically does not mean pursuit of this goal is straightforward. The consensus regarding critical thinking generally vanishes when the possibility arises that students will articulate conclusions that differ from mainstream or parental values. Critical thinking is commonly understood to be the use of reason in reaching judgments, while indoctrination is a process whereby ideologically committed instructors constrain reason in an effort to lead students to particular conclusions (Siegel 1988). The problem with this formulation is that it assumes a "neutral" ground exists. More exactly, this perspective obscures the ways the dominant culture and ideology are embedded in allegedly neutral reasoning.

Many critics of the kind of curriculum employed by Mills teachers and used during the progressive era, argue that these educators indoctrinate. They charge that the social reconstructionists' curriculum emphasizes liberal or left wing critiques of immigration policy, environmental policy, and the capitalist system. In one sense, these concerns have an empirical basis. No Mills students, for example, are engaged in a community-action project that would be considered politically conservative. Mills teachers, in fact, often struggled with this tension. A "debate" on immigration was retitled a "panel" on immigration after teachers grew concerned that the invited participants did not represent a broad spectrum of perspectives. These concerns led many educators, including many at Mills, to respond that they aim to be "value free" by presenting "all sides" of a given controversial subject.

This stance, however, fails to resolve the problem and encounters resistance from both the left and the right. A variety of conservative groups, for example, criticize "critical thinking" because they feel it "means teaching children to empty themselves of their own values (transmitted from parents, church, and culture)" (Simonds 1993/1994, 15). They argue that such curriculum, far from being "value free," often reflects a form of indoctrination toward "relativistic" and "secular humanist" values.

On the other hand, social reconstructionists and modern-day criticalists (McLaren and Pruyn 1996) argue that claims of "value neutrality" often function to obscure the mainstream values (the importance of individual autonomy and the efficacy of market incentives, for example) in which they are embedded. Educators may strive to tell "both sides of the story." They may seek balance or neutrality and hope students will then be free to form their own ideas about issues. But, as George Counts wrote in 1932, "neutrality with respect to the great issues that agitate society . . . is practically tantamount to giving support to the most powerful

forces engaged in the contest" (1932, 263). False notions of neutrality, Counts argued, can constrain critical thinking by failing to
make visible those "social forces" hidden by familiarity. It was this
concern that led Dewey, who criticized other aspects of Counts's
vision, to praise him nonetheless for making visible the "kind and
amount of indoctrination for a reactionary social order that goes
on in the schools" (cited in Graham 1967, 14).

Further, because the media and the broader culture dispro-
portionately reflect particular interests and perspectives and obscures others, there is no level playing field on which students can
discuss issues. Educators must therefore help students consider
the interests and power relations embedded in various perspectives—a formidable task. Such concerns motivated Harold Rugg's
curricular focus on the ways various powerful groups shaped the
development of institutions which in turn helped shape society.
This concern was also evident in Mills's learning challenges,
where study of "gang violence and ways to prevent it" led students
to consider how society might condone and encourage violence
through sports and the media. One teacher explained his stance
on "value neutrality" this way:

> What I'd like students to have is an open mind to things that
> are different from what they've experienced and an eagerness
> to find out about it. Not a lack of prejudice necessarily, but an
> awareness of where their prejudices lie.

In sum, critical thinking in relation to political issues requires
attention to situated ideas—ideas in the context of power relations and cultural norms. Students must learn how to respond to
social problems and also how certain problems come to the fore
while others remain unnamed. They must learn to evaluate legislative proposals and also the social and political dynamics that
favor one proposal over another.

CONCLUDING THOUGHTS

A clear vision exists for education that promotes participation
and action as well as a keen appreciation of the obstacles facing
educators pursuing this vision. On the one hand, the importance
of this task, and the thought and care with which Mills's teachers
and students pursue it, is inspiring. In terms of democratic edu-

cation, the social reconstructionists' stance may invite more controversy than efforts to validate students' experiences and interests or efforts to simulate the operations of courts and legislatures. But this approach is more exciting, because it is more of a stance: the social reconstructionists, unlike many of their progressive colleagues, provide a vision that aims directly at preparing youth to improve society.

On the other hand, it is doubtful that a significant number of teachers, let alone schools or districts, will pursue this goal. Not only are the talents and commitments necessary to pursue these priorities formidable, but the incentives to bypass these goals are significant. The curricular agenda described earlier breeds controversy, and controversy is not something schools handle well. In part, this is because they are governed democratically. Ironically, the civic community (parents and community members) that governs schools often sanctions those who implement curricula that engage the contentious issues a civic community must be able to engage for democracy to work. Administrators also work to avoid controversy. When a science class studying levels of radon at Mills discovered levels above the recommended standard, the school-district leaders grew concerned—not primarily with the levels of radon, but with the potential controversy and political pressures such findings might promote.

The policies and practices of teachers, schools, and districts can promote or constrain the degree to which students acquire the knowledge, skills, and attitudes necessary to function effectively as citizens in a democracy. The social reconstructionists and their modern-day colleagues at Mills and elsewhere may lack sufficient answers to important questions, and many roadblocks may constrain implementation of their vision, but they do provide a vision for a school curriculum that encourages participation, critical analysis, and action—pedagogical prerequisites for democracy. These educators offer not only a vision of education for action, but also important strategies for getting there.

REFERENCES

Berman, S. 1997. *Children's Social Consciousness and the Development of Social Responsibility.* New York: Teachers College Press.

Counts, G. 1932. Dare progressive education be progressive? *Progressive Education* 9:257–63.

Dewey, J. (1900–1956). "The School and Society" in *The Child and the Curriculum and the School and Society*. Chicago: University of Chicago Press.

Dewey, J. 1931. *The way out of educational confusion*. In *John Dewey: The Later Works, 1925–53*, edited by A. Boydston. Vol. 6. Carbondale, IL: Southern Illinois University Press.

Driver, R., H. Asoko, J. Leach, E. Mortimer, and P. Scott. 1994. Constructing scientific knowledge in the classroom. *Educational Researcher* 23(7):5–12.

Dynneson, T. L., and R. E. Gross, eds. 1991. *Social Science Perspectives on Citizenship Education*. New York: Teachers College Press.

Fine, M. 1995. *Habits of Mind: Struggling Over Values in America's Classrooms*. San Francisco: Jossy-Bass.

Giles, H. H., S. P. McCutchen, and A. N. Zechiel. 1942. *Adventure in American Education. (Volume II). Exploring the Curriculum: The Work of the Thirty From the Viewpoint of Curriculum Consultants*. New York: Harper & Brothers.

Graham, P. A. 1967. *Progressive Education, from Arcady to Academe: A History of the Progressive Education Association, 1919–1955*. New York: Colombia University, Teachers College.

Hanna, P. R. 1932. The need for teacher training. *Progressive Education* 9:273–74.

McLaren, P. and M. Pruyn. 1996. Indoctrination. *Philosophy of Education: An Encyclopedia*. New York: Garland.

Meier, D. 1995. The Power of Their Ideas. Beacon Press.

Moos, E. 1932. Steps toward the American dream. *Progressive Education* 9:264–65.

Rugg, H. 1921. Reconstructing the curriculum: An open letter to Professor Henry Johnson commenting on committee procedure as illustrated by the report of the joint committee on history and education for citizenship. In (1996) *Educating the Democratic Mind*, edited by W. Parker. New York: State University of New York Press.

Siegel, H. 1988. *Educating for Reason: Rationality, Critical Thinking, and Education*. New York: Routledge.

Simonds, R. 1994. A plea for the children. *Educational Leadership* 51(4):12–15.

Varelas, M. 1996. Between theory and data in a 7th grade science class. *Journal of Research in Science Teaching* 33(3):229–63.

Westheimer, J. In press, 1998. *Among Schoolteachers: Autonomy, Community, and Ideology*. New York: Teachers College Press.

Wigginton, E. 1986. *Sometimes a Shining Moment: The Foxfire Experience*. Garden City, N.Y.: Anchor Press/Doubleday Books.

Wood, G. 1992. *Schools That Work: America's Most Innovative Public Education Programs*. New York: Dutton.

2—The Human Lives Behind the Labels
The Global Sweatshop, Nike, and the Race to the Bottom

Bill Bigelow

I began the lesson with a beat-up soccer ball. The ball sat balanced in a plastic container on a stool in the middle of the circle of student desks. "I'd like you to write a description of this soccer ball," I told my high school Global Studies class. "Feel free to get up and look at it. There is no right or wrong. Just describe the ball however you'd like."

Looks of puzzlement and annoyance greeted me. "It's just a soccer ball," someone said.

Students must have wondered what I had to do with Global Studies class. "I'm not asking for an essay," I said, "just a paragraph or two."

As I'd anticipated, their accounts were straightforward—accurate if uninspired. Few students accepted the offer to examine the ball up close. A soccer ball is a soccer ball. They sat and wrote. Afterwards, a few students read their descriptions aloud. Brian's is typical:

> The ball is a sphere which has white hexagons and black pentagons. The black pentagons contain red stars, sloppily outlined in silver . . . One of the hexagons contains a green rabbit wearing a soccer uniform with "Euro 88" written parallel to the rabbit's body. This hexagon seems to be cracking. Another hexagon has the number 32 in green standing for the number of patches that the ball contains.

But something was missing. There was a deeper social reality associated with this ball—a reality that advertising and the consumption-oriented rhythms of U.S. daily life discouraged students from considering. "Made in Pakistan" was stenciled in small print on the ball, but very few students thought that significant enough to include in their descriptions. However, these three tiny words offered the most important clue to the human lives hidden in "just a soccer ball"—a clue to the invisible Pakistanis whose hands crafted the ball sitting in the middle of the classroom.

I distributed and read aloud Bertolt Brecht's poem "Questions From a Worker Who Reads" as a tool to pry behind the soccer-ball-as-thing:

> Who built the seven gates of Thebes?
> The books are filled with names of
> kings.
> Was it kings who hauled the craggy
> blocks of stone? . . .
> In the evening when the Chinese wall
> was finished
> Where did the masons go? Imperial
> Rome
> Is full of arcs of triumph. Who reared
> them up? . . .
> Young Alexander conquered India.
> He alone?
> Caesar beat the Gauls.
> Was there not even a cook in his
> army? . . .
>
> Each page a victory.
> At whose expense the victory ball?
> Every ten years a great man,
> Who paid the piper?

"Keeping Brecht's questions in mind," I said, after reading the poem, "I want you to *resee* this soccer ball. If you like, you can write from the point of view of the ball, you can ask the ball questions, but I want you to look at it deeply. What did we miss the first time around? It's not 'just a soccer ball.'" With not much more than these words for guidance—although students had some familiarity with working conditions in poor countries—they drew a line beneath their original descriptions and began again.

Versions one and two were night and day. With Brecht's prompting, Pakistan as the country of origin became more important. Tim wrote in part: "Who built this soccer ball? The ball answers with Pakistan. There are no real names, just labels. Where did the real people go after it was made?" Nicole also posed questions: "If this ball could talk, what kinds of things would it be able to tell you? It would tell me about the lives of the people who made it in Pakistan . . . But if it could talk, would you listen?" Maisha played with its colors and the "32" stamped on the ball: "Who painted the entrapped black, the brilliant bloody red, and the shimmering silver? Was it made for the existence of a family 32?" And Sarah imagined herself as the soccer ball worker. "I sew together these shapes of leather. I stab my finger with my needle. I feel a small pain, but nothing much, because my fingers are so calloused. Everyday I sew these soccer balls together for 5 cents, but I've never once had a chance to play soccer with my friends. I sew and sew all day long to have these balls shipped to another place where they represent fun. Here, they represent the hard work of everyday life." When students began to consider the human lives behind the ball-as-object, their writing also came alive.

Geoffrey, an aspiring actor, singer, and writer, wrote his as a conversation between himself and the ball:

> "So who was he?" I asked.
>
> "A young boy, Wacim, I think," it seemed to reply.
>
> I got up to take a closer look. Even though the soccer ball looked old and its hexagons and other geometric patterns were cracked, the sturdy and intricate stitching still held together.
>
> "What that child must've gone through," I said.
>
> "His father was killed and his mother was working. Wacim died so young . . . It's just too hard, I can't contain these memories any longer." The soccer ball let out a cry and leaked his air out and lay there, crumpled on the stool. Like his master, lying on the floor, uncared for, and somehow overlooked and forgotten.

Students had begun to imagine the humanity inside the ball; their pieces were vivid and curious. The importance of making visible the invisible, of looking behind the masks presented by everyday consumer goods, became a central theme in my first-time effort to teach about the "global sweatshop" and child labor in poor countries. [I did an abbreviated version of this unit with my U.S. history classes. Some of the student writing here is theirs.]

TEACHING ABOUT THE GLOBAL
SWEATSHOP

The paired soccer ball writing assignment was a spur-of-the-moment classroom introduction to Sydney Schanberg's June 1996 *Life* magazine article, "Six Cents an Hour." Schanberg, best known for his *New York Times* investigations of Cambodia's "killing fields," had traveled to Pakistan and posed as a soccer ball exporter. There, he was offered children for $150 to $180 who would labor for him as virtual slaves. As Schanberg reports, in Pakistan, children as young as six are "sold and resold like furniture, branded, beaten, blinded as punishment for wanting to go home, rendered speechless by the trauma of their enslavement." For pennies an hour, these children work in dank sheds stitching soccer balls with the familiar Nike swoosh and logos of other transnational athletic equipment companies.

Nike spokesperson, Donna Gibbs, defended her company's failure to eliminate child labor in the manufacture of soccer balls: "It's an ages-old practice," she was quoted as saying in Schanberg's article, "and the process of change is going to take time." But as Max White, an activist with the "Justice. Do It NIKE!" coalition, said when he visited my global studies class last month, "Nike knew exactly what it was doing when it went to Pakistan. That's why they located there. They went because they *knew* child labor was an 'ages-old practice.'"

My initial impulse had been to teach a unit on child labor. I thought that my students would empathize with young people around the globe, whose play and education had been forcibly replaced with the drudgery of repetitive work—and that the unit would engage them in thinking about inequities in the global division of labor. Perhaps it might provoke them to take action on behalf of child workers in poor countries.

But I was also concerned that we shouldn't reduce the growing inequalities between rich and poor countries to the issue of child labor. Child labor could be entirely eliminated and that wouldn't affect the miserably low wages paid to adult workers, the repression of trade unions and democratic movements, the increasing environmental degradation, and the resulting Third World squalor sanitized by terms like "Globalization" and "free trade." Child labor is one spoke on the wheel of global capitalism, and I wanted to present students with a broader framework to reflect on its here-and-now dynamics. What I share here is a sketch of my unit's first draft—an invitation to reflect on how best to engage students in these issues.

THE TRANSNATIONAL CAPITAL AUCTION

It seemed to me that the central metaphor for economic globalization was the auction: governments beckoning transnational corporations to come hither—in competition with one another—by establishing attractive investment climates (e.g., by maintaining low-wage/weak-union havens and not pressing environmental concerns.) So I wrote what I called "The Transnational Capital Auction: A Game of Survival." I divided students into seven different "countries," each of which would compete with all the others to accumulate "friendly to Capital points"—the more points earned, the more likely Capital would locate in that country. In five silent auction rounds, each group would submit bids for minimum wage, child labor laws, environmental regulations, conditions for worker organizing, and corporate tax rates. For example, a corporate tax rate of 75% won no points for the round, but a zero tax rate won 100 points. (There were penalty points for "racing to the bottom" too quickly, risking popular rebellion, and thus "instability" in the corporate lexicon.)

I played "Capital" and egged them on: "Come on group three, you think I'm going to locate in your country with a ridiculous minimum wage like $5 an hour. I might as well locate in the United States. Next round, let's not see any more sorry bids like that one." A bit crass, but so is the real-world downward spiral simulated in the activity.

At the game's conclusion, every country's bids hovered near the bottom: no corporate taxes, no child labor laws, no environmental regulations, pennies an hour minimum wage rates, union organizers jailed, and the military used to crush strikes. As I'd anticipated, students had breathed life into the expressions "downward leveling" and "race to the bottom." In the frenzied competition of the auction, they'd created some pretty nasty conditions, because the game rewarded those who lost sight of the human and environmental consequences of their actions. I asked them to step back from the activity and to write on the kind of place their country would become should transnational Capital decide to accept their bids and locate there. I also wanted them to reflect on the glib premise that underlies so much contemporary economic discussion that foreign investment in poor countries is automatically a good thing. And finally I hoped that they would consider the impact that the race to the bottom has on their lives, especially their future work prospects. (That week's *Oregonian* carried articles about the Pendleton Co.'s decision to pull much of its production from Oregon and relocate to Mexico.) I gave them several quotes to reflect on as they responded:

- "It is not that foreigners are stealing our jobs, it is that we are all facing one another's competition."
  William Baumol, Princeton University economist
- "Downward leveling is like a cancer that is destroying its host organism—the earth and its people."
  Jeremy Brecher and Tim Costello, authors Global Village or Global Pillage
- "Globalization has depressed the wage growth of low-wage workers [in the United States]. It's been a reason for the increasing wage gap between high-wage and low-wage workers."
  Laura Tyson, Chair, U.S. Council of Economic Advisers

Many global issues courses are structured as "area studies," with units focusing on South America, sub-Saharan Africa, or the Middle East. There are obvious advantages to this region-by-region progression, but I worried that if I organized my global studies curriculum this way, students might miss how countries oceans apart, such as Indonesia and Haiti, are affected by the same economic processes. I wanted students to see globalization as, well, global—that there were myriad and far-flung runners in the race to the bottom.

This auction among poor countries to attract Capital was the essential context my students needed in order to recognize patterns in such seemingly diverse phenomena as child labor and increased immigration to the world's so-called developed nations. However, I worried that the simulation might be too convincing, corporate power depicted as too overwhelming. The auction metaphor was accurate but inexorable: Students could conclude that if transnational Capital is as effective an "auctioneer" as I was in the simulation, the situation for poor countries must be hopeless. In the follow-up writing assignment, I asked what if anything people in these countries could do to stop the race to the bottom, the "downward leveling." By and large, students' responses weren't as bleak as I feared. Kara wrote: "Maybe if all the countries come together and raise the standard of living or become 'capital unfriendly' then capital would have no choice but to take what they receive. Although it wouldn't be easy, it would be dramatically better." Adrian suggested that "people could go on an area-wide strike against downward leveling and stand firm to let capital know that they won't go for it." And Matt wrote simply, "revolt, strike." Tessa proposed that people here could "boycott products made in countries or by companies that exploit workers."

But others were less hopeful. Lisa wrote, "I can't see where there is much the people in poor countries can do to stop this 'race to the bottom.' If the people refuse to work under those conditions the companies will go elsewhere. The people have so little and could starve if they didn't accept the conditions they have to work under." Sara wrote, "I don't think a country can get themselves out of this because companies aren't generous enough to help them because they wouldn't get anything out of it."

What I should have done is obvious to me now. After discussing their thoughts on the auction, I should have regrouped students and started the auction all over again. Having considered various alternative responses to the downward spiral of economic and environmental conditions, students could have practiced organizing with each other, could have tested the potential for solidarity across borders. At the least, replaying the auction would have suggested that people in Third World countries aren't purely victims; there are possible routes for action, albeit enormously difficult ones.

T-SHIRTS, BARBIE DOLLS, AND BASEBALLS

We followed the auction with a "global clothes hunt." I asked students to: "find at least ten items of clothing or toys at home. These can be anything: T-shirts, pants, skirts, dress shirts, shoes, Barbie dolls, baseballs, soccer balls, etc.," and to list each item and country of manufacture. In addition, I wanted them to attach geographic location to the place names, some of which many students had never heard of (for example, Sri Lanka, Macau, El Salvador, and Bangladesh). So in class they made collages of drawings or magazine clippings of the objects they'd found, and with the assistance of an atlas, drew lines on a world map connecting these images with the countries where the items were produced.

We posted their collage/maps around the classroom, and I asked students to wander around looking at these to search for patterns for which kinds of goods were produced in which kinds of countries. Some students noticed that electronic toys tended to be produced in Taiwan and Korea; that more expensive shoes, like Doc Martens, were manufactured in Great Britain or Italy; athletic shoes were made mostly in Indonesia or China. On their "finding patterns" write-up, just about everyone commented that China was the country that appeared most frequently on people's lists. A few kids noted that most of the people in the manufacturing countries were not white. As Sandee wrote, "The more expensive products seem to be manufactured in countries with a higher number of white people. Cheaper products are often from places with other races than white." People in countries with concentrations of people of color "tend to be poorer so they work for less." We'd spent the early part of the year studying European colonialism, and some students noticed that many of the manufacturing countries were former colonies. I wanted students to see that every time they put on clothes or kick a soccer ball they are making a connection, if hidden, with people around the world— especially in the Third World countries—and that these connections are rooted in historical patterns of global inequality.

From here on, I saturated students with articles and videos that explored the working conditions and life choices confronting workers in poor countries. Some of the resources I found most helpful included: *Mickey Mouse Goes to Haiti,* a video critiquing the Walt Disney Co.'s exploitation of workers in Haiti's garment industry (workers there, mostly women, make 28 cents an hour; Disney claims it can't afford the 58 cents an hour workers say they could live on); CBS *48 Hours* exposé of conditions for women workers in Nike factories in Vietnam, reported by Roberta Baskin; several Bob Herbert "In America" *New York Times* columns; a November 3, 1996, *Washington Post* article, "Boot Camp at the Shoe Factory Where Taiwanese Bosses Drill Chinese Workers to

Make Sneakers for American Joggers," by Anita Chan; *Tomorrow We Will Finish* a UNICEF-produced video about the anguish and solidarity of girls forced into the rug-weaving industry in Nepal and India; and an invaluable collection of articles called a "Production Primer," collected by "Justice: Do It NIKE!," a coalition of Oregon labor, peace, and justice groups.

I indicated above that the advantage of this curricular globe-trotting was that students could see that issues of transnational corporate investment, child labor, worker exploitation, poverty, etc. were not isolated in one particular geographic region. The disadvantage was that students didn't get much appreciation for the peculiar conditions in each country we touched on. And I'm afraid that, after awhile, people in different societies began to appear as generic global victims. This was not entirely the fault of my decision to bounce from country to country, but was also a reflection of the narrow victim orientation of many of the materials available.

I was somewhat unaware of the limits of these resources until I previewed a 25-minute video produced by Global Exchange, *Indonesia: Islands on Fire.* One segment features Sadisah, an Indonesian ex-Nike worker, who, with dignity and defiance, describes conditions for workers there and what she wants done about them. I found her presence, however brief, a stark contrast to most of the videos I'd shown in class that feature white commentators with Third World workers presented as objects of sympathy. Although students generated excellent writing during the unit, much of it tended to miss the humor and determination suggested in the *Island on Fire* segment and concentrated on workers' victimization.

CRITIQUE WITHOUT CARICATURE

Two concerns remained throughout the unit. On the one hand, I had no desire to feign neutrality—to hide my conviction that people here need to care about and to act in solidarity with workers around the world in their struggles for better lives. To pretend that I was a mere dispenser of information would be dishonest, but worse, it would imply that being a spectator is an ethical response to injustice. It would model a stance of moral apathy. I wanted students to know these issues were important to me, that I cared enough to do something about them.

On the other hand, I never want my social concerns to suffocate student inquiry or to prevent students from thoughtfully considering opposing views. I wanted to present the positions of transnational corporations critically, but without caricature.

Here, too, it might have been useful to focus on one country in order for students to evaluate corporate claims—e.g., "Nike's production can help build thriving economies in developing nations." I'd considered writing a role play about foreign investment in Indonesia with roles for Nike management as well as Korean and Taiwanese subcontractors. (Nike itself owns none of its own production facilities in poor countries.) This would have provoked a classroom debate on corporate statements, where students could have assessed how terms like "thriving economies" may have different meanings for different social groups.

Instead, I tried in vain to get a spokesperson from Nike, in nearby Beaverton, to address the class; I hoped that at least the company might send me a video allowing students to glean the corporate perspective. No luck. They sent me a PR packet of Phil Knight speeches, and their "Code of Conduct," but stopped returning my phone calls requesting a speaker. I copied the Nike materials for students, and they read with special care the Nike Code of Conduct and did a "loophole search"—discovering, among other things, that Nike promises to abide by local minimum wage laws, but never promises to pay a *living* wage; they promise to obey "local environmental regulations" without acknowledging how inadequate these often are. Having raced themselves to the bottom in the Transnational Capital Auction, students were especially alert to the frequent appearance of the term "local government regulations" in the Nike materials. Each might as well have carried a sticker reading WEASEL WORDS.

I reminded students of our soccer ball exercise, how we'd missed the humanity in the object until we read Bertolt Brecht's poem. I asked them to write a "work poem" that captured some aspect of the human lives connected to the products we use everyday. They could draw on any situation, product, individual, or relationship we'd encountered in the unit. As prompts, I gave them other work poems that my students had produced over the years [for example, see Joel Gunz's poem, "Diamond," included in my South Africa curriculum, *Strangers in Their Own Country*]. Students brainstormed ways they might complete the assignment: from the point of view of one of the objects produced, or that of one of the workers; a dialogue poem from the point of view of worker and owner, or worker and consumer; a letter to one of the products, or to one of the owners (like Oregon-based Phil Knight, CEO of Nike). Cameron Robinson's poem, below, expressed the essence of what I was driving at with the assignment. Some others are included on pages 36–8.

MASKS

Michael Jordan soars through the air,
on shoes of unpaid labor.
a boy kicks a soccer ball,
the bloody hands are forgotten.

An excited girl combs the hair of her Barbie,
an over-worked girl makes it.
A child receives a teddy bear,
Made in China has no meaning.

The words "hand made" are printed,
whose hands were used to make them?
A six year old in America starts his
first day of school,
A six year old in Pakistan starts his
first day of work.

They want us to see the ball,
not to see the millions of ball stitchers.
The world is full of many masks.
the hard part is seeing beneath them.

As we read our pieces aloud (I wrote one, too) I asked students to record lines or images that they found particularly striking and to note themes that recurred. They also gave positive feedback to one another after each person read. Sandee wrote: "I liked the line in Maisha's paper that said, 'My life left me the day I stitched the first stitch . . .' I like Antoinette's paper because of the voice. It showed more than just pain, it also reflected a dream"— an ironic dream of a sweatshop worker who wants to flee her country for the "freedom" of the United States. Dirk had written a harshly-worded piece from the point of view of a worker for a transnational company; it drew comments from just about every-one. Elizabeth appreciated it because "he used real language to express the feelings of the workers. As he put it, I doubt that the only thing going through their minds is 'I hate this job.'" As a whole the writings were a lot angrier than they were hopeful; if I'd missed it in their pieces, this came across loud and clear in stu-dents' "common themes" remarks. As Jessica wrote, "One of the things I noticed was that none of the [papers] had a solution to the situation they were writing about." Maisha agreed: "Each pa-per only showed animosity . . ."

I expected the unit to generate anger, but I hoped to push beyond it. From the very beginning, I told students that it was not my intention merely to expose the world's abuse and exploita-tion. A broader aim was to make a positive difference. For their final project, I wanted students to do something with their knowledge—I wanted to give them the opportunity to act on behalf of the invisible others whose lives are intertwined in so many ways with their own. I wasn't trying to push a particular organization, or even a particular form of "action." I wanted them simply to feel some social efficacy, to sense that no matter how overwhelming a global injustice, there's always something to be done.

The assignment sheet required students to take their learning "outside the walls of the classroom and into the real world." They could write letters to Phil Knight, Michael Jordan, or President Clinton. They could write news articles or design presentations to other classes. I didn't want them to urge a particular position if they didn't feel comfortable with that kind of advocacy; so in a letter they might simply ask questions of an individual.

They responded with an explosion of creativity: three groups of students designed presentations for elementary school kids or for other classes at Franklin; one student wrote an article on child labor to submit to the *Franklin Post*, the school newspaper; four students wrote Phil Knight, two wrote Michael Jordan, and one each wrote the Disney Co., President Clinton, and local activist Max White.

Jonathan Parker borrowed an idea from an editorial cartoon included in the "Justice: Do It NIKE!" reader. He found an old Nike shoe and painstakingly constructed a wooden house snuggled inside, complete with painted shingles and stairway. He accompanied it with a poem that reads in part:

There is a young girl who lives in a shoe.
Phil Knight makes six million she makes just two.

When Nike says "just do it" she springs to her feet,
stringing the needle and stitching their sneaks.
With Nike on the tongue, the swoosh on the side,
the sole to the bottom, she's done for the night . . .
When will it stop? When will it end? Must I, she says,
toil for Nike again?

The "sculpture" and poem have been displayed in my class-room, and have sparked curiosity and discussion in other classes, but Jonathan hopes also to have it featured in the display case outside the school library.

Cameron, a multisport athlete, was inspired by a *Los Angeles Times* article by Lucille Renwick, "Teens' Efforts Give Soccer Balls the Boot," about Monroe High School students in L.A. who became incensed that all of their school's soccer balls came from Pakistan, a child labor haven. The Monroe kids got the L.A. school board there to agree to a policy to purchase soccer balls only from countries that enforce a prohibition on child labor.

Cameron decided to do a little detective work of his own, and discovered that at the five Portland schools he checked, 60% of the soccer balls were made in Pakistan. He wrote a letter to the school district's athletic director alerting him to his findings, describing conditions under which the balls are made, and asking him what he intended to do about it. Cameron enclosed copies of Sydney Schanberg's "Six Cents an Hour" article, as well as the one describing the students' organizing in Los Angeles—hinting further action if school officials didn't rethink their purchasing policies.

One student, Daneeka, bristled at the assignment, and felt that regardless of what the project sheet said, I was actually forcing them to take a position. She boycotted the assignment and enlisted her mother to come in during parent conferences to support her complaint. Her mother talked with me, read the assignment sheet, and—to her daughter's chagrin—told her to do the project. Daneeka and I held further negotiations and agreed that she could take her learning "outside the walls of the classroom" by "visiting" on-line chat rooms where she could discuss global sweatshop issues and describe these conversations in a paper. But after letting the assignment steep a bit longer, she found a more personal connection to the issues. Daneeka decided to write Nike about their use of child labor in Pakistan as described in the Schanberg article. "When I was first confronted with this assignment," she wrote in her letter, "it really didn't disturb me. But as I have thought about it for several weeks, child labor is a form of slavery. As a young black person, slavery is a disturbing issue, and to know that Nike could participate in slavery is even more disturbing." Later in her letter, Daneeka acknowledges that she is a "kid" and wants to stay in fashion. "Even I will continue to wear your shoes, but will you gain a conscience?"

"JUST GO WITH THE FLOW"

At the end of the global sweatshop unit, I added a brief curricular parenthesis on the role of advertising in U.S. society. Throughout the unit, I returned again and again to Cameron Robinson's "masks" metaphor:

> The world is full of many masks,
> the hard part is seeing beneath them.

I'd received a wonderful video earlier in the year, *The Ad and the Ego,* that, among other things, examines the "masking" role of advertising—how ads hide the reality of where a product comes from and the environmental consequences of mass consumption. The video's narrative is dense, but because of its subject matter, humor, and MTV-like format, students were able to follow its argument so long as I frequently stopped the VCR. At the end of part one, I asked students to comment on any of the quotes from the video and to write other thoughts they felt were relevant. One young woman I'll call Marie, wrote in part: "I am actually tired of analyzing everything that goes on around me. I am tired of looking at things at a deeper level. I want to just go with the flow and relax."

I'd like to think that Marie's frustration grew from intellectual exhaustion, from my continually exhorting students to "think deep," to look beneath the surface—in other words, from my academic rigor. But from speaking with her outside of class, my sense is that the truer cause of her weariness came from constantly seeing people around the world as victims, from Haiti to Pakistan to Nepal to China. By and large, the materials I was able to locate (and chose to use) too frequently presented people as stick figures, mere symbols of a relationship of domination and subordination between rich and poor countries. I couldn't locate resources—letters, diary entries, short stories, etc.—that presented people's work lives in the context of their families and societies. And I wasn't able to show adequately how people in those societies struggle in big and little ways for better lives. The overall impression my students may have been left with was of the unit as an invitation to pity and help unfortunate others, rather than as an invitation to join with diverse groups and individuals in a global movement for social justice—a movement already underway.

Another wish-I'd-done-better, that may also be linked to Marie's comment, is the tendency for a unit like this to drift toward good guys and bad guys. In my view, Nike is a "bad guy," insofar as it reaps enormous profits as it pays workers wages that it knows full well cannot provide a decent standard of living. They're shameless and they're arrogant. As one top Nike executive in Vietnam told Portland's *Business Journal*, "Sure we're chasing cheap labor, but that's business and that's the way it's going to be"—a comment that lends ominous meaning to the Nike slogan, "There is no finish line." My students' writing often angrily targeted billionaire Nike CEO Phil Knight and paired corporate luxury with Third World poverty. But corporations are players in an economic "game" with rules to maximize profits, and rewards and punishments for how well those rules are obeyed. I hoped that students would come to see the "bad guys" less as the individual players in the game than as the structure, profit imperatives, and ideological justifications of the game itself. Opening with the Transnational Capital Auction was a good start, but the unit didn't consistently build on this essential systemic framework.

Finally, there is a current of self-righteousness in U.S. social discourse that insists that "we" have it good and "they" have it bad. A unit like this can settle too comfortably into that wrong-headed dichotomy and even reinforce it. Teaching about injustice and poverty "over there" in Third World countries may implicitly establish U.S. society as the standard of justice and affluence. There is poverty and exploitation of workers here, too. And both "we" and "they" are stratified based especially on race, class, and gender. "We" here benefit very unequally from today's frantic pace of globalization. As well, there are elites in the Third World with lots more wealth and power than most people in this society. Over the year, my global studies curriculum attempted to confront these complexities of inequality. But it's a crucial postscript that I want to emphasize as I edit my "race to the bottom" curriculum for future classes.

Enough doubt and self-criticism. By and large, students worked hard, wrote with insight and empathy, and took action for justice—however small. They were poets, artists, essayists, political analysts, and teachers. And next time around, we'll all do better.

STUDENT POETRY ON THE GLOBAL SWEATSHOP: "HOPE TOMORROW WILL BE BETTER"

Number one in moneymaking.
Number one in sweatshop, overworked, and underpaid labor.

Increasing prices of products.
Increasing the number of factories.

Killing new styles promoted on TV.
Killing Pakistani kids' lives producing those products.

Eager to be paid millions of dollars.
Eager to be paid to survive winters and summers.

—Tara Wyatt
11th grade

THE STITCHING SHED

Day by day
Sit in the stitching shed.
Stitch by stitch.
Hope I could do faster,
Do faster to earn money,
Do faster so my brother
won't cry because of hunger,

Do faster so my family can
survive.

Stitch by stitch.
One by one.
I want to cry out,
But can't do that.
Family still there.
I want to give up.
But can't do that.
My family needs food!!
Can't do it faster.
My hands hurt.
I hear the voices through the winds.
They tell me to let go of the pain.
Oh, God! I am too young to give up.
The hope eases my pain.
Hope tomorrow will be better.

—Tho Dong
11th grade

DEAR BARBIE

Dear Barbie

How are you? What will you do today?
Will you work all day for pennies an hour?
Or will you play in your dreamhouse
made from the sore hands of little girls?
Barbie, will you make up your perfect,
pretty face that has become more
important than the sad faces
that made you who you are?
Are you too good, Barbie?
So good that the very hands that put
you together will never have
you for their own?
Do you even care?
Dear, dear Barbie.

—Sandee Harris
10th grade

TO THE DAN DEE COMPANY:

To whom should I pay the money for this Valentine bear in a can? To you? For every careful, perfectly sewn-in thread that the under-aged, underpaid children sew day after day? Yet you get the profits and make a living off this trinket. And every time you sit at the table with your family and eat the food paid for by your Valentine profits, your children are eating the pain and agony and time it took to make this trinket. Tasting the poisonous fumes the little Chinese girl inhaled, destroying cells which could have been used in school for her education. Whom should I pay? The girl, for the four mile daily walk, for the sores and blisters on her feet as she walks barefoot? Or maybe I should pay you for taking your time to place your name on this gift? And to the company of Dan Dee: I would just like to know whom I should pay? You?

—Nailah Roaché

Note: At their request, some of the students' names used in this article have been changed.

3—Writing the Word and the World

Linda Christensen

I've heard that Alice Walker said if we write long enough and hard enough, we'll heal ourselves. Maybe that's true. But I've come to see that it's not enough.

I've watched kids write through rapes, parental abuse, the humiliation of the SATs and tracking, the daily bombardment of "you are not pretty enough, strong enough, smart enough" messages from commercials, budget cuts that mean they won't get any loans or scholarships for college—but these same kids passed through this room every day and headed back into the world that wounded them. I was patching them up and sending them out without tools to understand—or stop—the brawl they lived with.

For the past fifteen years I've worked toward empowering students to use their own voices, to plumb their lives for stories, poems, essays, to engage them in a dialogue with their peers about their writing and about literature. And I've succeeded.

Students learned to sing their lives through writing. They used writing to take the power out of their pain. Listen as Arne begins to understand his parents' divorce:

> Mom carried his name around
> like a phantom pain until she had him
> amputated
> to cut off what doesn't exist takes paperwork
>
> Now I see things after the break
> were burrs
> clinging to her flesh
> Maybe she smelled his carpenter sweat
> in the sheets and winced
> Maybe the little memories
> were sand in her shoes
> I see now
> Every chance to dismantle a memory
> was taken—
> a painting of the wall
> love poems slipped under things

maybe one side of a record
she doesn't listen to anymore

There is a time
to cut off fingers when
holding hands is wind
on chapped lips

I tried to stay with Father
and never saw why she didn't too
Now I see my mother as a lover
and the name she dropped
a phantom

Whitney, a "remedial" freshman, bopped in and out of class, and in and out of school, chose cigarette breaks over English for the first semester, but discovered a community where she could write, and hence talk, about her life and people would listen. This is what Whitney wrote after reading a short story about a mother who verbally abused her daughter:

My mother's not an alcoholic. Well, she likes to drink when she gets home from work at night because she's tired and the wine helps her relax . . . I don't like it when she drinks too much and comes into my room late at night and shakes me out of bed with her anger.

Rochelle, a junior in my Literature in American History class, wrote and shared stories from her family and her neighborhood. We grew to love her old Aunt Macy who handed down wisdom about sex, fried chicken, microwaves, and tardies: "Chile, you just don't know how easy you got it."

These kids can write. They are honest. They are truth tellers. They have discovered the power of writing down their stories. Admittedly, Gayleen didn't join in and neither did Marcus, but most students learned to love writing and sharing their lives.

When students read their pieces to the class, we gave them warm and sympathetic responses. We discussed where the writing "worked"; we elected lines we particularly liked; we noted how Justine used active verbs; the strong voice in Margo's piece; we asked questions in places where the writer needed to do more work, more thinking. And this was successful: students felt they were part of a community that cared about them. They learned something about style by hearing other student models and discussing the techniques in those pieces, and they began to understand how the published writers we read in class wrote their novels, short stories, poems.

In my classes today, we continue to look at our lives and we still respond on both the technical and the human level to each other's writing, but we also study those essays, stories, and poems as a text to get at the social roots of our feelings of alienation and inadequacy, as well as our possibility for joy and resistance (see Shor, Freire and Macedo 1987).

What emerged from students' writing over the years is that often their problems are experienced individually. Any failure or shortcoming appears to be the result of a personal deficiency. Sometimes it is—but often it is not. For example, in Literature in American History, a class I coteach with Bill Bigelow, students came back devastated after taking the PSAT. As far as they were concerned there was no need to go to college because this test confirmed their stupidity.

Rochelle said, "The words on that test had letters arranged in ways I'd never seen before. There were math problems that Mr. Chappelle hadn't taught us, formulas my pencil had never scratched out. I just wanted someone to give me a cool drink of water and let me go on my way."

Students blamed themselves for their poor performance or blamed their teachers. "Well, if you'd taught us subject-verb agreement instead of writing, I'd have a better score on the verbal section."

Because so much feeling was generated around the test, we said, "Okay. Let's look at what these tests are all about. Write about some test you've taken. It might have been the PSAT or a math or English test or the yearly Portland Achievement Levels Test. Choose either a good or bad testing experience. Think back to the experience and try to re-create it. What was the test on? How were you prepared for it? What did you feel like before you took the test? During the test? After the test? Tell it as a story or use the anecdote as your entrance into an essay on testing. Be sure to pay attention to the kinds of feelings you experienced around the testing situation." We wrote in silence for the rest of the period.

The next day the students, Bill, and I sat in a circle and read our papers. (Bill and I write each assignment and share our papers—good, bad, and mediocre—along with the rest of the class. This is an important point. If we didn't write and share, we would hold ourselves above and beyond the community we are trying to establish.) As we read, we took notes on the common themes that emerged from our stories. We asked students to listen for how the tests made people feel about themselves, their peers, and those in authority—the test givers. It became obvious that Joseph's problem was Claire's problem was Mindy's problem. Students who were privately stung with humiliation discovered that they weren't alone, although where or with whom they placed the blame differed sharply. After all the papers were shared, we read over our notes and quickly wrote summaries on the similarities and differences between our pieces.

This discussion circle, or "read-around" as it's become known, is the heart of our class. Here the crucible melts students' lives and society together. Here the tools are forged to understand the brawl and what must be done to end it. Here the students' experiences of joy and resistance became a collective text from which to discuss the possibilities of social change. In previous years, students would have shared their stories and learned that they weren't the only ones who felt stupid after taking the tests, but since we left our sharing at that point, they might have gone home saying, "Boy, I'm sure in a class with a bunch of dummies" or "Well, I didn't do so hot on my PSAT, but then neither did Bea and she's supposed to be so smart."

In the discussion circle, kids understand they aren't alone, but they also learn to ask why they had these similar experiences. After the testing paper, we began to question why they all came away from their test experiences feeling threatened and stupid.

Trisa opened the discussion by reading her summary: "[Tests] caused us to feel nervous, made us feel stupid, conditioned us to testing and to being told what to do without questioning, made us compete against each other, fostered an 'I'm better than you attitude,' appeared fair, but made us internalize the fault."

Students wrestled with their feelings and their stories. Matthew picked examples from classmates' papers to show how tests and schools foster competition, how grades are used as rewards or punishments instead of measuring how much was leaned. Elan referred back to Christen's and Amy's papers to show how some of us had internalized the blame—if only we'd worked harder we'd have done a better job or received a higher score. Students continued to call on each other and to raise questions for the rest of the period.

As productive as this discussion was, it left students without a broader context in which to locate their feelings and new understandings. They needed to explore where these so-called aptitude and achievement tests originated and whose interests they served. These youngsters, still smarting from their private battle with ETS's brainchild, were introduced to Carl Brigham and other testing gurus in David Owens's chapter "The Cult of Mental Measurement" from his book *None of the Above.* In "dialogue journals" students read and fought with Brigham, who was hired by the college board in 1925 to develop an intelligence test for college admissions (see Owens 1985).

Students were shocked by what they discovered about Brigham: He published in the same journal as Adolph Hitler and was convinced that there should be stronger immigration laws to protect the "contamination of the American intellect" by "Catholics, Greeks, Hungarians, Italians, Jews, Poles, Russians, Turks, and—especially—Negroes." The selections printed below are taken from student dialogue journals. They first quote from Owens's book and argue, agree, paraphrase, or question it in the comments that follow. Christen, a thoughtful young black woman, began to see connections between the present:

> In his book he [Brigham] argued passionately for stricter immigration laws, and within American borders for an end to the "infiltration of white blood into the Negro."
> This struck me because even though slavery has been over, they enslave us differently so that we will still be seen as dumb.
> Brigham reserved most of his considerable scorn for Blacks, whose arrival in America he described as the "most sinister development in the history of this continent."
> They could have kept us where we were in the first place. As far as I'm concerned we were better off.

Omar took offense at Brigham assuming he had the right or knowledge to control some else's life:

> . . . the problem of eliminating "defective strains in the present population" remained. One solution, Brigham believed, was intelligence testing. By carefully sampling the mental power of the nation's young people, it would be possible to

identify and reward those citizens whose racial inheritance had granted them a superior intellect endowment.

How does he know defective? Who appointed him population watchdog? Sounds like Hitler!

Omar also questioned the items appearing on Brigham's early Army Mental Tests which were used to assign recruits jobs during World War I:

Look at the Alpha Test 8!
The Pierce Arrow car is made in:
Buffalo Detroit Toledo Flint

This sounds like Trivial Pursuit! It's also very racist, no real thinking required, just trivia.

In another excerpt, Margo bites back:

Brigham did not advocate the reestablishment of human bondage. He did believe that Blacks should be barred from mixing freely in White society.

What does this mean? What's the difference? Is he but trying to be a nice bigot?

In recent years the College Board and Educational Testing Service have described Brigham's virulent racism as a sort of irrelevant eccentricity.

His racism is by no means irrelevant. He has a strong grasp on who goes to college and therefore a grasp on the future of the country. I would say that is fairly relevant.

The dialogue journal allowed students to critique and question Brigham and ETS. In some cases they related it to their own experiences. A number of their questions echoed Omar's: "Who appointed him watchdog?"

Who indeed? It would be misleading for students to lay all blame for the inequities of testing at Brigham's doorstep. Through role plays, film, and source readings, we explored the changes in mass education in the early twentieth century and looked critically at those groups needing Brigham's tests as a sorting mechanism to preserve the status quo (see Bowles and Gintis 1976; Nasaw 1979).

We followed up this historical study by analyzing correlations between today's income levels and SAT scores: on average, the higher the parent's income, the higher the score a student "earned" on the SAT. Then we looked at some of the sample vocabulary used in typical analogy questions:

HEIRLOOM: INHERITANCE:
(A) payment: currency
(B) belongings: receipt
(C) land: construction
(D) legacy:bill
(E) booty: plunder.

After we pulled a few analogies apart and made some of our own from each other's background and neighborhood experiences, it became clear to students that the SAT questions measured access to upper-class experience, not ability to make appropriate analogies. The test vocabulary did not reflect the everyday experience of these inner-city kids, and they said so. Through class discussion, it became evident that the test was biased toward the privileged and functioned to segregate students on the basis of social class.

After scrutinizing the test, the students concluded that Brigham's grandchild didn't measure their intelligence nor would it predict their success in college. When the test became demystified, when it was no longer a bogeyman, when the kids saw it as an obstacle, ETS no longer held the same kind of power over them.

Trisa and her classmates became skeptical of tests, of any measure or device used to include some and exclude others. Beyond that, they sharpened their analysis of who would want devices which promoted and protected inequality.

When students see either their lives or history as inevitable, they are not encouraged to work for change. By studying problems in their lives and by rooting those problems historically, students are able to diagnose this society, uncover inequality, and explore the reasons for its existence.

At our end-of-the-year class evaluation, Elan said, "Before I took this class, I hated school. I never tried. I'd never written a poem or story. I accepted what teachers told, what I read. Now I question everything. And I write stories and poems for the fun of it."

And Justine, who argued all year with us, said, "I thought, god dammit, I don't want to be conscious. I just want to eat candy and ride the swings. But I learned how to think."

Claire said, "I learned from everyone in the class . . . I learned how to think differently by listening to other people's stories, by seeing their growth."

Now all of this sounds great, but a problem remains. While kids learned to question, while they broke down their senses of isolation and alienation, while they pushed toward a greater knowledge of how this society functions, they were moved less often to hope and action and more often to awareness and despair than I felt comfortable with.

During the class evaluation, Amy, who plans on becoming a teacher so she can "help change the world," sat quietly and didn't volunteer her feelings about the class. After everyone else shared, I asked her what she'd thought of this course. She offered one of the strongest critiques. "You need to include some more positive aspects. We can't live in a world where it's all negative. I became overwhelmed and angry. I felt like I couldn't take it."

When Bill and I talked with her after class, she said she could see our optimism and hope, but she didn't see where it originated. She wanted to know who else was working to make it a better world. She wanted to hear those people speak, to find out what vision they had for a different society. As she spoke, I began drafting changes for next year's classes, ones that put kids in touch with real people who haven't lost their hope, who still fight and who plan to win.

Sometimes I remind myself that I'm an English teacher and I question whether I'm straying too far afield. I know my pasture is broader than nouns and verbs, stories, poems and essays. Where does the world begin that is within my terrain? How can I teach *House of the Spirits* without teaching about Chile's socialist President Salvador Allende and General Pinochet's coup which ended that country's democracy? My students now reach beyond the beauty, power, and seduction of their descriptive writing; they are probing for the whys and asking, "Is this the way it has to be?" I'm no longer tranquilizing their pain through writing; I'm helping them develop the tools to understand the causes of those wounds. Now I want to work toward hope and transformation. I haven't lost optimism. Like Amy, I teach because I want to change the world.

REFERENCES

Bowles, S. and H. Gintis. 1976. *Schooling Capitalist America: Educational Reform and the Contradictions of Economic Life.* New York: Basic Books.

Freire, P. and D. Macedo. 1987. *Literacy: Reading the Word and the World.* Massachusetts: Bergin and Garvey Publishers, Inc.

Nasaw, D. 1979. *Schooled to Order: A Social History of Public Schooling in the United States.* New York: Oxford University Press.

Owens, D. 1985. *None of the Above: Behind the Myth of Scholastic Aptitude.* Boston: Houghton Mifflin Company.

Shor, I. 1987. *Freire for the Classroom.* Portsmouth: Heinemann.

Shor, I. and P. Freire. 1987. *A Pedagogy for Liberation.* Massachusetts: Bergin & Garvey Publishers, Inc.

AN ACTIVIST FORUM I:
AWAKENING JUSTICE

Haywood Burns

Haywood Burns, courtesy of
Democracy and Education

When my grandfather was a boy, it was against the law—a crime against the state—to teach him to read. It was not without reasoned self-interest that so many American states carried on their books such penal statutes relating to African Americans. Frederick Douglass, the former slave and great human rights leader, marks his success in cleverly evading such laws as one of the key turning points on his road to liberation and the fight for the liberation of others. And so it has been and is for so many young children dreaming, reading, discovering, and awakening in our nation's ghettos, barrios, and reservations, and among the wretched of the earth around the world. Once they understand, they will never be the same.

And so it is that as a teacher I always put a great deal of emphasis on history. Educating others about the past is a necessary precondition to their understanding our present and appreciating how we have come to this sorry state of inequality and injustice. Helping others whom I teach and with whom I learn to this threshold permits them to understand better whether, when, and how they cross over and enter into action. The teaching is never solely about how the oppressed have become victims, though it is about that; it is also always about how people individually and in concert have made a difference and changed their situations. Thus, I teach not only about the roots of racial, sexual, class, and other forms of oppression, but also about the triumphs of the abolitionists; the suffragettes; the labor, civil rights, and antiwar movements; and all those who, with the knowledge of their condition, were able to change it for the better.

Caroline Heller

Caroline Heller, courtesy of
Therese Quinn

During a particularly intense discussion in one of the first classes I ever taught at an urban university—a course on literacy and society—one of my students, a young woman who taught first grade, said that she thought it was ridiculous for us to be talking on and on about the importance of literacy. She said that in our racist society, no matter how literate her first graders—all of them poor and black—would become, they'd still have a brutally difficult chance of finding comfort and safety and hope in their lives; while affluent white children, even those with low levels of literacy, would probably fare pretty well. Suddenly she was in tears.

The next day I had the opportunity to observe my student in her own classroom. She was a phenomenal teacher. The morning opened with a gathering on the rug during which her first graders talked about what had happened in their lives the day before. My student talked with them about her own previous day's struggles and triumphs—getting through a quarrel with her husband, watching her teenaged daughter play soccer. She showed her students a storybook called *Insects Are My Life!* that she'd just discovered at the library, explaining that she was drawn to the book because her youngest son loved insects and wanted one day to study them for a living. After reading it with them, she invited her students to write stories about their own passions or, if they hadn't yet mastered the alphabet, to dictate stories to parents visiting their classroom that day. Later that morning, she read their stories out loud, showering her first graders with compliments on the precision of their word choices and on the pride and vitality of their messages.

When I'm asked to describe what it means to teach for social justice, I guess—bottom line—that's it. My student, like thousands of teachers each day, has a covenant with her own students. The covenant is something akin to what James Baldwin called faith in "evidence of things not seen." In spite of raging doubt about the fairness of our society, my student lives her classroom life by a belief that a sense of decency might yet live in the American soul. Daily, in the particulars of classroom life, she and her students are staking their claim for that day and perhaps, just perhaps, are causing it to come sooner by cultivating their own classroom community, their affection and understanding for themselves and each other, their own precise and passionate voices.

Lisa Delpit

Lisa Delpit, courtesy of Studio 1210, Baltimore, Maryland

Recently, I've had conversations with several educators concerned about issues of social justice who are questioning just what their roles should be. What's more important, they ask, teaching skills and content or working to create a just society? I suppose my answer would have to be that for teachers, the teaching has to be primary. After all, no revolutionary society would have much use for a physician who was committed to social change but couldn't keep any patients alive!

I believe that teaching the skills and perspectives needed for real participation in a democratic society is one of the most revolutionary tasks that an educator committed to social justice can undertake. It is only through such education that we can hope to create a truly just society where the most disenfranchised of our citizens can gain access to the political power needed to change the world.

Mike Rose

Mike Rose, courtesy of *Democracy and Education*

Let me begin with an anecdote. I was talking recently with a talented young teacher—a third-grade teacher—who was complaining about a fifth-grade teacher in her school who, it seems, was a stickler for "standards": could children spell, punctuate, indicate paragraph breaks, and so on. This teacher made known her displeasure when children came out of the earlier grades without these skills somewhat in command. "My class," the third-grade teacher told me, "is not about academics. It is about student empowerment and building one community." She continued, positioning herself as an advocate for social justice and defining one fifth-grade teacher's concerns as conservative.

Now, of course, that fifth-grade teacher may well hold values that a lot of us would find offensive, and there are probably other things going on that play into the conflict. But what struck me—for I read and hear variations of it so frequently—is the way a number of educators on the Left have begun defining concerns for academic standards, disciplinary knowledge, and intellectual rigor as conservative. Put another way, we have allowed conservatives to appropriate those concerns, make them their own, and define them in their terms.

The irony in the case I just sketched was that the third-grade teacher, in fact, ran a classroom rich in reading, writing, and thoughtful discussion—a wonderful place. Yet, in the context of her school and the broader *political* context surrounding it, she virtually defined "academics" as *antithetical* to her mission. I think those of us concerned with social justice need to take back the discussion of "standards," "rigor," and "academics" from conservative spokespeople and reframe it in a way consonant with a social justice agenda.

Barbara T. Bowman

Barbara Bowman, courtesy of
Democracy and Education

Identification with others who share race, religion, or culture is as human as laughter and tears. Its value is particularly apparent when individuals feel vulnerable and underappreciated. For many, self-respect depends on and is filtered through the strength of the group: they gain power from the mantle of belonging. Ethnocentrism—or tribalism—grips people's emotions and gains their loyalties. It is a potent tool for building confidence and mobilizing energy.

Many teachers, recognizing the importance of pride in group membership, have become supporters of multicultural and ethnocentric curricula. However, sometimes they forget that prejudice is as easily learned as self-respect. Bigotry and intolerance are often the handmaidens of a high group esteem. If we are to have a civil society, teachers must understand not only the benefits of tribal identity but the evils of tribalism. Throughout the world we have ample evidence that when one's own group identity is given free range to denigrate that of others, the whole society suffers.

—Portraits: In The Raindrop

> In the raindrop, the ocean . . .
> Lao Tze

E very child born is infinite. Every moment, pregnant. Even now, we each have all-important possibility and potential, still: Take a breath, you are the universe.

Teacher. Warmer than the term "educator," more intimate: To call someone a teacher is to point to people touching people. Teachers open people to the world. They reveal the universe below the surface, the ocean in the raindrop. And if they are inspired, passionate, and persevering, they may show us the ways that we are each a spark of infinite possibility. The paths they illumine for us will not be stumble-free—we will still face the twists, and pits put there, the boulders, as well, that we drag along. But light starts the journey.

The bittersweet of a teacher and a moment of inspiration is this: A flash might leave just a lingering glow. Just memory, and no moving toward action. The flashes are indispensable—they can chart courses, fan spark into flame, at least leave dreams like afterglow. The best moments happen when some latent possibility roars forward, breathing something smoldering into combustion—someone silent speaks, a specific woman reveals her oceanic whole, a child claims space, ordinary people feel the keys in their hands. Some people join hands. Then all the world looms as possible home, to be loved and refurbished, nurtured and corrected. Teachers can move us to this recognition.

The challenge for teachers moving legions toward some more just place is to sail out from familiar harbors into the wild, deep, and unboundaried sea. Pressing past their knowns, our teachers pull us past ours, too. Audre Lorde (1984) asks, why accept "the mockeries of separations that have been imposed on us and which we so often accept as our own" (43)? Why, indeed, when the ocean in each of us will open unendingly, and best, when we move together as lusty and united as an army of lovers? And to and from each other as our lives thicken with that knowing. A teacher will be there at the beginning.

In this section—Portraits—all these stories are told. We see lights, fall into potholes, scrape against the rusty limits of our cells, and emerge, in a journey wrought by brave teachers telling stories about brave teachers who have changed and are changing this world. Leave your harbor, the whole wide ocean awaits.

REFERENCE

Lorde, A. 1984. *Sister Outsider.* Crossing Press: Freedom, CA.

4—School Days

Nelson Peery

Nelson Peery from *Centralian Year Book*, 1942
Background, left to right: H. Franklin, N. Peery,
P. Dvorak, J. Dyste, C. Curry, B. Beed, D. Ditschler
in foreground.

This is the story of three black youths whose lives changed for a moment in 1941 because of two democratic and outstanding teachers. Their commitment to the students and to teaching could not begin to breach those ramparts concretized from the muck of three hundred years of slavery, poverty, and discrimination. Their commitment, though, illuminated the possible—and that possibility was a beautiful contrast to that terrible time of segregation and violence.

Chuck, Hank, and I attended Central High in Minneapolis, Minnesota. Central was a solidly working-class school. More than half of the 4,500 students attended first-rate shop classes that prepared them to go on to technical schools or to enter the semi-skilled and skilled sectors of the working class. Those who had the financial wherewithal or outstanding grades went to college preparatory classes.

The twelve black students who attended Central High that year were scattered through the grades. There were only the three of us—plus one young black woman in our class. Ignored by the students and the teachers, the sense of isolation that most teenagers feel was intensified to the nth degree by our poverty and the all-pervasive, if unofficial, segregation. The students were not hostile toward us. We were not in their world. There was no common space where we could get to know one another. As for the teachers, 1941 was the apex of "a white man's country" ideology and most of them expressed it consciously or not. The white students were trained for white men's jobs and, tolerated so long as we knew and kept our place, black students trained for black folks' jobs.

We could not join the Hi-Y or the drama club. We could not attend the Friday afternoon hop. Except for sports, the school excluded us from extracurricular activities. Our participation in the sports program was in the interest of the school and some of it was open to us. Our tiny group dominated the football, track, basketball, and boxing teams. We knew better than to try out for tennis, swimming, or any activity that tended toward social closeness or equality.

A few of the black students, including my older brother who retired as an astrophysicist, had their goals in mind when they were sixteen. Some of them kept their grades up and made it into university prep classes. Chuck and Hank and I, like most of the black students, attended shop classes. There, we would learn the necessary reading, writing, and arithmetic to put us on the labor market with the entrance skills to become good workers.

Chuck, Hank, and I had been together since seventh grade. We were preparing to enter our senior year with very little direction as to where to go from there. We did not realize it at the time, but our long, if loose friendship grew from our individual strivings to express ourselves culturally. Throughout our school years, no one looked for any special talent in us and there was no way for us to ask if they saw any.

Moody, sometimes choked up with asthma, often violent, Chuck was a talented artist. The most sensitive of our group, he felt the social oppression more acutely and reacted with the impotence of black youth. He withdrew behind the barricade of social hostility. His grades were terrible and he was always on the verge of expulsion from school. Chuck lived with his parents, brother, and six sisters in a big, ramshackle house on our block. His mother, recognizing his artistic need to be alone, assigned the attic with its one bare bulb to him. He would detach himself from us for days and, secluded in his attic hideaway, draw or patiently carve wood or linoleum cuts.

Hank lived in another black enclave about six blocks from us. Introspective, quiet, studious, and brilliant, the only child of his widowed mother, his secret love was poetry. We knew he liked to read and write poetry, but he never discussed it with us for fear we would think him a sissy. Hank got good grades. He studied hard and believed more than the rest of us that somehow he would find an opening.

I lived with my parents, grandmother, and six brothers. My father, a railway mail clerk, had as good and as stable a job as a black man could expect. My mother, a former teacher, spread herself thin trying to run the household and guide each of us onto the path of education. I was adrift, with no idea where I was going or why. I got A's in the classes I liked and failed those I didn't—which were the majority.

Our day began with the black students gathering near my house. It wasn't for physical protection. Our little black neighborhood had grown until it reached within a few blocks of the school. We knew that the ten or twelve of us appeared threatening simply by being together. Our walk to school was a ritual of solidarity and a bit of defiance to sustain us during the day.

Central High was just one of our schools. Another was the corner where we hung out, soaking up the street wisdom of the older guys. They were hanging out on the corner because they were without jobs. With plenty of time to talk, and no power to change anything, they were our philosophers. As discriminatory and racist as the city was, their inability to find work made it seem even worse. That want of confidence in the future cut away at whatever secret belief we might still have held that if we studied and got good grades, we would have a chance at success.

Our street-corner school was life itself. Not a day went by but we learned an object lesson as to our social worth. By the time we were fifteen, we had already learned what was meant by white men's jobs and colored men's jobs. Even the lowest of occupations reflected this. The white man drove the coal truck; the black man carried the coal. It was more than making a mockery of education. It engendered in us a defiance expressed as Why get an education when petty criminals had more money and more social respect than the college graduate who sorted mail at the post office?

Entering our senior year, we could choose an elective course. After talking it over, Hank and I signed up for a class in Shakespeare. He had already developed a love for the plays and the sonnets. I think I took the class because Paul Robeson made such a hit playing Othello in England. His triumph made Shakespeare appear democratic or at least color-blind. Then too, in our street corner culture, it would be nice to be able to drop a quote when it was effective. Partly, I simply wanted to learn why so many people loved Shakespeare and why his works have endured for so long.

It was an elite, elective class. As far as we knew, no black student had ever taken the course before. When we entered the classroom, heads turned. The teacher scowled at us, then looked at the class roster. Realizing that we belonged there, he coldly indicated empty seats in the back of the room. No one had to tell us we were in the wrong place, or ask why black kids were in Shakespeare instead of shop.

There were many teachers who practically ignored us. This teacher was different. He was vicious. He never called on me except to embarrass me. We were reading *Hamlet* and going through a soliloquy in Act I. As one student finished, he looked about the room. His eyes settled on me, and he nodded that I should continue the reading.

"Within a month,
Ere yet the salt of most unrighteous tears
Had left the flushing in her galled eyes,
She married. O, most wicked speed, to post
With such dexterity to incestuous sheets!"

"Now, Nelson, tell the class what you think that means."

I thought for a moment. If I answered the way every student understood it, it would prove how vulgar we blacks were. If I didn't answer, he would give me a fail for the day. I took the second option.

"I don't know."

"If you intend to stay in this class, you are going to have to come prepared to answer questions. That's fail for the day."

I knew he wanted me out of the class and there was no way for me to pass the course. I began to skip the class, or sit there reading a book or gazing out the window.

Hank fared a little better. Thin, quiet, and light-skinned, perhaps he didn't seem quite the "surly Negro" that I exemplified. However, I stayed in the class, partly because dropping out would have meant fail and partly because I liked reading the plays despite the teacher.

They were reading *Macbeth* when I sauntered into the class late and slumped into my seat. I suddenly realized there was a new teacher. She glanced at the roll book and said softly, "Please take one of the seats up front where we can hear you."

She sounded friendly enough. I went to the second row and opening my book, slumped into the chair.

"Will you read from page 30, line 11."

"Methought I heard a voice cry Sleep no more!
Macbeth does murder sleep—the innocent sleep,
Sleep that gathers up the raveled sleave of care."

She held up her hand for me to stop.

"I think this is the most beautiful metaphor in the English language. Doesn't it call to mind the safety of home and mother who gathers up and mends the raveled sweater to keep you warm?"

I nodded. She smiled. It was a beautiful thought. I smiled at her and suddenly I loved Shakespeare and metaphors.

Miss Setterburg was born to teach Shakespeare. She looked the part: blue-veined, blond—to me, pure English. She taught as if her mission was to teach us to love the things she loved. Her class was a turning point for me. Suddenly, I wanted not only to read what others wrote, but to write, too.

Posted on the bulletin board of every classroom, everyone knew about the national scholastic contests. When Chuck saw the categories for the competition in art, he wanted to enter some of his work. He wasn't sure how since he didn't have the grade average to be in the art class. He got bad grades because he didn't see any reason to get good grades. His bad grades automatically routed him to the shop classes. He didn't do any better in shop classes. He didn't want to learn to be a good machinist. He was an artist, though neither he nor anyone else understood this. Besides, he knew very well there was no work for black youths, no matter what school preparation they had. Finally, he took a few of his woodcuts to the art instructor who dutifully sent them in to the contest. He won first prize and the embarrassed school administration transferred him into the art class.

If Chuck could do it with very little help, maybe we could do something too. Encouraged, Hank and I told Miss Setterberg of our desire to learn to write. Delighted, she encouraged us to enter a writing class. Hank and I applied for, and after struggling with the school administration, joined the creative writing class.

The teacher, Abigail O'Leary, reoriented the lives of many

students during her career. For me, perhaps more than for Hank, her class was a watershed. I began to understand Chuck as Miss O'Leary forced me to deal with myself. His aggressiveness covered his lack of self-confidence. His seeming lack of ambition covered the fact that he, and most of us, had given up just at the point where we should have begun. His aloof and withdrawn attitude covered his conviction that he could not compete with those whom the schools, from first grade on, guaranteed scholastic success. Perhaps his teachers felt they should spend all possible time with those who were ahead and trying to stay ahead. Chuck met their seeming disregard for him with a scathing, withdrawn "leave me alone" attitude. They could not understand or did not want to understand that the black kids were in school because they wanted to learn. Taught in a thousand not too subtle ways that they couldn't learn, they very often didn't.

The few teachers who earnestly tried to develop some of the more promising but backward black students did not realize what an integrated, ramified set of problems they faced. Each problem positioned to prevent the resolution of another, this complex of problems appeared as a dichotomy. This complex of problems appeared irresolvable without wholehearted effort by the student. This dichotomy became a part of the social outlook of the student, and even when the teachers wanted to help, they very often couldn't.

Miss O'Leary attacked these attitudes one at a time. She knew I wanted to do it, or I wouldn't have been there. The first thing I had to learn was that I could do it. She accomplished this by alternate praise, harsh criticism, threats and praise again. She knew that once assured of their worth, students would rather be beaten than ignored.

Chuck didn't have it as good. After the brief glory of winning the art contest, the old pattern reemerged. Ignored at Central, after being assured of his worthlessness, he never recovered. His teachers ignored him and he ignored them. Not paying attention in class escalated into skipping school. He began hanging out on the corner where they still congratulated him on his achievements in the scholastic world and, increasingly, in the street. He listened and learned from the petty criminals as they laughingly recounted their adventures.

Hank quietly integrated himself into the writing class. Considered a model student, he wrote poetry and handed his assignments in on time.

I tried to divide my time between the demands of school, especially the writing class, and hanging out with our little group of black Central High students. I knew I could not keep doing both, but was reluctant to give up either.

The high point of our writing class came when we organized to publish our literary magazine, *Quest*. The writing class gathered together and Miss O'Leary went over the mechanics of putting out the magazine. Elected by the students, Hank became business manager. I became assistant literary editor and Miss O'Leary asked the art teacher to allow Chuck to become the art editor. After warning her that Chuck was a troublemaker—a student with a low I.Q. who happened to have a narrow talent—the teacher released him.

The males on the editorial board were black, all the females were white. We understood that the hopes of all the black students, and Miss O'Leary's reputation (and perhaps her future) depended on what we did and did not do and what kind of magazine we published.

The three of us changed during that period—especially Chuck. Never satisfied with his work, he spent days in his attic. Even after we approved them, he threw away sketches and woodcuts and started again. Hank wrote, penny pinched, and recorded every cent. I read everything I could find on short stories and essays. We stayed after school and worked. *Quest* was our tiny window to a new life. Miss O'Leary beamed and encouraged us and generally let us find our way.

We met all the deadlines, and sent the magazine to the printer. Then the tensions eased. For the next two weeks, we anxiously awaited the announcements from Columbia University. They came Monday morning as scheduled. For the nineteenth consecutive year, National Scholastic chose *Quest* as the best high school literary magazine in the country. In addition, Hank's concise, terse poetry won a first prize. My short story and essay took first prize. Chuck's woodcut and ink sketch took first prizes. Every high school in the city was aware of the composition of our board and the prizes we won.

The congratulations finally ended and we settled back into our school routine. Chuck, who hadn't missed a day of school for over a month, began hanging out on the corner. It seemed as if the brief moment of fame followed by a return to teachers who clearly disliked him and subjects that were alien to his world, was the final straw. Chuck dropped out of school six months before graduation. He probably would not have made it. Hank graduated with honors. I graduated primarily because the Army Reserve called me up and all members of the armed forces graduated.

Asthma kept Chuck out of the war against the Axis. Instead, he deepened his private war with society. Denied a place in America, step by step he sank into the wartime underworld of prostitution. He became a pimp, and from what I gathered after the war, a brutal one. At any rate, shortly before the end of the war, two of his women decided they had had enough and murdered him. The coup de grace was an ice pick through the eye. A life so full of promise at seventeen ended in disgrace at twenty-three.

Hank, drafted into the all-black, segregated 92nd Infantry Division, went overseas to fight in Italy. Wounded in 1944, he spent a few months in the hospital and returned to combat. Hank was a poet, not a foot soldier. His letters were full of resentment of the white Southern officers, the segregation and the coarseness of army life. Finally discharged in 1945, he returned home totally crushed by war and a brutal world of discrimination that was not in the least interested in poetry. Staggering through a series of disastrous marriages and declining jobs, Hank ended up changing tires at a filling station. A gentle, talented life so full of promise at eighteen ended unnoticed at forty-five.

As for myself, I served four years in the infantry—in the all-black, segregated 93rd Division. In the twenty months I was in the South Pacific, I earned three campaign ribbons and four battle stars. I returned home a committed revolutionary and desperately plunged into the movement. Apart from deep socialist convictions, I hated the resurgent racism and growing fascist danger. Only later in life did I realize how much I needed the movement's discipline and sense of purpose. It stabilized me in my postwar battle with depression, alcohol, and its social consequences. At the time, I did not know how common that struggle was among combat veterans. By the time that battle was won, I was ideologically and theoretically committed to the movement and it had become the center of my life.

I often look back at those few months fifty-five years ago when two teachers gave the three of us a vision of social worth and contribution. Those few months were too short a time to make a difference. Perhaps if we could have had more time with them, things might have been different with Chuck and Hank. Maybe not—but we loved them for helping us create that beautiful moment.

5—"We'd All Be Holding Hands"—A Reentry Women's Learning Community

Diane Horwitz

> *I had a real traumatic childhood and I sort of escaped in reading, and reading was my security. When it got to be too much, or I just wanted to hide, I would spend the whole summer days in the library, because it was cool and it was quiet and I could escape the chaos and the heat. They didn't have air-conditioned libraries, but I remember how wonderful it would be: high ceilings, and they would have these big fans and you would walk in and feel instantaneous coolness and peace. It was like church to me.*
>
> *Judy Nowicki, age 38*

> *Reading was the greatest pleasure in life. I can remember when I was about four or five years old, and I don't know where I read my first book, but my cousin came and she said, "Next time I come I'm going to bring you a book," and we were way out in the country, so it was maybe a month that she came back, and she brought me a Little Golden Book, you know, the Mother Goose Books. I could not believe it. I treasured the book. I read it over and over.*
>
> *Cherie Davis, age 46*

Two women talking today about the act of reading with awe and reverence, each a high school dropout returned to school in middle age. Cherie, an African-American woman, grew up in the South. As a teenager, her family became part of the great black migration to the North. In their case, it was the need for a quick escape after her grandfather, an outspoken preacher, was "found in a ditch with a bag over his head and wire around his neck."

She remembers her high school on the south side of Chicago: "I don't think anybody even knew I was there. I was just quiet and to myself." And as for her parents when she told them of her decision to drop out: "It was just the daily trying to live that had their attention."

For Judy, growing up on the southwest side of Chicago, high school memories are vivid recollections of the desegregation struggles at her school, and of her mother and neighbors organizing school boycotts to oppose the movement. She recalls her mother saying: "Okay, fine, if you insist on the black kids being there, then our children will not." She was kept out of school for months, uneasy but listening "to mommy and all my friends' mommies and all the neighborhood moms that you grew up with that you trusted. They bandaged your knees when you fell down and your mom wasn't there, so how can you tell them what you're doing is wrong?" By the time the white children went back, Judy was weeks behind; unable to catch up, she left school and "went sort of downhill after that."

By the late 1980s, after pregnancies, marriages, low-wage jobs, unemployment, and, for one, a divorce and a period of time on Aid to Families With Dependent Children (AFDC), and following persistent efforts to get their high school general equivalency diplomas (GEDs), both women found themselves at a community college, about to enter formal schooling once again. But this time they began with the support of a women's community for learning program.

I started teaching at Moraine Valley Community College in 1971, and for several years I observed increasing numbers of adult women students in classes. They came into classes anxious and fearful. How could they possibly keep up with the younger students? How would their new role affect family relationships? They were worried about taking exams, being able to read and concentrate, finding their way around the campus, feeling old and out of place. Once settled into the school routine, however, these same women became the most active, serious, and challenging students. They built strong connections to the other adult women students in their classes. They frequently set the academic standards, wondered why the younger students were not as serious, and were appreciated by the faculty who valued their earnestness.

With this in mind, I initiated the Returning Women's Program in 1975 to provide support for reentry women and to create a space where adult women students could develop their intellectual talents in community with other women. I drew on a lifetime of activism in antiwar and civil rights struggles. My first involvement with the women's liberation movement was in a consciousness-raising group in New York City in 1968. Fifteen women met weekly, talking about everything: our childhoods and our work, our love and our sex lives, relationships with other women, and most of all, politics. We were all involved in the radical movements of the day: community organizing, antiwar activism, civil rights work. With thousands of other women, we discovered that "the personal was political": the everyday experiences of each person's life were situated deeply in a social context, and understanding this could be the stuff of a transformative education. Four years earlier in a different setting, miles away in Meridian, Mississippi, I had my first teaching experience in a Freedom School. I taught reading and writing to small children, typing to teenagers and adults. The school and my work were totally joined with the goals and dreams of a society free of racism.

My hope and confidence in the possibilities of democratic social change developed here; my understanding the importance of people organizing on their own behalf and learning to make decisions collectively concretized. I brought to education the values of collectivity, community, risk taking, respect for differences, and challenges to conventional ways of thinking. As a feminist, I place great value on women coming together to consider thoughtfully their experiences and the social forces that shape them. I know the energizing intellectual and personal growth that can take place in such groups. Like many other feminist teachers, I wanted to enable women students to participate in this adventure and wondered if this experience could be translated into more formal, institutional settings.

In the Returning Women's Program, students spend three mornings (or two evenings) together taking a block of three-credit courses: An Introduction to Communications, Introduction to Sociology, and Human Potentials. The classes complement each other. The communications course is basic freshman English, to help every reentry woman build her confidence and skill in more formal, standard writing. In sociology, we study the impact of the larger society on individual lives. We initiate extensive discussion of women's roles: talks about women's work inside and out of the home, about the changing nature of the family, about parenting in a world often unfriendly to children. Our far-ranging conversations explore the growing inequality in our society, the impact of poverty on people's lives, how jobs are changing, whether participation in voting is worthwhile. Students practice their writing skills in essays reflecting on these issues.

Human Potentials is an introductory psychology course that attempts to tie experiences in the program together by challenging women to examine and develop their potential, both academically and personally. It is here that much of the personal talk goes on: conversations about personal histories, academic worries, the difficulties in marriages, hopes and dreams. The women develop study skills, learn how to conquer test anxiety, try to figure out a plan for the coming years of their lives, and get support for difficult personal decisions. While the sociology course gives them a broad overview of structural barriers to women's lives, in psychology the daily meaning of those barriers are confronted. Here, too, writing skills are sharpened as women work on composing autobiographies. The faculty work together as a team to monitor progress of individual women, to integrate our curriculum, and to evaluate the program.

Feminist elements in the design and implementation of the program are central to its conception: building a women's community for support, the use of personal experiences both as starting points in the curriculum and throughout, discussion of women's roles, reading women authors, and teachers who are empathetic to adult women's issues. All of this draws on the power of women's self-organized consciousness-raising groups and the tradition of women's studies. Although many community colleges offer personal growth and reentry workshops for women, as well as a range of counseling and support services, this program integrates services (counseling, career development, referral services, tutoring, a child care center) with women's crucial first academic experience in college.

The Returning Women's Program provides opportunities for women to tell their stories, and for me, their teacher and increasingly their student, opportunities to listen and learn.

When Judy and Cherie came into the program, they found twenty-five other women in their class with shared memories of screwing up in high school, putting in little effort, getting poor grades, and failure. Many had hated school; few could remember teachers who were encouraging. For most, higher education for young women was viewed with suspicion, unnecessary, a waste. They were drawn to the Returning Women's Program because "it sounded comfy"; "you'll be going to the three classes together; it sounded like we'd all be holding hands." Judy, using the language of her children's elementary school, envisioned the program as a "contained classroom," staying with the same group all the time, a feeling of security, "kind of like a family."

Cherie felt invisible and silent in her high school, but she vividly recalls the first day in the women's program—chairs in a circle, each woman telling a story of why she is back in school, moving accounts of the past ten or thirty years of their lives in a few minutes. Another woman who had worried about not having a "road map or bread crumbs" to find her way around—or back home—thought after these first day disclosures: "Ahhh, I'm not out in that life raft alone."

As a teacher, I respect the process of introductions and I admire the risks taken—the chance to become visible and be heard, coupled with the danger of being exposed, vulnerable. Reentry students' stories are similar to Judy's and Cherie's. So many women who come to the community college are trying to rebuild their lives: women who want a second chance and a new direction; women claiming a place for themselves after years of raising families; women struggling off welfare, women whose marriages are falling apart; women who want to escape the poverty of dead-end, low-wage jobs; women who are victims of domestic violence. Education, they hope, may be a way up and a way out.

The bonds that begin to develop on the very first day grow and deepen over the course of a semester as the group engages in their common enterprise of shared work and learning. "It was like a little cocoon for me," observed another student, Sharon, "but the idea of being in a cocoon is that you are going through changes while you're in there, and then you spread your wings, and that's exactly what I think happened to each one of us."

I arrive at class to find that many women have been here for a half hour already, sitting and talking, creating a breathing space after the children are off to school. Phone trees were made and circulated. Students talk after school, on the weekends, at night when their kids are put to sleep. They know what it is like to miss class because of a child's school performance or illness. And they support each other, helping everyone to cope and keep going. Judy says, "We met at the library and we shared notes, and if you were sick or your kids were sick and you weren't in class, the copy machine was going big time and you made sure you wrote real well that day, so the person could understand your notes."

Study groups were formed; everyone had at least one other person to collaborate with; usually it was four or five. They worked together, pulling each other through hurdles:

Sharon: We would meet somewhere in the building—those little clusters of chairs they have out in the hallways—we would go over and quiz each other.

Renee: The day of the test, four people crammed me, and I got a B.

Mary: Didn't that feel good!

Evelyn: That brain was working big time.

Renee: It was four brains actually.

Kathy: Five, five!

Betty describes a way to remember information for an exam: The day before the test we were all there helping one another go over the bits and pieces that we were afraid we would forget and then when I would take a test, I would look at a question and remember who was telling me how to remember it, and I would look at that person, like they were going to actually sit there and tell me the answer. Okay, then I would write it down, because I would have the vision of her repeating it to me.

Commitment to each other grew as commitment to the learning process intensified; work was the link between them, the glue of their bonds, a kinship of like minds. So often I hear: "I'm hungry to learn." Their tales tell of nourishing and stimulating their brains ("My brain is like a sponge"), of the powerful intellectual experiences of ideas coming together, of discovering as Kathy laughed, "School could be fun." For the high school dropouts, Judy and Cherie, the passion for knowledge is powerful.

Judy: "I love the learning. I love to do the research. I could just spend hours reading and researching. When I have free time on my hands now, other women, my friends, they go to the mall. I go to the library. People think I'm nuts."

Cherie: "Once I understood it, it was like the overall picture. I started to like it, and before it was over, I fell madly in love with it. "

Passionate encounters with learning—what one woman described as "exhilaration"— reoriented student intentions. Sally came back because she knew her husband was going to leave the family and she had to be prepared for a job "in a hurry." She says: "But that wasn't the reason I did my work after a while. It was a whole world opened up for me. I was going to take a typing course or two, and then get a job. Then it just made me hungry for everything." The women's community fostered for her and others a sense of purpose and pleasure in intellectual adventure.

Conversation in the reentry women's classes is dynamic and propulsive—women reinforce and feed off of each other's ideas, often interrupting and finishing each other's sentences, idea building on idea. The talk is punctuated with laughter, often hilarity. "Ooh" and "aah" and "yes" and "that's right" and "I know what you mean" sprinkle the dialogue, infusing an affirming and supportive affection. "I love it!" "Great!" "Wonderful!"—exclamations of attestation, of recognition, of confirmation. The talk in class is often intense, emotional. There are frequent nonverbal gestures of support—a hand on someone's shoulder, an expression of recognition. Discussion is exploratory, dialogic, question posing. Women check things out. I notice in my own talk phrases such as "How's it going so far?" "Is this okay?" "What I'm hearing is"—words that establish connection, confirm understanding.

Voicing uncertainty, recognition that evolving thought is always tentative, raising questions—these are signs of involved learners. Empathy, caring, emotion, and connectedness in such discussions is a way of learning that can foster more equitable classrooms based on the cooperative development of ideas. A questioning voice encourages elaboration, gives space for another tentative student to enter the conversation. Cherie points out: "You know, even something as simple as going someplace. Directions—a man will simply *not* stop and ask directions. Even if he's lost, he just keeps on going . . . The first thing I think about is, let's stop and ask somebody and find out where we're at." The cliché about men not stopping to ask for directions is a metaphor for women's vulnerability, the possibility of not knowing, of uncertainty, of needing help, perhaps an openness to new information and a questioning spirit.

The Returning Women's Program creates a nurturing environment for learning; a women's community that is safe, personal, supportive; an intellectual community as well, one that is student-centered, holistic, collaborative, and challenging. And soon, women begin to feel they are "starting to get smart"—women who had sat silently in high school classes, who accepted C's from indifferent and hostile schools. "My skills kicked back in." "I realized I learned a lot from life." "I could do it!" Sally realizes she has the "answers": "I found out that I was starting to know the answers, whether I spoke or I didn't. When we were studying together I found out I had a mind. And I didn't just accept things that I thought I had no control over or no say."

The beginning of speaking up may have been as simple as realizing that when someone else spoke the same question was in her mind, or perhaps it was the first time a hand was raised. Judy declares: "I grew more in that semester than I had grown in all of my twenties and early thirties. I grew by leaps and bounds. Before I had all these self-doubts and all of a sudden, it was not just 'I'm going to do this program,' but 'I'm going to continue on.' It's not just going to be a two-year thing, but to go for four years."

After a semester in the program, women are "mainstreamed" (their word, not mine), integrated into the varied age and mixed-gender classrooms at the college. To keep the connections and support, many sign up for classes together.

Judy: "My second semester in a communications class, it was pretty much returning women but we had a couple of eighteen-year-old girls who needed a class at that time, and I think they felt this is going to be a piece of cake. We worked our butts off, and we really showed them, and they came out of there and said, 'How do you people do this?'"

They also began to see themselves through the eyes of their instructors. Judy continues: "And sometimes the instructors would rely on you and lean on you and always call on you. Or when they would throw out a question and there was a dead silence for two minutes, they would give you a pleading look." I recognize "that pleading look," my visual connection with the adult student who I can always count on to spark a discussion. Coming to school with feelings of insecurity about their abilities, inadequacies that came from being out of school for many years, with memories of indifferent high school classes and teachers, and low expectations from family, they were often surprised to discover that they were people as Judy says "who could cut it." For some women, it meant the beginning of questioning authority and experts. "Where did you get your stats?" one woman demanded. "Why was that question on the test?" another challenged a teacher.

One day, Evelyn asks the group, "Do you sit in the front row? I'm a front-rower. Here's the teacher; here's me." (She shows us with her hands; they are a few feet apart). It turns out that they are all "front-rowers." They are "naming" a phenomenon for me that I had observed for many years—in mixed-age classes, adults sit in front. They are taking a risk—of connection to the teacher, of opening themselves to dialogue and public interaction. For the reentry women, it is a statement of engagement, of seriousness. And serious they are. Judy calls herself a "maniac studier": "I was like a maniac. If you said read such and such chapter, I read and read it until I was quoting it in my sleep. I would study for tests in the shower in the morning." Sharon echoes this activity: "I would study when I was cooking dinner, and study when everyone else had gone to bed, and even after I went to bed at night. I can remember asking myself all these questions in my sleep." They packed their kids off to their mothers, took their books to their children's sports practice, read by the light in the car at the baseball field.

Some suffer from "A-tis." This was another naming event for me. Judy describes the phenomenon:

Wanda ties lived experience to "naming," to the deepening of consciousness: "Suddenly all these things I had been living all these years, I put labels on them. It was really making me face reality. When we got into poverty things, and you started putting up charts, it was like I was up here last year, and I'm way down here this year. This really hit home probably because it was so real. It made me look."

And Sally also describes this awakening: "My husband is mentally ill. I knew all the living with him, all the conditions, and all the horrible things, but when I would read it, I would say, 'That's it.' 'That's it!' I was learning the words to apply with my life; saying it almost makes what you've experienced real. Before you didn't know, because it was more personal."

And for Cherie: "When I saw some of the things, that the system has really oppressed people,and it wasn't all my fault. I had always felt ashamed of my race of peoples, because we were always down at the bottom of the barrel. So it gave me a totally new way of looking at it. It wasn't just isolated. Finding out how society was set up, class systems and how people were treated. I remember finding out about things that I had sort of thought about, but never really knew about."

I suggested to her that "You lived it, you know." Cherie replied, "But I couldn't put it into words!" They tell me that the words they learn in class now leap out at them from the newspaper, the television, in conversations at work. The words are everywhere, but they hadn't noticed them before. "It was just personal." Like me understanding the "pleading look," being able to identify the social character of an individual experience allows us to see our lives in a different way. As Toni Morrison accepted her Nobel Prize for Literature she noted: "It is words that empower meditation, that fend off the scariness of things with no names and that ease the burden of oppression. And in the end, it is words that enable us to make some sense of our existence by allowing us to stand aside to narrate it."

In the summer of 1997, Cherie is working at a social service agency, providing counseling and supportive services for previously homeless women now living in transitional housing. After the Returning Women's Program, she completed her Associates of Art (the two-year community college degree) as well as both undergraduate and graduate degrees in social work. "Originally when I came in, I was planning to take typing and get a little certificate." This narrow goal was defined by Project Chance, a program for women on AFDC. She says later, "All my life, I wanted to be in some area where I could help others." As part of my sociology class, she visited various women's community projects. She continues: "And it just struck me, this is what you've been wanting to do all your life!" She has found a calling where her strengths, her interests and her life experiences are entwined and enacted in the strengthening of others.

Judy has moved with her family to California where she is working on her last year of courses toward her goal of becoming a high school history teacher. Her experiences in the program led her to question her children's schooling:

"And then it was sort of looking at different ways of teaching. I always thought you sat at a desk, and your hands were folded and you nodded or took notes and whatever the teacher said, you ingested. I kind of hoped college would be a little different. But I always thought school was just absorbing everything that was thrown at you. And what I really liked about the Returning Women's Program was that, my God, we were able to talk and converse. We did get off on tangents, but some of them were great tangents, and then I started looking at my own kids' education, and my kids were in a parochial school and the majority of their classes was sitting at their desks with their hands folded and saying, 'Yes sir' and 'No sir,' and I thought . . . well, you know . . . is this really the best?"

This is a glimpse into a vibrant kaleidoscope of stories from returning women; stories of hope and courage, of pride and confidence; funny stories next to tales of grand passion. These stories command my attention, deepen my understanding and caring for my students as I discover more about the complexity of their lives. These insiders' accounts, students' reflections on their learning experiences, provide lessons for students and teacher alike.

We need to build academic learning communities in community colleges and other settings—places where students can find support, personal contact, and visibility, rather than experiencing anonymity and disconnection in large impersonal institutions. Students at community colleges commute; they rush from classes to jobs to families. Most adult students are part time, juggling multiple responsibilities; their schedules and lives are complicated and busy. I see fragmentation and isolation as characteristic of many of my students' experiences, particularly when they begin schooling. Who do you talk to about your worries? How do you learn of possible opportunities and options? Who can you share your emerging sense of intellectual excitement with?

Perhaps the Returning Women's Program can point toward such a community—learning initially in a "contained classroom" with a team of teachers working together, integrated support services which can provide nurturance, challenge, and personal connections. Even by conventional yardsticks, such a program has served not only the students but the college well. Women who participated in this program have both the highest retention and degree completion rates. As an example, over a five-year period, between 78 percent and 90 percent of the Returning Women's Program students registered for classes the semester following their enrollment in the program. The return rate for all students during the same time frame ranged between 51 percent and 64 percent. A small-schools approach might have a dramatic impact on both retention and degree completion.

So many women speak of their high school experiences with indifference, antipathy, often hostility. They did not find validation, intellectual excitement, or challenge. They were not taken seriously, yet years later they are serious and passionate students. Why did they silently sit back then? Why was school such a chore? I think of the Judys and Cheries and others in today's high schools—girls who are marginal, silent, invisible, alienated. Do they have to wait twenty years for a passionate learning experience? How can their schools encourage a "hunger to learn"? A personalized, supportive, yet challenging experience like the Returning Women's Program, building on the strengths of young women, and encouraging new self-conceptions of female identity, might be an alternative to conventional modes of high school practice.

What would have happened to Cherie if she were trying to complete her education while temporarily supporting herself on AFDC today? The passage of the so-called welfare reform legislation would have insisted that instead she "take typing, get a little certificate," and head for a dead-end job. Educational opportunities for poor women are being eliminated. In California, where Judy lives, the passage of Proposition 209 (outlawing any preferences on the basis of gender, race, or ethnicity) would put a Returning Women's Program on the shelf. There is a climate of anger toward women who are seen as marginal—poor women, African-American and immigrant women, young women, single mothers, women in low-wage work. While they want them to take responsibility for their lives, the political powers simultaneously remove all possible supports, keeping women "in their place."

The stories from reentry women here point us in a different direction. Just in this one small program, hundreds of women changed their lives. The presence of adult women students at community colleges, arriving in classrooms with years of rich experience and wisdom from daily living, "hungry to learn," demanding attention to and respect for the multiple roles they play, serious and outspoken, becomes a challenge to regressive social policies as well as an invitation to rethink education. They have experienced the beginning of claiming knowledge, too long denied these opportunities by a culture that devalues their wisdom and voice.

College faculty can be advocates for supportive spaces for reentry women—for alternative programs that make it possible for students to juggle their multiple responsibilities, that provide nurturance and challenge—workshops on returning to school, organizations of adult women students, and building schools within the school such as the Returning Women's Program. In many colleges, reentry women on public assistance are seeing their educational careers threatened. Together with these students, teachers have an important role to play in stopping the assault on welfare mothers' right to an education. College teach-ins on the impact of the welfare legislation on educational opportunity could be a way to educate the campus community and build support for these students. Links to social service agencies, as well as alliances with women's organizations in the community, need to be built. Together with teachers who are concerned with social justice, adult women reentry students can be a powerful force for the right to a robust and vital education for women.

6—A Grassroots Think Tank—Linking Writing and Community Building

Hal Adams

In a small wooden structure in the blacktop playground, across from their children's elementary school, a handful of adults smoke cigarettes, eat doughnuts, drink coffee, and talk about their lives. The focus of the discussion is a short piece one of them wrote last weekend.

The author is twenty-three years old, pregnant with her third child. Her oldest is seven. She has no husband, no job, little formal education, and uncertain housing. Because of her situation, she thinks she is a failure. Her writing is self-critical. She fears she has violated God's plan for her life. She is weeping as she responds to others' comments, though the comments are gentle. They say it is not God's plan she has violated, but her own. They say she is following God's plan by preparing for her baby's arrival and providing for her other children as best she can. The conversation alternately focuses on her writing, offering her emotional support, and debating religion. She begins to reconsider her writing and her views.

Sometimes these meetings unfold as literary criticism sessions, other times as church revivals, coffee klatches, therapy groups, or political caucuses. But mostly they are writing workshops, which turn out to be a kaleidoscope of possibilities and enactments. The participants are preparing their work for publication in a magazine that will be distributed in their school and community. The magazine is called the *Journal of Ordinary Thought*.

For three years I have been offering a parent writing program in local elementary schools in Chicago. The purpose of the program is to increase community involvement in the schools and demonstrate the link between education and community life. This is the story of that effort in one school. It began as a writing class for parents and grew into a community-building program that called itself a grassroots think tank.

EVERY PERSON IS A PHILOSOPHER

The school is in Austin, a poor black neighborhood on the west side of Chicago. Everybody in the group lives in the neighborhood, most of them all their lives. Two mornings a week we gather, usually ten or twelve of us, to write and talk about life. It was not always relaxed, especially not the first day. People were anxious then. They had come because they wanted to help their children with their schoolwork. Only a couple viewed themselves as writers, and here I was, the outsider from the university, under scrutiny, asking everyone to write freely about their experiences. I insisted that each of them had stories worth writing. Even strangers would be interested, I told them. They were doubtful, but polite. I persisted.

Every person is a philosopher, I said, thinking of the Italian Marxist Antonio Gramsci, who thought people with power maintain dominion over ordinary people through the control of ideas as much as through the exertion or threat of force. If ordinary people develop confidence in their own ideas, Gramsci reasoned, they can challenge the control others hold over them. I was thinking also of the Brazilian educator Paulo Freire, who thought ordinary people limit themselves by rejecting ideas that grow from personal experience and instead adopt ideas from the class that rules them. These ideas tend to justify class and race privilege. If ordinary people learn to recognize the alien ideas they have adopted, they are able to discard them and act in their own interest. Last, I was thinking of the Caribbean revolutionary C. L. R. James, who thought the artistic expressions of ordinary people contain truths essential for social change. If ordinary people recognize the truths within their art, James concluded, they are more likely to trust their capacity to make a better world.

The ideas of these three thinkers can be summarized like this: ordinary people hold the key to a better world; experience is the best guide to thinking and action; to achieve social progress people must think for themselves and reach their goals through self-activity rather than rely on outside authority to think or act for them; it is the responsibility of everyone to strive for a better world; those who are not political in this broad sense are illiterate, no matter how well they read and write.

I was in a poor neighborhood on Chicago's west side, facing ten mothers and grandmothers who had vast experience in raising their families while keeping life and limb together under harsh conditions. Gramsci's, Freire's, and James' emphasis on the experience and thinking of ordinary people was compelling. The parents were intrigued by the idea that it is people leading ordinary lives who understand the world most clearly and create the truest meaning of their situation. Heads began to nod.

Near the end of the first session, having discussed lofty ideas about the importance of experience and the role of the ordinary person in creating a better world, the parents wrote what was on their minds. "Use your own language," I urged, "don't worry about spelling and grammar. If you don't know a word, leave a blank space; we'll figure it out later." Everyone gave me something.

The papers were so brief and cautious I was tempted to dismiss them as shy attempts to "get over" on the first day, to avoid drawing attention to themselves. Perhaps the good stuff would come later. But more was there than immediately apparent. Several papers, for instance, made reference to religious practices and beliefs. Looked at as a whole, they formed a religious theme that could not be denied. I typed all the submissions and distributed them at the next meeting. The group focused its attention on one, which read, in its entirety: "I went to church Sunday. I had a good time."

"If the author were to write more about this topic," I asked, "what would you as a reader like to know?" They gently began to ask questions aimed partly at the author, partly at the group. Why do you go to church? How did you choose this church? Do your children like it? What happened in church Sunday that made it a "good time"? Each question sparked discussion. People offered opinions on the differences between churches, the role of pastors, how churches have changed, their importance in African-American communities, disputes and disagreements within churches, and so on. They talked about how church communities and religious beliefs had helped them in everyday living and during crises.

From a simple two-sentence piece of writing I had nearly dismissed as "getting over" grew a discussion about how people create institutions to deal with the difficulties they face and how articles of belief influence everyday life. The discussion had its effect. The author had new directions to pursue, and others who were stimulated by the piece began writing ideas of their own.

The lessons were not lost on the group:

1. Even apparently simple writing contains meaning for the group.
2. The group helps develop the meaning in a piece of writing.
3. Writers develop their work by discussing it with others.
4. Writing by one person stimulates writing by another.

PRIMACY OF EXPERIENCE

The writing group was a place to identify questions from the gritty reality of life experience and to address them in discussion and writing. Nothing in these meetings took precedence over the experiences of the members. The parents took to this idea quickly. It was as if it affirmed an approach to learning they already had intuitively accepted, namely, that life is the best teacher. Within a few months, armed with the confidence that its perspectives on the community were valid, the group would begin to take action on issues raised in the writing.

The meetings were run as writing workshops. I collected the writing, commented on it, and photocopied some for the class to read and discuss in future sessions. All discussion started with a member's writing. Discussion often went off in disparate directions, but inevitably it returned to the writing.

Mary was a leader but she was not a confident reader or writer. Each meeting the group would encourage her to write, but to no avail. A tape recorder and individual attention helped, but she still refused to write. One day, months later, she appeared with a piece of writing and proudly distributed it to the group. She had written it over the weekend with help from her teenage daughter and two of her daughter's friends. The four of them were lounging about in Mary's bedroom one night discussing their relationships with men. Mary asked the others if they would help her write something summarizing their discussion. Mary spoke while her daughter wrote and the others made suggestions. This grim piece, the result of that cross-generation writing session, clicked immediately with the writing group and brought expressions of understanding that came from places formerly kept secret. An old bond was deepened between Mary and her daughter in the writing of the piece, and a new bond was forged in the group with the reading and the discussion of it:

Males obsession over females. It starts with friendship, then they fall in love. The relationship begins wonderful; the nice secrets they share, gifts, romantic dinners, and the first time they make love. That's when the changes begin. The female is not allowed to have other male companions, no going out with her friends. All she can do is sit at home and wait on him. Then they have children and it really gets bad. The crying and fighting starts. All of a sudden the female loses interest and breaks the relationship off. Some get away, others can't. They are chased, harassed, and some even get killed in the process. Then all the male can say is, "If I can't have her, no one else can." Don't ever think you have made the right choice because you never know.

This story, based on the experiences of Mary and her young friends, prompted others to tell similar stories about sexual relationships. A furious discussion followed about the oppressive conditions under which black men and women live in the United States and the stress these conditions place on intimacy between black men and women.

The group members brought new writing every session. They wrote about commonplace and extraordinary experiences: bus rides, kids getting ready for school, funny episodes, scary times, childhood memories, illness, death. The group discussions that followed the reading of these pieces always demonstrated the complexity of experience, including experiences that appeared trivial at first. It became second nature for the group to explore each story for its broader implications.

One mother wrote about taking a summer trip as a teenager with her mother and aunt to the southern United States. She was surprised that life in the rural South was so different from the northern city life she had always known. She disliked being in the South because there was nothing for her to do. After the others read her story, they identified words they considered to be essential to it, even words the author did not use: surprised, different, peaceful, safe, friendly, boring, caring, violence, drugs. Using these key words as a point of departure, the parents discussed the difference between northern urban and southern rural life. How did values differ in the two regions? Was life safer in the South than the North? Were families closer in the South? Was the educational system better? Did it cost less money to live in the South?

The parents' attention was rapt during the reading of these

experience-based stories, and the ensuing discussions were intense. The stories rolled on, about family life, raising children,
relations between the sexes, living amid violence, finding afford-
able housing, dealing with the public aid system, and surviving as
women. The mothers first came to the writing group because they
wanted to learn how to help their children with schoolwork. They
returned for the chance to explore the meaning they had gleaned
from lives lived under stress of poverty, and because it was comforting to make explicit to each other the common struggle they
shared.

PUBLISHING

Inside the front cover of the *Journal of Ordinary Thought* (*JOT*) is
its statement of purpose: "The *Journal of Ordinary Thought* publishes reflections people make on their personal histories and
everyday experiences. It is founded on the propositions that every
person is a philosopher, expressing one's thoughts fosters creativity and change, and taking control of life requires people to think
about the world and communicate the thoughts to others. *JOT*
strives to be a vehicle for reflection, communication, and
change."

It was time to publish writing from the parent group. I had
previously published *JOT* in other settings: a public assistance
office and a single residency hotel for formerly homeless people.
The writing group's response to these earlier issues was positive.
They liked the plainly written style and the stories by people who
lived lives similar to their own. They were fascinated by the prospect of seeing their names in print. The decision to publish was
unanimous.

A few weeks later the group published an issue of *JOT* featuring writing by its members. The magazine's appearance in the
dead of winter must have taken some bite from the Chicago wind,
because group members were dashing without coats between the
school and the little back building where we met, waving copies.
It was high drama. They were celebrating having published a
magazine that would cast them in a new light in the community,
as writers and thinkers to be taken seriously.

The magazine contained several stories about family life and,
as a portent of what was to come later, a few about violence in the

community. The family, troubled as it may be, was viewed in the writing group as a buffer against the harsh outside world. Charlene's piece reflected both of these themes and, by implication, suggested a relationship between them. She foreshadowed the strong fear of violence other group members would pursue later in their writing. The security of her home, described in the opening, three-sentence paragraph, allowed her the psychological protection one evening to reflect on this disturbing experience:

> I have put my kids to bed, finally. My house is peaceful, quiet. I will do some writing.
>
> Two weeks ago I was standing at the bus stop. I noticed a guy walking up wearing house shoes. There were three other ladies standing there too. He was standing there looking at everyone's purses. He was moving a little closer every second, so I moved up a little closer to the pole at the bus stop. My heart was really pumping hard. I turned to the left to see if the bus was coming. It was, thank God. The bus pulled up and I rushed to the door as it opened. I did not want to be the last person to enter, but the lady behind jumped in front of me. I entered the bus gripping my purse real hard. As I sat at my seat I asked the lady why she jumped in front of me. She told me she too was frightened that she was going to have her purse taken. I finally felt at ease for a while.

The story, interesting in its own right, opened the door for others to write later of experiences more frightening than Charlene's. The group began to explore the violence that, while it surrounded them, did not overwhelm them.

Alberta, like Charlene, introduced a topic that would become a theme for the group as time passed. In only a few lines, she explored tension within the family, between men and women in particular.

"My brother called. He wants some money. I want to give it to him, but he don't work like he could. I wish he could get the right job and clean himself up. He only had one real job, and then didn't do so well. I don't want to give him money to waste up on something else.

"The world is such a mess, not like it used to be. I know it has to change."

The explicit recognition by the group of the tension between men and women, introduced here by Alberta, was a primary factor in establishing a separate writing group for men within a few months. Starting the men's group and openly discussing the tensions eventually increased the potential for men and women from the neighborhood to collaborate as the group evolved toward community action.

Publishing the magazine changed the group. Commitment to the writing sessions soared as almost nothing took precedence over the writing class. Membership grew. The group was asked to speak at several university classes. The children's teachers began to take notice of the parents' writing.

INFLUENCING THE CLASSROOM

The stories the group published were not primarily about children, nor were they written primarily for children. From the beginning the authors wrote for themselves and each other, which is good because honest self-expression is the best way for adults to win children's respect and attention. Children learned from seeing adults tell stories about lives fully lived. The parents' history was the children's history, and committing it to writing demonstrated the truth in the adage that people are accumulated history. It was good to convey to children that experience counts, and that we are all philosophers interpreting the experience that forms our lives. There was wisdom in the stories for anyone in the community who read them, including children. Children grasped the meaning of some of the stories, while the meaning of others eluded them. Even stories beyond their reach, however, made a point with the children: there were stories from the neighborhood worthy of publication, and there were adults close to the school who cared enough to write them.

The parents began visiting primary-grade classes as guest authors. The purpose was to show the children that adults familiar to them were writing and publishing, reinforcing the idea that literacy was an everyday, important part of their community. The children enjoyed seeing familiar faces in the magazine, and gave close attention when the mothers read their work. Karen read her piece to her daughter's first-grade class.

> Let me tell you what a bad day I had. First I woke up late. The kids were hungry. I had to iron. I had washed only one of every sock. Finally we got out the door and wouldn't you know

it, we missed the bus. So, I walked to get my check, but the lady said it was not there. My caseworker said I missed my appointment, which I didn't know about, and I had only one day to get my medical card. I got to the doctor, but he was gone for the day. Then I got some money to go to the store only to find that what I wanted was not on sale anymore. So I went home and cooked what I had. There was not enough for me, so I went to bed hungry. Now that's a bad day, but everybody has them.

The first graders gave it a positive review. The children's comments showed an understanding of the subtle message of Karen's story: Bad days are hard, but they can be handled. It was tiring and difficult to run around town with your kids, the children agreed, and scary to go bed hungry, but at the same time it was pretty funny that only one sock from each pair had been washed. The children emerged from Karen's reading with an understanding that one can survive a bad day with dignity and humor. Equally important, they developed new respect for Karen for having written about her bad day.

A MEN'S GROUP

The inclusion of men in the writing group on a regular basis was problematic for several reasons. The school had become the almost exclusive place for the women to meet socially; men in live-in relationships with women receiving public aid often remained in the background for fear their known presence would reduce the women's already meager public aid checks; most importantly, living in poverty strained the relations between the sexes because men were unable to find decent jobs to support their families, often leaving women with the sole responsibility for raising children.

It was gratifying, then, when two young men from the neighborhood asked to start a men's writing group. They had seen *JOT* and thought they could recruit several men to a group to work toward publishing a men's magazine. The women and the school administration enthusiastically agreed to have the men meet at the school once a week. Four men attended the first meeting, but the group quickly grew to twelve. All were in their late teens and twenties; some were former or current gang members; most were not employed; and only one had a secure, well-paying job. The group met for a year and published two issues of a magazine called *Through the Eyes of a Villain*.

I objected to the title at first, arguing that it made them sound evil. "That's the point," they explained. "That's the irony. We are seen as evil. Our music strikes people as evil; our appearance strikes people as evil. They have to listen carefully to rap music to discover it is far more complex than 'bitches' and 'hoes' and violence. They will have to read the magazine to see beyond their fears, to realize we are men thinking about the world and how to remake it."

One piece in *Through the Eyes of a Villain* described the author as waking up one morning "unemployed, but not without work to do." It was an important phrase because this author and his writing group were taking a new look at their community. The men approached this task by offering highly personal critiques of two cultures—mainstream U.S. culture and the street culture of their neighborhood. Their critique of the mainstream was angry. Their critique of the street was poignant. Both cultures, the mainstream and the street, have ravaged the lives of these young men. The men expressed surprise that they had survived the racist violence of the mainstream and the street violence of the neighborhood. Here we are, they said with some surprise, in our twenties, still alive and out of jail. Who would have thought? As Derrick put it:

> Growing up on the Westside is a task all people can't do. There is a fear of death that haunts the neighborhood. Many people are scared because of drive-by shootings and drug sales on the corner, to come outside or even let their children play in front of their own houses. I can see where they're coming from. Sometimes I feel like that, because I'm a Black man on the Westside of Chicago that about seen everything from group beat downs to getting shot, to getting cut, to shooting first, to seeing murder, to kicking it with murderers. I ain't saying that I'm a bad guy or a nice guy, but I came a long way. All the things I did in my life, I'm surprised I didn't go to jail or die, but I know I came a long way. I got a long way to go. Looking back through all the madness, I believe I was possessed, but now I feel peace and blessed and the demons have left and I can start with my self-evolution, evolving to a peaceful state.

The men wrote about what most men think about—what does it take to be a man? Existing on the outside of the only two cultures they knew, they faced a void they sought to fill with their manhood. They recognized the tremendous potential in the world and in their own lives for creativity on one hand and for barbarism on the other. At this point in their lives, like C. L. R. James, they were seeking an artistic solution to the crisis. Most of them made rap music, and they all wrote. It was no escapist art in which they were involved. It was art that told the truth, for them the only path to being human and to manhood. Kevin wrote:

"Life, it's a hard subject to talk about because I'm having a hard time dealing with it. A buddy of mine was smoked about a month and a half ago on the South Side. It was gang related. Another one of my homies had his picture taken with a 12 gauge. The last thing he saw was the flash. It was drug related. When I lived in California one of my boys got beat down by some Bloods over his truck . . . I could go on and on with these types of stories, but it's hard, especially when it's one of your boys. Each time I heard the bad news I wanted to strap up and take care of business. But who gives me the right to kill another muthafucker just cause he killed my boy? Like I said in the beginning, life, it's hard to talk about. We're becoming extinct, being hunted by our own kind. . . ."

A GRASSROOTS THINK TANK

Before the men's group was formed, the women had become more active in the school. Writing and group discussion seemed to make them more free to offer public opinions about school policy. Several ran for the local school council, which in Chicago has considerable power in neighborhood schools. As their confidence grew, some parents who had previously viewed their classroom volunteer role as primarily disciplinary began to take a different initiative with students. Linda contributed to the discussion of this process with "Parent Volunteer":

"There is a child in the classroom where I volunteer. His name is Marvin. He is so cute. He has a problem reading, but he is trying hard. He also has a problem with adding and subtraction, but he is learning. When the teacher passes out the homework he gets his and puts it in his bag. The next day she asks the kids to bring up their homework, and she asks Marvin for his. He says,

'My mom wouldn't help me.' So, I suggest, 'Marvin, do the best you can. Try by yourself, and if you can't get some part, leave it blank.' For a while he wasn't bringing in any homework, but boy, now he's doing it and turning it in. . . ."

The discussion of Linda's piece, where members reassessed their roles as parents in the classrooms, was part of a larger discussion about the relationship of neighborhood culture to the educational process. The physical environment, family traditions, educational expectations, child-rearing practices, family structure, and community institutions were described in writing from a personal perspective.

Toward the beginning of its second year of existence, the writing group began to discuss taking action on issues that had arisen in the writing. As members continued to write about the experience of living in the community, the group expressed an awareness that the community environment was related closely to the quality of education their children received in school. They convened a meeting to discuss the matter with about thirty neighbors. To get the ball rolling, members of the writing group read selections from writing in progress. Three authors who subsequently published their works in *JOT* caught the attention of the meeting.

Paulette went first with a piece she called, "Abandoned Buildings": "I imagine people staying around abandoned buildings. Sometimes you have to pass these buildings. You're actually scared to walk by them because you never know who might be inside. Sometimes you know they are inside watching you come by, but you don't know who is there. It might be a drug addict or someone to kill you. So when you pass these buildings, you have to watch carefully."

Joyce followed with "Dangerous World": "It is a dangerous world today. Something I wonder about a lot is how my children will live in this world. I know it's coming to an end one day. I hope and pray I will live to see my children grow up and make something out of themselves.

"So much is happening out there every day of their lives. I see things and hear things—people and deaths, and so many young people killing one another over nothing. That's why I worry about a lot of things. I pray to God every day that nothing will happen to my kids. I tell him, don't forget us down here. Just keep watching over us and everybody in the world."

Theresa read last with an untitled piece: "Most everywhere you go in the 29th ward there is a vacant building. Some are torn halfway down or boarded up. Some were boarded up but the drug dealers have taken the boards down and made the buildings into spots to sell drugs, or they take someone in there to rape or kill.

One night I was going to work. After taking the kids to the baby-sitter, I was on my way back to Central and Washington to catch the bus when I happened to walk by a vacant building and heard a lady screaming. I did not stop because I was the only one walking on the street that night. I was frightened. I ran fast and prayed—just get me to the bus stop and then, please bus, hurry up!"

Each author's story was greeted with nods and murmurs of approval. As it happens, there was a large abandoned apartment building next to the school playground. At the time of the community meeting it was well known as a center for drug activity, and a few years earlier a woman had been raped in the building. It is no wonder the three essays struck a responsive chord.

It was agreed that the group would do something to stop drug activity near the school, but there were no illusions about the limited effect a victory would achieve. Everyone knew if the dealers were removed from the school area, they simply would set up shop in another place, but at least parents would not have to worry about their children passing by drug deals on their way to school. People understood the complex nature of the problem. The deeper social and economic problems would not be solved by removing drug activity from the school area or, for that matter, even by eliminating drugs from the entire neighborhood. Many expressed sympathy for the young people selling drugs. There was strong sentiment in the discussion for the group not to take an unalterable position against the desperate people, some of whom were acquaintances, who had turned to selling drugs as a last resort. What appeared on the surface to be a simplistic solution (get drug sales away from the school) was in fact a solution that took into account complex social factors beyond the comprehension of many people not from the community. The lesson here is that long-term solutions to the complex problems of poor communities cannot be found without the broad, realistic perspectives that can be developed only by community residents.

At least once a month for the next year the writing group met not as a writing group, but as the Austin Grassroots Think Tank. The think tank was an organization committed to planning community action based on ideas that grew from the writing of ordinary citizens who lived in the area. During think tank meetings, the group discussed what to do about the abandoned building next door. They took pictures of the many vacant buildings in the area and wrote stories about their experiences with them. They called in the police to discuss increased security (to little avail) and invited the city housing department staff to explain procedures for addressing the matter. They discovered how to do a title search to identify the owners of abandoned buildings. They learned about housing court. They sent representatives to testify in court several times during the year, and on two occasions rented buses to carry groups of people to the downtown courtroom. They invited building owners to meetings to discuss the threat their buildings posed to the children. With pressure from the court and the think tank, the owners of the building next to the school agreed to secure their building, post a guard during school hours, clean the area, and report to the school office each day.

THE MEN'S AND WOMEN'S GROUPS UNITE (SOMETIMES)

As time passed, the men's writing group joined the think tank sessions. The effect was significant as both sexes shared their often differing perspectives on common problems. At one meeting, for instance, Detrich read a piece in which she asserted that black women coped better than men with drugs, poverty, and violence. She concluded that it was difficult to find "a good Black man." Joe uncurled his long limbs, reached for a paper of his and said, "Yeah, women go through a lot we don't understand, but we go through things women don't understand. Check this out." He began to read about hanging out with his buddies after a writing group session:

". . . An hour later I smoked a blunt and drank a couple of brews with my buddies in the alley behind my house. I turned to walk away and there was an unmarked police car flying towards me. In my neighborhood cops like to hit you, so I was hoping they would drive right by. All four doors flew open and the car screeched to a stop. I took a step back and threw my hands up. I was snatched and thrown roughly against the gate alongside my buddies. . . . One cop [started yelling], 'Hit him, hit him, hit him, hit him! One of you fuckers is going to jail.' . . . one [of the cops] reached into my underwear looking for dope. My cousin came out of the house to see what was going on. 'What the fuck do you want,' one of the officers asked . . . 'you're going to jail too, motherfucker, put that bag of dope on him. . . .'

"I got angry at myself. I felt like a sellout. I was afraid. It was five of them with guns, but that was no consolation. I kept quiet because I was afraid they'd make good on their threats. They left as suddenly as they came. 'Get out of the alley,' they warned, leaving us spread eagle against the fence.

". . . I think I've been searched by the police at least a hundred times, but I've never gotten used to it. Each time it's like being raped. Sometimes they even do it with a gun to my head or ribs. I told my mom what happened and she said I shouldn't hang with my friends. My aunt called and told me to stay out of the alley. My alley! . . ."

A heated discussion followed the reading of Detrich's and Joe's papers, with all the men and some of the women initially siding with Joe and most of the women taking the position of Joe's mother and aunt that Joe should not be hanging out in the alley. Eventually the group decided there was an overriding matter that concerned everyone in the room: the tension in the community regarding its diverse expectations of the police. At the time of this writing, the think tank is debating a program to address this issue.

By becoming more active in the school as volunteers and policy makers, by addressing community issues that have an impact on education, and by basing these actions on experiential writing, the Grassroots Think Tank has taken beginning steps toward realizing the visions of Gramsci, Freire, and James, who imagined a primary role for ordinary people in changing society. The steps are encouraging when one considers the pressure in contemporary society against such political initiative. (Gramsci called it self-activity.) Democracy has been reduced in popular consciousness to the occasional casting of a ballot. True community action based on collective deliberation is rare, and those who engage in it are often viewed cynically as being naive. The think tank and the *Journal of Ordinary Thought* are instances of participatory democracy in practice.

LOOKING AHEAD

The Grassroots Think Tank would like to expand the concept of a writing-based community organization beyond its current location in one school. It would like to establish writing groups around the neighborhood in different settings: housing complexes, churches, libraries, public aid offices, and so on. Each group will be responsible for publishing its writing. Periodically the expanded organization will convene forums where the writing groups will make their work available to each other. Ad hoc action committees with participation from several writing centers will form around shared community concerns. In this way people from several community bases will be working on issues of common interest.

The early success of the think tank was largely a function of its nonhierarchical, informal, organizational character. Individual, experiential writing and group discussion drive the think tank. Thus, it relies simultaneously on both highly independent and highly collective activity. Any expanded version of the program must preserve this mode of operation to preserve the intimate atmosphere. Otherwise, new, honest writing about personal experience will not be forthcoming.

Moving from writing groups to action groups is both the most promising and most problematic aspect of an expanded Grassroots Think Tank. It is promising because the movement from writing to action will be based on perceptions of the community by people at its roots, a condition implicit in the ideas of Gramsci, Freire, and James. It is problematic because there will be no central staff to assume responsibility for organizing action programs and moving them forward—but one cannot simultaneously have self-activity by community residents and central control of them. Central control often discourages ordinary citizens and otherwise weakens their initiative. It is the philosophy behind the think tank's organizational approach that people will be more likely to take control of their community if they are not expected to hand over their initiatives to a central administrative body.

We propose to set in motion a process whereby residents of the community can examine with each other the weighty matters of family, community, and economic development. The process will rely heavily on writing and publishing by community residents.

We do this to demonstrate the critical role literacy plays in community development, and because community writing is an effective way to reveal the profound wisdom and understanding residents can develop by examining their community experiences.

The time is ripe for such initiatives in poor communities where people often are discouraged by their chronically limited economic prospects. It is clear that help from the outside is not immediately forthcoming. Self-activity is now the only real alternative. A writing-based community project offers a practical way for citizens to be involved at the center of a process that will address their own futures. The precise direction the community will take in the process is not certain, but that is the nature of self-direction, and it is part of the reason it appeals to people who have long since become skeptical of solutions imposed from the outside.

REFERENCES

Buhle, P. 1988. *C. L. R. James: The Artist as Revolutionary.* New York: Verso.
Freire, P. 1964. *Pedagogy of the Oppressed.* New York: Continuum Publishing.
Gramsci, A. 1971. *Selections From the Prison Notebooks.* New York: International Publishers.
Grimshaw, Anna, ed. 1992. *The C. L. R. James Reader.* Oxford, UK: Blackwell Publishers.

7—Roses and Daggers

Patrick McMahon

SPRING

"Look at what I have for you, Mr. McMahon."

I don't want to look. It's Uriel. He always has something he wants me to see: a Ninja star, an unusual bottle cap, a minor hurt. Sometimes I have time for him, more often I don't. This morning I'm finishing lesson plans for the day while my third graders file into the classroom. I've forgotten to lock the door, and my precious preparation time is being threatened. I try to concentrate on my plans but something in Uriel's voice tugs me away, and at last I look up into his ten-year-old face, all freckles and anticipation, gray-green eyes wide open, ever watchful for love or assault. Satisfied that he has my attention, he unzips his jacket halfway, peeks inside dramatically, and . . . pulls out a rose. Of course! This is May, when children bring their teachers, not apples, but flowers.

The smile on Uriel's face as he holds out his crimson joy is its own blossom. I rummage around in myself for a vase worthy to hold it. Meanwhile I search under the washstand and find a mason jar. As Uriel fills it with water, I clear a spot on my desk. We place it, a splash of color among teacher's manuals and unfinished plans, and he runs out to play for the remaining minutes before class begins. With pencil poised, I fall to musing over the gift and the giver.

Earlier this spring Uriel stole twenty-five dollars from me. I'd naively left the wallet in my jacket, on my chair during lunch hour. I was devastated. Uriel is my favorite kid. After the storm of truth telling, the thunder of my indignation, and the tears of his shame, we came to a settlement. He would pay me back with earnings from recycling. With ten weeks of school remaining until summer vacation, at a modest $3 a week, it seemed doable. We wrote out a contract, shook hands, and that was that. But as of this morning, I've received only a single solitary dollar bill toward the debt. When I've asked Uriel about our contract, his eyes widen with worry. When I threaten to call his parents, he flinches. I suspect he's already been beaten. Our agreement, I realize now, was wishful thinking. If Uriel earns anything, it's going to go for food or toilet paper or candy.

Kiss that money good-bye, I say to myself. The relevant currency here, after all, isn't cash, but pain, and by that standard the debt has surely been long paid off. I can let go of the whole affair—but can Uriel? In order to clear himself with himself, it seems he must give me something of value, however nonmonetary. Clean up my room every afternoon? Turn over to me his collection of bottle caps? The bell interrupts my thoughts. As I rise from my desk to meet another day, the flash of red on my desktop cuts through the knot of my moral dilemma. I've got it! Later that morning I take Uriel aside. "Remember our deal about the money you took?" I pull out the contract, and the envelope containing its single bill. "Well I want to change it a little." I point to the rose: "Can you bring me more of these?" He nods his head vigorously. Yes, his mother has roses, his neighbors have roses, the whole town is blooming with roses. "Well, how about if you bring me a rose instead of a dollar, every day until the end of school?" I pull out my calendar and we count the days. Nineteen. "Bring me a rose each day, and how much will you still owe me in the end?" (Always the teacher, on the prowl for real-life math problems.)

He counts on his fingers. "Six dollars?" he offers, then corrects himself: "No, five. Remember?" He points to the envelope with its one dollar. But then he lights up with an inspiration which blows away all petty calculations: "Mr. McMahon, I can bring you a BIG bag of roses." He opens his hands to show me how big. "A big bag, Uriel, and we're even." We write a new contract and shake. I watch as he bounces back to his seat. Just one dilemma remains: how am I going to find a vase big enough to hold them all?

FALL

Making back-to-school purchases in a teacher's supply store recently, I noticed on the checkout counter a tray of tattoo decals. In these last weeks of summer I'm open to omens. In the mix of hearts and dragons there seemed to be something for me, something I'd put out of mind, now seeking shape. I came across an image that arrested me: a rose twining about a dagger. I had to have it. It wasn't until I had it transferred to my shoulder that I understood the reason.

Late last spring, with just a few weeks of school remaining, I found myself locked out of my classroom, the latest episode in a years-long dispute with my principal. We saw the means and ends of education differently, and in the politics of power I was losing. One night I received a phone call from the personnel office informing me that my teaching credential had elapsed and that a substitute teacher had been ordered for the next day. I was to return to my room to clear out personal belongings, and after that was to stay away "until you've rectified the situation." Later that night, when my heart had stopped pounding, I saw my mistake. In neglecting the paperwork aspect of my job, I had played right into my adversary's hands. This was the weak point for which she'd be waiting.

Under any circumstances I would have been upset, but with the year coming to an end, I was wild with the prospect of not finishing it out with my students. But, forward! The next day I set my shoulder to the wheel of my dilemma, enough to see that it was going to take time to get things moving. I returned to my classroom long enough to tell my students what I could. As I was leaving, Uriel raised his hand: "I have something to tell you, Mr. McMahon." Following his pointing finger, I spotted what, in my preoccupation with my own drama, I'd missed: his big bag of roses, which apparently the substitute had helped him transfer to a gallon jar.

I took those roses home. In the coming week they confirmed again and again, even as they dropped their petals, that in the whole mess something was working, that in any conflict, there was an alternative to blame and punishment. "One mistake after another," as Zen Master Suzuki Shunryu said about his own life. One recovery after another. The roses gave me hope.

I fought my way back into my room with one week of school remaining to the year. But where was Uriel? "He brought a knife to school," my students told me. "He was suspended." The story that emerged was that in the time I was gone Uriel had been bullied by a bigger kid. Now this is the stuff of school life, and stuff I take seriously, and I've put in place a conflict resolution process, in the safety of which these kinds of disputes can at least surface. But in my absence, and in the absence of a similar school-wide process, he'd been left to his own limited solutions.

He was, indeed, suspended, and for the rest of the year. As a kid, he hadn't had my resources. That wasn't the only difference between the outcome of my suspension and his. Worse, the police had been called in. Preoccupied with my own drama, I'd lost him to the System.

Fortunately, he came back after school one afternoon the last week of school to retrieve something left behind. His black eyes, usually wide open to the next thing coming his way, were closed down. Yes, I thought to myself, I failed you. Outwardly I thanked him again for the roses. "At least you and I are even now, aren't we?" I asked hopefully, hopelessly. He looked at me quickly, and rode off on his bike. I wasn't fast enough to call after him, "You're a good kid, don't let anyone tell you different."

Now, with the summer vacation coming to a close, I'm carrying back to school the scar of that memory on my shoulder, as a rose twined around a dagger. But wait a minute—weren't there a pair of rose daggers in that package? With any luck, Uriel will be back in school again, a fourth grader now. He'll love that tattoo.

A version of this originally published in *Turning Wheel:* Journal of the Buddhist Peace Fellowship, P.O. Box 4650, Berkeley, CA 94704. Reprinted by permission of author.

8—No Little I's and No Little You's—Language and Equality in an Adult Literacy Community

Kate Power

> *I know it is not the English language that hurts me, but what the oppressors do with it, how they shape it to become a territory that limits and defines, how they make it a weapon that can shame, humiliate, and colonize.*
>
> —bell hooks, *Teaching to Transgress* (168)

THAT WAS THEN . . .

When I was in Miss Johnson's first-grade class in Baltimore, Maryland, circa 1968, the monotony of our reading lessons lulled me into a comfortable rhythm. Divided into three groups, class members would alternate between seat work and oral reading in a circle with the teacher. Reading aloud was the only thing that split this sameness with brief bursts of terror. This was my trick: I'd sit in the circle quietly counting off the paragraphs, calculating precisely which paragraph I'd be assigned. I would rehearse the paragraph furtively in my head until my turn was announced, and then the words would spill out in a torrent of relief.

We never talked much about what we read. Our reading books were of the Dick and Jane variety, not the kind that would inspire laughter, tears, or a vigorous debate, even for those of us who looked at Dick or Jane and saw children much like ourselves. Talking of any sort was frowned on. "Sit down and be quiet!"— these were our perennial instructions. When we were really bad, when we talked too much, Miss Johnson would stride to the light switch and flick the lights off and on in rapid succession to capture our wayward attention. "Heads Down!" she would roar. We would stop whatever we were doing and put our heads down on the desks. "You'll keep them there," she promised, "until you're ready to behave like good little boys and girls."

I fit in well in this kind of environment. I liked structure and silence. I liked knowing what to expect. I enjoyed the feel of the cold desk against my cheek and the opportunity it gave me to rest and allow my mind to drift miles away from the confines of the classroom. I preferred not to speak anyway. Then, and for many years afterward, I was afraid to speak in front of any group. My heart would pound with relentless anxiety, my throat would tighten, and my lips would quiver. My mind would go blank. I still feel like that sometimes.

More than twenty years later, I found myself working as an untrained reading teacher in an alternative program for high school dropouts in Chicago. Faced with a group of students and a text I wanted them to read, I slipped into this pattern of oral reading like a comfortable old shoe. I found it a useful way to "get through the material" and noticed that my students seemed to expect and like it. Like many teachers before me, I came to appreciate the usefulness of oral reading as a classroom management tool. Whenever I used this technique, the students were docile and "on task." As it turned out, I valued this kind of behavior. I had as little tolerance for loud talking as my own first-grade teacher. Fortunately for me, the bland and unconnected passages we read in class from a variety of GED workbooks were as uninspiring for a group of African-American adolescents in Chicago in the eighties as Dick and Jane had been for a white girl in Baltimore in the sixties. There was little to discuss in my class.

As I continued to work with the students in the program, I started to be troubled by their lack of progress. Disturbingly, many of them elected to drop out again. Those that stayed did not look like they were learning. Although there was nothing that I could put my finger on at the time, I knew that the instruction we were providing was inadequate and unmotivating. Plagued by these continuing failures, I decided to return to school and pursue a master's degree. I wanted to learn as much as I could about how to teach reading.

While in graduate school I found the words to name my favorite instructional technique. It is called round-robin reading. I also learned that it is bad. Round-robin reading, I learned, places an undue emphasis on decoding, distracting students from the meaning-centered nature of the reading process. Round-robin reading can also be humiliating for struggling readers, forcing them to air their problems in the public domain. I learned some other things, too. I learned that talking is important to the process of literacy development. I learned that all of the communication processes are interconnected and that building strength in one can bolster the others. When I found all this out, I felt sheepish. I had adopted round-robin reading unquestioningly, ignoring the fact that I had learned to read in first grade more in spite of than because of my classroom instruction. I was embarrassed that as a novice teacher I had been relying on methods discredited by my own experience.

Equipped with a teaching credential and a repertoire of alternatives for teaching reading at all levels, I swore to myself that I would never again use round-robin reading, that the voices of my students would be heard in other ways in my classroom. I had also picked up a few other ideas about the best ways to teach reading. When I think of them now, I visualize them as a list of edicts chiseled on a stone tablet. I stored these edicts in my brain with linear clarity and could rattle them off with an evangelical fervor. Statements such as "Teachers should use the oral strengths of the students to build bridges to written language," "Literacy instruction should be relevant to the cultures of the learners," "Learning is a social process," and "Teacher must share control of the curriculum with the learners" slipped from my lips like so many pearls.

What I was not prepared for was how complicated interpreting and implementing these edicts could be with real live students. What I had not considered was how ubiquitous traditional methodologies like round-robin reading still are in the schools and how tenaciously my students would cling to them. What I was not prepared for was how challenges to my new-found expertise about curricular and methodological issues would make me feel about myself as a teacher.

The most perplexing example of this (at least at the time) came in the summer of 1993 when I accepted a three-month assignment teaching in a GED program for high school dropouts from sixteen to twenty-one. The program gave these young people the opportunity to earn money and study for the General Educational Development Tests as part of the Mayor's Summer Youth Jobs program. The group of about twenty-five who gathered that summer in the Albany Park neighborhood classroom in Chicago were mixed in terms of race, ethnicity, language, and gender; all had to produce evidence of economic hardship in order to qualify for the program. The two teachers were white, female, and middle class.

In planning the language arts curriculum for that summer, I borrowed heavily from Atwell's (1989) reading and writing workshop approach. I organized the summer around two or three interlocking units in which students would choose their own books and topics for writing. My goal as a teacher would be to facilitate the workshops and teach the students "strategies" to help them better comprehend and improve their writing. To get the ball rolling, my plan was to read an entire book aloud—modeling fluent and engaged reading, directly teaching the comprehension strategies the students should later apply to their independent reading.

I started reading through the book out loud with all of the expression and fluency I could muster, but within days a number of the students started to complain long and loud about the method I was using. How could they learn to read, they wanted to know, if I was the one who was doing all the reading? Besides, their other teacher relied on round-robin reading to get through content material; why was I doing things differently? One fiery young African-American woman was clear about what the problem was. "You think we're stupid! You think we can't read. And I can read!" she shouted at me. Not all of the students felt as she did, but the ones that did were vocal. Before too long, the summer GED group was split into two camps: those who loved my class and those who hated it. The latter camp was none too pleased with my plan for them to choose their own books and essay topics, either. One young woman did appreciate the dialogue journals which I gave them. It provided a place for her to give me feedback about my teaching: "Dear Kate, I want GED workbooks. You think that I and the class do not read or write enough. I am trying but I want to know when we can get some spelling books?"

I tried to explain my methodological choices to the dissenters over the early weeks of the summer, but they stood their ground. Ultimately, I gave in and split the students into the two groups that had formed naturally along methodological preferences. We came together in an uneasy alliance, although our common ground felt in no way to me like a collaborative place.

In a classroom like the one that I tried to create that summer, the teacher tries to break down the power differential between teacher and student, positioning herself as a facilitator and co-learner. I was only halfway successful in doing this. While half of the students liked to learn in an autonomous way, the other half wondered aloud what my purpose was when they had to make all of the choices and do most of the work. Ironically, their resistance to my pedagogy backed me into a corner where I felt that rather than letting them break down my authority I needed to assert it. I felt I had to convince my students that I knew better than they did what they needed. At the time I had the sensation that some of the students wanted to hate school, that they had a need to try to re-create the negative relationships and empty teaching methods that they had known in the past. Given my defensive reaction to their resistance, I also came to the uncomfortable conclusion that playing the role of the authoritarian teacher was too easy for me to slip into. We were all playing roles. At the time I blamed the schools for brainwashing the students, but I knew that I was implicated in some way.

An experience near the end of that summer forced me to stop for a minute and consider the way my students saw me. I was sitting alone in a classroom chatting with a female student. She had been one of the resisters who had opted to be in the round-robin reading group. After we had spoken for a while, she grabbed my wrist and looked down at my left hand. "Let me take a look at this ring," she said, pointing toward my wedding and engagement ring set, "since everyone else has been talking about it." For a moment I whooshed up and out of my body and felt myself looking down on me, and I imagined how I looked to my students—white, thirtyish, married, college educated, spoiled, the nonchalant owner of a thing which symbolizes arrival for the middle-class heterosexual female: the one-carat diamond engagement ring and wedding band set. It was then I realized that our struggle to define how and what we would learn was more complicated than I imagined.

I had always been attracted to the notions of democratic education and liberatory teaching methods that I had encountered primarily through writings by and about Paulo Freire (1972). In fact, that is what I thought I was trying to do that summer. But teaching reading and writing in a way that I imagined would give my students choice, voice, and autonomy was not as simple as I imagined. I learned that whenever you are in the classroom—and especially when you are a white, middle-class teacher teaching a multiracial, multilevel group—you must think through the meanings of democracy, authority, and control. The contradictions inherent in the ideals of equality and liberty, respect for individual differences and the ethos of the group, the need for leadership and the need to share power pose as serious a challenge within a classroom as they do in the larger society.

. . . AND THIS IS NOW

Most recently, I have been doing some unpaid teaching with a small group of adult women who attend a literacy program near the university where I am currently working toward a Ph.D. I entered the doctoral program in the fall of 1993, on the heels of my summer teaching experience, looking for a way to reconcile the contradictions that had emerged for me as a teacher.

I selected the program on the basis of a friendship with the lead teacher, a dynamic black woman named Ophelia Rogers. All of the regular students are female, African American, and residents of nearby housing projects. I had a number of conversations with Ophelia that convinced me that she was poised right at the edge of working out some of the tensions I have already described. In April of 1994 I interviewed Ophelia and asked her what her theory of teaching black women consisted of. She replied: "[To] Not always let society dictate and define everything about us. What's good, what's bad, what's successful and what's unsuccessful and just have a place . . . We're all in the universe and sometimes if no one gives you a place, you have to take it!" I was thrilled to find a place where a teacher was articulating and attempting to enact a way of teaching black women that was liberatory. I asked and she granted her permission to visit the program on a regular basis. Since January of 1994, I have spent more than 150 hours at METRO engaged in a variety of activities: talking to Ophelia, tutoring students, participating in a weekly women's group, and facilitating small reading and writing classes.

It is tempting to describe in greater detail Ophelia's beliefs about teaching and the journey that I have traveled as a teacher over the two-year span I have worked at METRO, but the vignettes that I will share here relate to only one of the reading and writing classes that I taught. This one took place from February to April 1995, after Ophelia had left the job and moved out of state. This was a difficult rupture for the students, and I was hoping that I could make the transition less painful by extending my class and using what I had learned from Ophelia to continue to seize an educational space for black women.

By this time my ideas about what this would take had been complicated—not only through my involvement with the women and my conversations with Ophelia, but by the reading that I did as a student. I have been particularly influenced by some black writers (Delpit 1988, 1995; Walker 1992) who agree that the experiences of black students must be placed at the center of the literacy curriculum, but assert that these experiences must be used to build a bridge to the literacy valued by the dominant culture. Students want and have a right to this, they argue. For the students I have taught who have dropped out of high school, the most powerful symbol of and obstacle to access to dominant culture is the GED test. Balancing the challenge of preparing students to pass the test with the idea of putting the experiences of the students at the center of the curriculum, the progressive white literacy teacher might feel trapped in a conundrum of competing goals. According to Lisa Delpit (1995), some white teachers give up in the face of this contradiction. This abdication is a more insidious form of domination (and not unconnected to my failure to reach all of the students in the summer GED program). My readings have convinced me that I do not have to feel conflicted about these two equally important goals, but this does not make them any easier to reconcile.

In the pages that follow, I will introduce the context of the METRO Literacy Initiative and the women who attended my group. I will present five chronological vignettes of class life excerpted from the fourteen-week, two-hour classes I taught, culled from field notes and audio tapes. I selected the vignettes to represent a sampling of typical practice and to illustrate certain key themes. These vignettes will be presented baldly, without much embellishment or interpretation. Finally, I will pull together these themes to shed light on how "the language of the master can be used toward liberatory ends" (Delpit 1995, 165). My discussion of teaching language and literacy will show how this is a context that shapes and is shaped by issues of content and social relationships. This web of concerns is central to the effort of any teacher trying to live a pedagogy of liberation.

CLASSROOM VIGNETTES

The METRO Literacy Initiative

The METRO Literacy Initiative is not much to look at. It occupies a tiny, cluttered room in the uppermost corner of a recreation facility. When you come to METRO to teach, you never know what to expect. The atmosphere is charged with a certain looniness. Student attendance and punctuality are mercurial things, impinged on by family demands, health crises, and last-minute emergencies. The agency that houses METRO is unsupportive, misdirecting first-time visitors and occasionally closing the program down without advance notice. My group was scheduled to meet every Tuesday morning for two hours during the months of February to April. During that time the coordinator called me six times to cancel for a variety of reasons connected to the contingencies listed above. When I did teach the group, the temperature within the room fluctuated wildly. Most days heat gushed out of the radiators; we opened windows and stripped down to T-shirts and jeans. For a few sessions, however, the heat was mysteriously turned off all together. We sat around the table in our coats clutching hot drinks.

Each group of students is unique. Each woman brought with her a special set of strengths and challenges. Our relationships with each other made for a particular dynamic. Briefly, here are the women you will get to know better through the classroom vignettes:

Rochelle. Rochelle is the person assigned to substitute in the position of coordinator/lead teacher after Ophelia's departure. She is twenty-four years old, the youngest person in our circle. She is married and has two young daughters. Her position at METRO is temporary, and she hopes to return soon to the other literacy program from which she came and where she has many students she cares about. She is usually quiet. She becomes most animated when she talks about her daughters, whom she wants "to raise right . . . keep them in the books and away from the TV."

Rowena. Rowena is one of the few holdovers who stayed after Ophelia left. She is in her mid-forties. She lives in the METRO housing projects with her two teenage children. Of all the students in the literacy project, she has the farthest to go in terms of developing her literacy abilities, something that she knows. She told me that she was in a program for students labeled Educably Mentally Handicapped when she did attend public schools. "All my life I been called slow," she explains. Since she decided to go back to school about five years ago, she has bounced around from program to program as the city colleges closed down satellite sites in the communities. Despite these setbacks, Rowena describes herself as somebody with a "made-up mind" who will never be content to sit at home and watch soap operas like some of the other women she knows. She attends the literacy program almost every day and works furiously, although her progress is painfully slow. When she thinks about her future, she says: "I always said that if I ever finish and get my GED, the first thing that was on my mind is no resting . . . non-stop. I'm just going to sign up and go straight to nursing school. . . . Ever since I was little . . . you know I had my own little dream, where I used to pretend I'm a nurse and my dog was my sick patient and I would tend to her and say, 'well, everything's going to get better, keep your chin up.'"

Bell. Bell is in her mid-forties, with strong traces of her Mississippi background in her molasses voice. She is a pastor in her church and frequently talks about the need to "have faith." She had enrolled in the program in March of 1994, when she had to leave her job as a nurse's aide in a nursing home because of foot and back problems. She decided to return to school to get her GED so that she could advance in her nursing career and get a job where she would not have to do heavy lifting, clean bedpans, and change diapers. She continued attending the literacy program when Ophelia left, although she had been one of Ophelia's most loyal fans. In a discussion I had with her at the time of Ophelia's departure, she said, "You know, she's not dead. Life has to go on. I just don't let myself get too close to nobody. I keep my distance." But in the months immediately following Ophelia's departure, Bell's back problems took a turn for the worse. She started requiring a cane to walk and was prescribed a variety of medications. She was only able to attend two sessions this time around. She called Rochelle to tell her that her medications made her too drowsy to concentrate on schoolwork.

Miss Pearl. Miss Pearl had been a student of Ophelia's when Ophelia taught at a literacy program in a housing project neighboring the METRO complex. Her program had closed down in December, and she transferred over to METRO at the beginning of January. Like most of the other students, Miss Pearl is in her late forties. She is tall with a medium-brown complexion, large round glasses, and a number of teeth missing in the front. She carries herself in a stately fashion and enjoys speaking in front of a group. The formality of her title is an indication of her status among her peers. She talks a lot about the importance of getting up in the early morning and getting out and doing something with your life, of making something of yourself no matter what your age. One of her fondest memories is being selected to serve on a jury: "I told the judge that I couldn't read too good, but he said that's okay. So I sat up on that jury just like anyone else." In discussing her decision to sign up to take the GED test, she said, "You got to motivate yourself that I'm still going to get it even if I don't make it this time. I'm still going to go on and on and on. You got to go on no matter what. You can't say I'm tired or I was sleepy or I'm going to be late. Keep on, get what you can get. I'm like John the Baptist . . . I keep on going on and on and on."

Sherri. Sherri is a petite, wiry woman in her mid-thirties. Younger than most of the other women, she is also set apart by the fact that she already has a high school diploma. Besides me, she is also the only childless member of the METRO literacy project. She recently moved into public housing and has some scars to show for it, literally. About a year ago, she was scheduled to finish a clerical training program. Weeks away from graduation, she was attacked as she tried to open her door by a man who was smoking crack out of an antenna in her hallway. He slashed her hand with a knife and nearly severed one of her fingers. She had to have a number of operations and only recently has been able to come back to school: "I have to start all over again. I've got to get my typing speed back up, and then I'll move on." She hopes also to be able to move out of the projects: "This is my first time living in CHA. How can a federally-run establishment like CHA . . . have problems like that and be legal? It's legal for them to let the buildings deteriorate. It's legal for them to let people, who knows what they got . . . people just in your hallway . . ."

Miss Williams. Miss Williams is a stocky woman in her late forties. She has large, black-rimmed glasses and tucks her hair up underneath a black beret. Unlike many other women in the program, who started their lives in the South, she was born and bred on the west side of Chicago. She has fond memories of her growing-up years on Damen Avenue. She was a tomboy and used to bribe the boys ten cents to let her play sandlot baseball with them. "Here comes that Williams girl," the boys used to say when they would see her coming. She found out about the program from her neighbor Miss Pearl. She always sits next to Miss Pearl at the far end of the table that they have staked out as their own. She's much quieter than her gregarious friend and gets up from the table about every twenty minutes or so to fill a beige coffee cup with water, which she sips constantly.

Renee. Renee has been coming to the program for as long as I can remember, and before that as well. She is a small but heavy woman in her late twenties with wide-set eyes and a doleful look. Five years ago her boyfriend beat their infant son to death. He went to jail for the murder, and Renee has been fighting with the Department of Children and Family Services to get her other son back ever since. Her literacy level is probably as low as Rowena's, but her participation is extremely erratic and sometimes she seems to have trouble concentrating. She has participated faithfully for days at a time and then disappeared for months. She participated in the class in two out of the eight sessions.

The Power of the Word!

On the first day of the class, I selected an interview with Maya Angelou, from the book *Black Women Writers at Work,* to read with the women. Although I was still sensitive to issues of oral reading and control, I found that in this group my reading aloud was accepted and even enjoyed, provided they had a copy to follow along with and had other outlets to build their own oral reading in class.

After reading, I asked: "What do you remember from what we read? What jumped out at you and made you think?"

Rochelle launched the conversation: "What she said was that she liked every different kind of a poet, it wasn't just any particular kind of person, man or lady . . . I especially like in the first part when she said (reading aloud), 'We need to have these women preserved,' and she started naming them . . . I liked that."

Miss Pearl nodded vigorously and jumped into the conversation. As she spoke she moved her hands in front of her and alternated between reading aloud and paraphrasing. She added, "I like the part where she said 'Writing is a part of my life . . . Cooking is part of my life. Making love is part of my life. Walking down the street is a part of my life. Writing demands more time but it's all of these activities.' I like that part where she said it, because in life . . . the world don't see it that way when you write . . . but she's letting the interviewer know where these all fit . . . where these all fit into her life, and that's very important. She's talking about all the responsibilities . . . she says you got to be good . . . that she says I don't write what I feel and let it all hang out she says that's baloney! She said learning and language and gaining control of the language . . . the ability to make people weep, to make people laugh, make them feel love, make them go to war. The power of the word! I like that part."

Rowena added: "I like the part on page eight where she is very eager in her writing, that she gets up and she does it at a certain time, she does what she says she's going to do. So she puts in a lot of time. She would just write about her life history and what it was like for her coming up."

I ventured: "I like that part, too. I don't know about all of you, but I think writing is hard, and to get up at six o'clock and every day say I'm going to write, I don't know if I could do that."

Rochelle agreed: "I'm like you Kate . . . that's something, to even get me to write. To get up at six, six-thirty . . . it'll be twelve o'clock before I'm started."

Rowena added: "You know she's just like the type of person that she had a made-up mind and she knew just exactly what's she's going to do. And you know I am really proud of her and you know there's a lot of things that have happened to her in her life that she never had forgotten from her youth on up, the things that she had talked about when she first started out. It's taken a lot to remember all that and say I'm just going to write a book about my life."

I posed this question: "What she says about telling the truth . . . she says she doesn't write about everything in her life, that some things are just too painful and she can't write about them because she can't think of a way to write about them that wouldn't be melodramatic . . . that her books are about survival and they're about facing different challenges but not letting yourself be defeated by them. I thought that was really interesting, because it seems like she writes so honestly about things that are so painful, like in *Caged Bird* when she writes about being raped . . . I'm wondering what did she leave out?"

"You know what?" Miss Pearl jumped in, "She says all my work says you may encounter many defeats, but you will not be defeated. That means she's a strong woman. But when she said that there might have been something that just touched her too much," Miss Pearl gestured toward Rowena, "and then like she was saying to remember all that, because this is so much."

Rochelle wondered, "Maybe there is just a little bit that she did leave out . . ."

" 'Cause she's strong you know," Miss Pearl interjected. "Especially what you just said about the rape part. Yeah, when you can come out with that . . . 'cause most time when a person's being raped it seems like it's something . . . I have lived it so I know, it's a hard thing to live with 'cause you keep going over it in your mind sometimes."

"Remembering?" Rochelle queried.

Miss Pearl nodded and elaborated: "Yeah . . . so you got to be strong, that's why I say this is a strong woman! And then she can get up and write it . . . and do all these things 'cause sometimes this kind of stuff stops some people from going on in life . . . But she's a strong woman, a strong woman. She's going to survive . . . out of all the things that's going on in her life, she be going on and on and on and on."

"That's one thing that I want to say to you," I elaborated, "is that I may say let's try writing about this, let's try writing about that, but that doesn't mean that you . . . that I'm trying to say that you have to share everything with me or with anyone else . . . 'cause it's not anybody else's business. You don't have to do that. But the choices that you choose to make as a writer, the risks that you try to take, that's up to you to decide. It's always up to you because you're always the author."

Wherever You Go, She's Already Been There

The book *Black Women for Beginners* is a cross between a revisionist history text and a comic book. It is colloquial in its writing, but challenging in its ideas. After reading a section of this book aloud, I assigned a reading guide which asked the women to write down some notes about the things they found most interesting in the text.

When we came back together, I asked the students to meet in pairs to share what they had found most interesting in the book.

In some cases conversations were slow to percolate, but once they got going, partners were flipping eagerly through their copies of the book, pointing to illustrations and reading aloud the parts of the narrative that had excited them. After about fifteen minutes I asked everybody to reconvene and report back to the whole group.

Everyone had discovered something different. Rochelle had been struck by the theme of grandmothering that she saw in the text. Bell had been drawn to some of the evocative language describing the shades of black in the book. She read aloud this poetic list to us: "brown, low-brown, high-brown, nut-brown, lemon, maroon, olive, mauve, yellow balanced between black and white, black reaching beyond yellow. Almost white on the brink of change sucked down by the terribly sweet rhythm of black blood . . ." Rowena had been fascinated by some of the photos of sculptures from Southwest Asia that showed that black women had lived there around 5,000 years ago.

When it was her turn, Miss Pearl read this excerpt from the beginning of the book: "There are five hundred and ninety million, eight hundred and seventy thousand black women here on the planet earth. There's a Black Woman on each of the seven continents, in almost every country and in the space program. So no matter where you go she's already been there. She travels with forces greater than herself. Her presence is everywhere." Miss Pearl paused for effect and peered over her glasses at the group: "That's the part that I like."

"Why were you drawn to that?" I asked.

"Because it tells about the black women that we can be seen everywhere and anywhere . . ." Miss Pearl stopped reading and looked up from the page. "It's letting you know, when it comes to black women . . . heeeey, it's going on!" The other women responded to her comment with hand clapping and hoots of approval.

I then asked the women to turn their attention to a page that had confused us a bit when we read the text the first time. On the page there was a picture of three scientists arguing about whether or not the bones of the first woman in the world (named Sistuh Eve in the book) proved that she was black or white. I asked Bell, who is a pastor, to tell us if the Bible says whether or not Eve was white.

Sherri interjected: "The Bible don't say nothing about Eve's color!"

A smile played across Bell's lips before she spoke: "It doesn't say it."

I asked the women to talk about what they thought of this book. Rochelle opened the discussion: "It doesn't really . . . my history didn't go about it like this. Mine was a little, but not going deeper. This book it's like WHAT? Every page, I'm like, huh? REALLY?"

I asked the women, "What kinds of things did we learn in school about history and about culture?"

Miss Pearl piped up, "Most of mine was about fighting . . . about war!"

Rochelle agreed. "Uh-huh, World War I, World War II . . ."

Miss Pearl affirmed this: "Abraham Lincoln, George Washington, that's all I was told."

Rochelle went on to explain that when she was in high school there had been a lot of promises made about offering a black history class. When she was a junior they finally started the class, but in her words it was not that different: "You know, World War I, World War II, slavery, Crispus Attucks, . . . a little, just a little bit."

Ain't We Fine?

The women at METRO love reading the poetry of Maya Angelou, and I found her poetry especially useful for building fluency in oral reading. The poem "Ain't That Bad?" consists of eight four-line stanzas and a refrain that is repeated twice, lending itself well to choral reading. First I gave them time to read the poem silently. Then I assigned each woman a stanza to read aloud. I explained that we all would read the refrain in unison.

Miss Pearl volunteered to get us started and began somewhat formally. She stood up, straightened her clothes and threw back her shoulders, before announcing in a dulcet voice: "Our poem for today is 'Ain't That Bad?'" Then she started reading the first stanza.

Miss Pearl:
"Dancing the funky chicken-Eatin ribs and tips-Diggin all the latest sounds-And drinkin gin in sips."

Miss Williams:

"Puttin down that do-rag-Tightenin up my 'fro-Wrappin up in Blackness-Don't I shine and glow?"

Bell:

"Hearin Stevie Wonder-Cookin beans and rice-Goin to the opera-Checkin out Leontyne Price."

Rowena:

"Get down Jesse Jackson-Dance on Alvin Ailey-Talk Miss Barbara Jordan-Groove Miss Pearlie Bailey."

All:

"Now ain't they bad?-An' ain't they Black?-An ain't they Black?-An ain't they bad?-An ain't they Black?-An ain't they fine?"

Sherri:

"Black as the hour of the night-When your love turns and wriggles close to your side-Black as the earth which has given birth-To nations, and when all else is gone will abide."

Rochelle:

"Bad as the storm that leaps raging from the heavens-Bringing the welcome rain-Bad as the sun burning orange hot at midday-Lifting the waters again."

Me:

"Arthur Ashe on the tennis court-Muhummed Ali in the ring-Andre Watts and Andrew Young-Black men doing their thing."

Miss Pearl:

Dressing in purple and pinks and greens-Exotic as rum and cokes-Living our life with flash and style-Ain't we colorful folks?"

All:

"Now ain't we bad?-An ain't we black?-An ain't we bad?-An ain't we Black?-An ain't we fine?"

After reading, we collapsed into giggles and applause. We read through several more times to work on fluency and enjoyed our increasing syncopation: We sounded pretty good. I prepared a reading guide to go along with the poem, asking the women to sort out and elaborate on some of the components of black cultural life that Angelou writes of. We sat around the table and "talked through" the guide. As we worked, we let the conversation take us other places. We discussed hairstyles and music of yesteryear, and the women debated which recording artist had done the song that went along with the "Funky Chicken." Bell jumped up to demonstrate the "Bus Stop." "I shouldn't be doing this you know. Last time I did this I banged my knee on a stove!" she joked.

Author! Author!

One regular component of our writing instruction was the author's chair. I designated a certain chair for the honor and pulled it out from under the table, gesturing toward it with a flourish: "I know to all of you this might look like an average, everyday, ordinary chair, but when a writer sits in it and shares her writing, it become the author's chair!" I asked for volunteers to take the chair and share whatever draft they were currently working on. One by one we read our pieces and received feedback from the group.

Whenever Rowena sat down in the author's chair, her readings were accompanied by additional narrations and explanations. She was resistant to reading her writing aloud and said that "talking it out" helped her to work through her ideas.

On this day, Rowena started with an explanation of her writing process: "The first piece that I had did, I did concerning my grandma. When I was talking about it I had talked about the types of foods that she had prepared for the family which she loved like getting up early in the morning fixing hot biscuits and hog head souse and she would take the pig and grind it up and fix it up and put in the freezer then take it out and we would eat it. Her homemade ice cream . . . I misses that very much, and she was a God-fearing woman. And I wrote up another piece concerning that. Okay . . .

"My grandmother make very good ice cream on Sunday morning. People like her ice cream in the neighborhood. She sometimes sell her ice cream to the people in the neighborhood on Saturdays. I like her cakes and all the good foods that my grandmother make. Cakes, cookies, pies. You name it. It is good."

Rowena continued narrating her story beyond what she was able to commit to paper: "The people in the neighborhood, they would come to the house on every Sunday or Saturday mornings and they would spend their money on buying the ice cream. She would try to show all of her grandchildren how she does it and she would talk about her life story like when she was back on her farm. 'Cause back then, she had had her own farm which belonged to her. She had a lot of cows and chickens and I remember when I was a little girl how I used to . . . back then I was a tomboy where you know I didn't have to worry about wearing shoes like I do up here . . . I just loved that dirt, that red clay dirt which you could stick your toes down in and it'd feel so nice and cool. There was this one special little tree, I loved to climb it was like a hickory nut tree. I loved to pull the nuts off. She had showed me how to run as fast as a chicken and just to see how fast I could catch one. I remember when I was a little knothead little kid where I would run and fall and scratch my knee but I'll get right back up and say well no this little chicken is not going to get the best of me. I would catch the chicken and take it and wring its neck off and pop it."

Rowena paused to indicate the end of her formal presentation and we applauded supportively. I asked the others what feedback they had to give her.

Rochelle asked: "You said your grandmother made ice cream on Sundays?"

Rowena responded: "Oh yes, on Saturdays and Sundays, she would make ice cream and homemade yogurt with fresh strawberries."

"I bet it was good . . . ," Rochelle commented wistfully, and a murmur of agreement circulated around the table.

"Oh, yes," Rowena nodded, "It was very tasty."

"Did she make her own butter?" I wondered.

"Oh, yes, she had churned the butter when she was at home before she moved up here. I like the way she talked to her animals . . . her chickens. It seemed like they would know exactly what she's saying to them," Rowena expanded. "I could go on and on about this, but it'd take too long."

Renee chimed in: "Back then you could leave your door open 'cause everybody knew each other."

Rowena said, "I loved it down there. I would go there to visit and I learned to do a lot of things, how to do things, how to make things. And once you learn things you never forget."

Rochelle wondered, "Why did they leave the South and come to the city?"

Many overlapping voices responded: "To get jobs . . . There's lots of jobs back then . . . No jobs in the South."

Everyone began to discuss their personal knowledge of the black migration to the North. "My mother didn't want to come. She cried and cried," Miss Williams remembered.

Rowena was sympathetic: "It's hard when you have your own place to leave it."

Miss Pearl opined, "When I moved here it was the fifties. You could get jobs. There wasn't welfare. You could work. They had jobs. Welfare didn't start until the sixties."

"That's when DCFS got started too," Renee pointed out.

As Rowena exited the author's chair, I complimented her on the details she had added to her typed draft: "It made it come alive for me."

"Yeah, I wanted to finish it," she said. "Thank you."

Capitals

I knew that to improve their writing and GED scores, the women needed to build skills in the conventions of English grammar. One of the first hurdles that I attempted to tackle was capitalization. Rowena, Miss Pearl, and Miss Williams, my most regular students by this point, all had some difficulty with it, and I knew that there was always a certain percentage of capitalization questions on the exam. The GED test uses a confusing format to test the rules of grammar—planting, in sentences and passages, errors that the student must identify in a multiple-choice format. It is not enough simply to know how to do something correctly; you also must be able to recognize it when it is done incorrectly.

To prepare, I used some of the text from a standard GED preparation book and developed my own sentences with errors for the students to correct. I wrote them using sentences from the students' own writing and created some artificial sentences that were written about subjects that were closer to their experience than the sample sentences you usually find in GED preparation materials. My plan was to tack back and forth between exercises and writing activities—some that were more relevant and some that were more test-like.

Miss Pearl, Rowena, and Miss Williams sat around the table. We each took turns with a sentence and "talked through" the corrections, justifying our choices. The first sentence was: "maya angelou is one of the greatest poets that ever lived in the united states of america."

Miss Pearl went first. "Maya Angelou, Maya Angelou . . . 'm' supposed to be capitalized and 'a' supposed to be capitalized cause this is a name!"

"All right," I affirmed. Miss Williams and Rowena followed along and made the corrections on their copies.

Miss Pearl continued ". . . is one of the greatest poets that ever lived in the United States of America."

"United States of America is supposed to be capitalized!" Miss Williams interrupted.

Miss Pearl swiveled in her chair and looked at Miss Williams with mock irritation. "Shut up," she warned

"Oooo-oooo," we all laughed. I teased Miss Williams, "Miss Pearl wants to do this by herself."

We continued working around the circle, talking through sentences and discussing the rules of punctuation. When we finished the worksheet I had prepared, I asked the students to write their own trick sentences which I wrote on a piece of easel paper I taped to the wall. They could then choose who they wanted to make the corrections in their sentences. Tellingly, both Rowena and Miss Pearl seemed to relish assigning their teacher, Rochelle, to their trick sentences. Miss Pearl said, "You make us do it all the time. Now we get to do it to you!"

Language and Literacy

In all of the activities presented here, the boundaries between thinking, listening, speaking, reading, and writing are fluid. The teacher reads aloud, the students read orally and silently, we write in response to our readings, we practice skills, and we discuss the meanings of all of these endeavors with varying degrees of depth and structure.

We celebrate oral language in our group. The women are given ample time to talk through their ideas in relation to their reading and writing. I believe that students need this: to read aloud, to raise their voices, to testify to their presence and power in the world. This emphasis is essential to the literacy development of adult students and the most likely means to help women and African-American students (Foster 1992) seize control over the language of the dominant group while maintaining a connectedness to their own ways of thinking and speaking.

Content

When the black women in my class read and write, they need to read and write themselves. The writing of Maya Angelou, the book *Black Women for Beginners*, their own essays and grammar exercises crafted from their experiences serve this end. The themes that emerge from these readings—themes of survival, spirituality, the quest for social justice, self-definition, self-determination, and unsinkable style—allow these students to squeeze out a space in the curriculum that has been denied them for too long.

Social Relationships: No Little I's and No Little You's

In the liberatory classroom, the authority that usually comes from course content and the expertise of the teacher is dismantled, scrambled, and reconstructed. Because the content centers on the experiences of the students, the authority must be shared. I take responsibility for finding materials that I hope will be useful and relevant to the students, yet the decoding of these materials is always something that the students define. I encourage the students to realize their authority by quite literally requiring that they think of themselves as authors. Reading the interview with Maya Angelou, sharing their essays in the author's chair, and playfully assigning grammar exercises to the teacher illustrate this. I share in these experiences with them as a colearner, surprised by the readings, moved by their interpretations, and offering my own writing in the author's chair. But this does not mean that I abdicate my responsibility to teach directly the skills the women need to become more powerful readers and writers and to succeed on any test that they want to take.

I have found that the students at METRO prefer to learn in a collective fashion. Their "egalitarian ethos" (Foster 1992) and community spirit is something that runs throughout these vignettes as well, in the images of a group of women sitting around a table in circle, sharing supplies, teasing each other, and jumping up to demonstrate the "Bus Stop." I actively try to mirror this preference by creating opportunities for the students to work in pairs and encouraging collaborative completion of reading guides and grammar exercises.

I know that my race and class status place me in position of privilege that cannot be overlooked. Still, I have hope that through our communication we can join together in a common and liberatory project. Paulo Freire speaks of this when he says, "Through dialogue, the teacher-of-the-students and the students-of-the-teacher cease to exist and a new term emerges: teacher-student with student-teachers" (1972, 61).

I do believe in equality. I do believe in the power of the word. This is what our students believe in as well. I wonder if it is this ethic of equality that at least partially explains the American love affair with round-robin reading. This instructional technique feeds into our democratic impulses: the need to divide a text up evenly, ensuring that we all contribute, that we all raise our voices in a common project.

While I still believe there are more progressive ways to teach oral reading, we must listen to our students. Their vision of equality will lead us. I was pondering the meaning of equality when I stumbled onto one of Rowena's comments on a class transcript: "This school right here is more so where everybody loves one another and would help one another. It's no little Is and no little yous. Ain't nobody looking down on nobody. You know, it's a lot of love."

This impulse toward equality, this predisposition toward love, is why we teach. There is no better reason.

REFERENCES

Atwell, N. 1989. *In the Middle.* Portsmouth, N.H.: Heinemann.

Angelou, M. 1986. *Poems.* New York: Bantam Books.

Delpit, L. 1995. *Other People's Children.* New York: The New Press.

———. 1988. The silenced dialogue: Power and pedagogy in educating other people's children. *Harvard Educational Review,* 58(3):280–98.

Freire, P. 1972. *Pedagogy of the Oppressed.* London: Penguin Books.

Foster, M. 1992. Sociolinguistics and the African-American community: implications for literacy. In *Theory Into Practice,* edited by V. Gadson, 31(4):303–11.

Griffith, M., B. Jacobs, S. Wilson, and M. Dashiell. 1989. Changing the model: Working with underprepared students. *The Quarterly of the National Writing Project* 11(1):4–9.

hooks, b. 1994. *Teaching to Transgress.* New York: Routledge.

Sharp, S. 1993. *Black Women for Beginners.* New York: Writers and Readers Publishing, Inc.

Tate, C. 1984. *Black Women Writers at Work.* New York: Continuum.

Walker, E. S. 1992. Falling asleep and failure among African-American students: Rethinking assumptions about process teaching. In *Theory into Practice,* edited by V. Gadson, 31(4):321–27.

Weiler, K. 1991. Freire and a feminist pedagogy of difference. *Harvard Educational Review* 61(4):449–74.

—An Activist Forum II: Fault Lines

Anna Deavere Smith

Anna Deavere Smith, courtesy of Janette Beckman

Actors are very impressionable people, or, some would say, suggestible people. We are trained to develop aspects of our memories that are more emotional and sensory than intellectual. The general public often wonders how actors remember their lines. What's more remarkable to me, is how actors remember, recall, and reiterate feelings and sensations. The body has a memory just as the mind does. The heart has a memory just as the mind does. The act of speech is a physical act. It is powerful enough to create, with the rest of the body, a kind of cooperative dance. That dance is a sketch of something that is inside a person, and not fully revealed by the words alone. I came to realize that if I were able to record part of the dance—that is, the spoken part—and reenact it, the rest of the body would follow. I could then create the illusion of being another person by reenacting something they had said as they had said it. Using my grandfather's idea that if I said a word often enough it would become me, the reenactment, or the reiteration of a person's words would also teach me about that person . . .

Trying to do other-oriented work also raised some questions which may interest the general public. Any of us who engage in extroverted activities are aware of our inhibitions. I am interested in how inhibitions affect our ability to emphasize. If I have an inhibition about acting like a man, it may also point to an inhibition I have about seeing a man or hearing a man. To develop a voice one must develop an ear. To complete an action one must have a clear vision. Does the inability to empathize start with an inhibition, or a reluctance to see? Do racism and prejudice instruct those inhibitions? If I passed out a piece of poetry to be read by a racially mixed group and I asked them to read it with an English accent, most of them would try. If I passed out a piece of black poetry written in dialect, many would be inhibited and fearful of offending others. In a playwriting class, I gave an exercise called "gang writing." Students were asked to write short scenes about gangs inspired by gang writing. A student raised the question, "Isn't it offensive for us, here in our privileged environment, to write about gangs?" Does privilege mean one shouldn't see? At the same time, the standard for excellence is still a Eurocentric theater written by and for white men. Who else can participate? How? Does it mean new plays? Does it mean rethinking old plays? The mirrors of society do not mirror society.

Who has the right to see what? Who has the right to say what? Who has the right to speak for whom? These questions have plagued the contemporary theater. These questions address both issues of employment equity and issues of who is portrayed. These questions are the questions that unsettle and prohibit a democratic theater in America. If only a man can speak for a man, a woman for a woman, a black person for all black people, then we, once again, inhibit the spirit of theater, which lives in the bridge that makes unlikely aspects seem connected. The bridge doesn't make them the same, it merely displays how two unlikely aspects are related. These relationships of the unlikely, these connections of things that don't fit together are crucial to American theater and culture if theater and culture plan to help us assemble our obvious differences. The self-centered technique has taken the bridge out of the process of creating character, it has taken metaphor out of acting. It has made the heart smaller, the spirit less gregarious, and the mind less apt to be able to hold on to contradictions or opposition.

Therese Quinn

Therese Quinn, courtesy of
Patricia Guizzetti

When the ocean's lapping around your neck, tide rising, you have to grab the hands that reach toward you. Any hands. The first few that beckon are your instant community, and there's a great hope that they will be your home too, or at least a safe harbor or buoy for the time being.

This is how I started my gay life: secretly, through a dark bar's doors—the Casino Club let me bet some given-to-me plans against some real and present lusts (it was a steamy, lonely gamble)—and later through sensuous tongue lashings and ferocious wranglings toward identity. Gay or faggot? Dyke or lesbian? Who you calling queer? Who are my angels? Gay folks weren't welcome and invited guests anywhere, and we clung to each other like drifting, life-saving planks from wrecked ships. Marching fiercely into a nation of action, we were the parades and promise, too.

Every Gay Pride Day and parade felt good and necessary, with my head still reeling from first girl kisses and all the "outlaws together" bonding. It was my day and our procession. No crashing needed, entry was guaranteed. The lineups were inclusive and outrageous—the nasty fishnet-stocking Sisters of Perpetual Indulgence led by shirtless power dykes on motorbikes followed by Rapunzel-haired radical leather faeries all shouting and flouncing down the city's main drag. Membership was comforting. I thought I had found home.

But last year and the year before, and for some time before that, Gay Pride Day was a galling and bitter pill. The pride parade, my parade was lassoed by a few gay men for profit. Now the parade winds down a narrow and marginal street flanked by bars so that the same group of guys can sell a sea of beer to the rest of us. Who leads this procession? First, a flood of straight politicians—smarmy elected gals and gents who are only symbolically present and still take up too much space. The glad-handers are followed by bar floats and brewery trucks. Bottom line, alcohol isn't really a queer person's friend—for gay "pride" many of us smear our loneliness into shitty-drunk grins and get "bad" all day, in direct proportion to our rest-of-the-time squashedness. Who watches? Crowds of city ditchers in for the day, cheering and jeering between swigs. Diluted, the day serves a much-muted purpose, lounging somewhere below power and above titillation.

Gay pride isn't a unifier. Maybe never was, beyond the first blink of recognition or comfort fostered by our surprising numbers and diversity. We don't all start or end at the same place: In a wink and nod at separate but equal, my city has two gay days in one. It goes like this: (Mostly) white folks march in a parade and end up at a (mostly) white rally. Black folks meet at the lakefront, and stay there. What was an ad hoc and de facto protest by absence (of black gays and lesbians from a largely white-run march) is now the expected, incorporated and smiled on. Local queer rags herald both gatherings, and the "they have theirs and we have ours" mentality deepens. No problems addressed, all stunting and warping accommodated.

Further fracturing: Now a group of white lesbians call a "girl-cott" of the official parade on the grounds of sexist harassment and for the second year a dyke march takes the streets the night before the "official" gay event. To me, it's not like three good flavors and more fun—it's a depressing defeat. Three events, three groups of marginalized queer people, each now more entrenched in separation from the other.

Stolen and split, this queer twenty-four hours is still a day for something newly possible, a day for transgressive hand holding and loud love-ins, and a nodding toward new definitions and good sex. How can that be ignored? As we name ourselves, get visible, and march in throngs, we etch more deeply the grooves that our civil rights fighting mothers and fathers began to carve for us. Ignoring what they started is somehow worse than never beginning a move toward freedom—more hopeless. So I am beholden, and compelled to let my feet pound a sturdy poem into the streets as I claim my place at all three parties: Yes, I remember, take my hands, we're home.

Jonathan Silin

Jonathan Silin, courtesy of
Robert Giard

I have never developed the thick skin that would allow me to be a cool, dispassionate reader of student evaluations. Recently, some students have begun to say that I have an "agenda." Of course the students are right. I am clear from the first day of the semester that I bring to class a critical view of education in America, a demand for more socially relevant curricula in schools, and the experiences of a gay man who has participated in dramatic social changes over the last thirty-five years. To some, "having an agenda" is a description of a well-structured course; to others, an angry accusation about a lack of objectivity; and to just a few, a valued recognition that teachers may be committed intellectuals.

When I first started teaching undergraduates, my agenda was simpler. Then in 1984 I began to speak in class about being gay. I acted out of neither the desire to become a role model for lesbian and gay students nor the wish to promote greater tolerance among straight students. Rather, it simply seemed disingenuous to lecture prospective teachers about the connectedness of our personal and professional lives and *not* talk about being gay. It was a matter of integrity, of the authentic voices I hoped my students would assume in their own classrooms.

I teach that education is an ethical and political practice, a concept often difficult for students to accept. I am obligated to reveal the way that sexual identity informs my understanding of how public institutions function in our society. My gay history tells me that modern "science" normalizes some lives and pathologizes others, makes me suspicious of the role that experts play in our society, and aligns me with other groups who have experienced physical and psychological violence.

At Bank Street College where I currently teach, my story is no longer a coming-out story. But even in this progressive context, I do not underestimate the powerful ways in which ignorance is socially negotiated. Students often comment on my "radicalizing" politics and commitment to feminist viewpoints but never make direct reference to my sexual identity. What they do say is that I have created courses to address my "personal concerns" and that teaching seems to be a "very personal experience for this instructor."

But I believe that when I teach as an openly gay man, I do not reveal anything of a personal nature. Rather, I act to interrupt a social secret, the kind that one person tells another about a third party. I also interrupt the myth of the omniscient narrator and our ability to speak for other people. How can persons of privilege talk about the lives of those who are oppressed? How can men talk about women's lives? I want students to acquire an appreciation of the difference between talking *about* and talking *for* someone else. While we engage in lengthy epistemological debates about knowing others, I also want students to recognize the overriding ethical imperative to act against all forms of social injustice.

Speaking personally is not limited to matters of sexual orientation nor is it confined to my role as teacher. I ask students to write and share with the class narratives about their own childhoods. At the same time, I am aware that we live in a culture that thrives on personal narratives of the intimate. Television talk shows, bookstore shelves, and self-help groups are awash with stories in which people recount their struggles with addictions to substances, destructive relationships, and the effects of childhood abuses. I ask myself if classroom confessions are so very different? Have we sought undue intimacy with our students? Have we gained their participation in a culture of self-display?

I am arguing that storytelling is a necessary but not sufficient foundation of education for social justice. Individual self-expression must be part of a critical study of the larger social work. Stories link our lives to our cultures, offer maps for others, provide insights into sociopolitical realities. Our task as critical educators is to help students to recognize the differential effects of stories. We must all learn to ask: whose interests are served and whose silenced by this story? Who gains power and who loses power in this particular version of truth?

Stories are fictions that change over time and are transformed by the times. We constitute ourselves through the stories we tell and are constituted by the communities available to hear them. My gay story could not have been told before the 1970s when the contemporary lesbian and gay community began to take form, just as that community is strengthened every time someone tells her or his story.

In the classroom I want to create a community in which students can tell their own stories and trust that their differences will be heard. Democratic communities are based on differences. Real identifications are earned only when we struggle to make sense of the other and recognize that our knowledge is always partial and incomplete. By making teaching "a very personal experience" we give up being like our students or even being liked by them in order to foster authentic public dialogue.

There are other risks as well. Our words and our lives are misunderstood and misrepresented. Naming may confine and control but silence can be deadly.

Last semester a student wrote that I had an "excellent" command of the course content. "But," she added, "this material is clearly his baby." The "but" belies her assumptions about education. It suggests that real teaching occurs when we transmit material from which we are distanced and detached, rather than ideas to which we are connected as to a baby, through the immediate demands of the body. But the objective purveyor of truth, disembodied teller of other people's tales, is the one position that I am no longer willing to assume. And that, I suspect, is the most disturbing part of my agenda to students.

Kim Murray

Kim Murray, courtesy of
Tam Stuart

Imagine walking down the hall of the place in which you are expected to learn and not being able to go a day without being called such names as: psycho dyke, dyke bitch, homo, lesbo, and anything else a teenage imagination can come up with when referring to your known, suspected, or rumored sexual orientation. How about receiving little or no help from teachers or other adults because they could care less or are simply afraid of being labeled with the same tag as you? Imagine your classmates going as far as threatening your life if you dared going to your senior prom with the one you cared about.

I am a 1995 graduate of Plainfield High School in Plainfield, Illinois, and those are the conditions under which I attended school. Being the only "out" student in the school, I had several classmates who felt the need to come out to me. We literally had no safe haven to go to and be ourselves in the school. Considering that a large percent of lesbi-gay teens' lives end in suicide, I started a support group with a lot of help from my dear friend Eddie Walczak. The group started strong and the counselor seemed genuinely interested, but that was short-lived. She did little to help ensure that the harassment be looked into, accused us of trying to get special privileges, and created trouble in the homes of some youths in the group.

When I made the decision to take my current girlfriend to the prom, I received ridicule for wanting to wear a tux, wanting to dance with my date, and was accused of trying to make it my personal coming out party. A week or two before the prom, I had received extreme harassment from a particular heterosexual student couple regarding me even showing up. When a death threat appeared in my locker, I took it to the dean and mentioned the problems I had been having with the couple. His response to me a few days later, regarding the note and harassment, was that the guy was the star of his golf team and the student would have told him if he was the one who made the threat. Because he denied it, the dean had to believe him. At the prom, the couple made the last comment of the year, targeting me, and of course my date, and I had no help from the principal, counselor, or security. When Eddie and I graduated, the remaining "out" lesbi-gay students tried and failed to ensure some kind of safety be provided at the school. One particular girl was chased out of the school.

What this has shown me is a desperate need for an education about lesbi-gay life in our schools, not only for the students, but also for the teachers and staff. My school had different pride clubs for the racial groups, so why did they accuse us of wanting special privileges? Why were we forced to endure ridicule, fear, harassment, and embarrassment each day in a place that they expect us to learn in? We are human too. We need a safe haven when it gets to be more than we can take. We also need outside support groups made more accessible through our schools. Schools are where we need it all to start, so we won't have to say later that a lot of us are lucky to have even made it to adulthood. Please, give us role models and active support.

I feel I am one of the fortunate ones who found role models. Now I am on my way to a hopefully healthy, happy, adulthood. Today I join my elders in the fight to help lesbian and gay youth who are in need of someone to turn to.

Elizabeth Alexander

Elizabeth Alexander, courtesy of Barbara Kigozi

A poetry student of mine, a woman who wants to teach women's literature and who I am relatively sure would call herself a feminist, is frustrated by the way I am teaching her. She has asked me if she has "talent" and I have resisted, explaining that I do not wish to invest myself with the magic-wand authority that bestows talent on credulous students; that while I am excited by her work and its promise, I am trying to teach her to work for herself rather than for an endowment that I can't really give her anyway. Dorothy learns in *The Wizard of Oz* that the ability to go home has always been within her, not extrinsic, and all she needs to do is click her heels and she will be there; but the journey has been crucial. However corny, I want my student to understand this, to understand the bind of mentorship, that I can be encouraging without bestowing something on her and that my working with her in this way demonstrates my faith in her and her writing. I believe this and still do. I want my students to have something that keeps them going from within when no teachers are around saying "yes."

I know that she is angry with me. One day we are having a group conversation about the accouterments of writing—pens and paper and notebook and the like—and she offers her own beautifully covered journal for me to see. "Please, look," she says, and I riffle through the heavy, creamy paper. My eye catches the line, in her handwriting, "I think I am smarter than Liz Alexander." I shut the book quickly and give it back to her.

Now, first of all, "Liz"? Anyone who knows me knows that the diminutive of my name is simply not who I am. Or maybe it wasn't me at all. Maybe there is a Liz Alexander who sits next to her in chemistry. Maybe . . .

But probably not. At a university where I am the only black woman who teaches undergraduates, I cannot help but wonder if this challenge to my "authority" should be read not as necessary hubris from a young woman striving to find her place but rather as a much more profound inculcation of the ethos of a university that, at very least by its hiring practices but also by its curriculum, has as much as said: black women are not authorized here.

When I teach black women's autobiography, I find that many of my white women students are at first swept into the class and their experience of me as a teacher by a general sense of sisterhood. But when they listen to some of the hard challenges, explicit and not, that the works make to them as white women, they turn their prickliness on me, challenging my authority. I believe they are responding to feeling displaced in a room where the first-person voices of black women are primary and occupy the "woman" space that some of their feminist education has unfortunately taught them, however implicitly, is the rightful place of white women.

I want to inject them with a serum that makes them believe what I know: that speaking is crucial, that you have to tell your own story simultaneously as you hear and respond to the stories of others, that education is not something you passively consume. And I want, just for a sustained moment, the kind of unarticulated, enveloping mist that shrouds my male colleagues: respect that does not have to be earned over and over and over again.

9—On A Mission—Hazel Johnson and Marvin Garcia

Therese Quinn

> *I believe, absolutely, that if you do not break out in that sweat of fear when you write, then you have not gone far enough.*
>
> Dorothy Allison
> (217)

SURVIVAL'S SIGNATURE

Left by my mother at four, I've been looking for strong women to follow since I was a girl breathing in the talcum safety of my granny's girdle. Growing up poor meant I felt "the short end of the stick" and the festering anger that often stunts possibility, and is sometimes a painful motivator. My family lesson was: alcohol is anger's anesthesia. Anger is survival's signature. It is a secret constant sore, but I think that spark is better than numb. I want to feel my whole life. Can someone teach me how to transform anger into fuel?

All passion is a powerful magnet. I'm drawn to women who make a way out of no way, and teach others that they can do the same. Women who teach me about survival, in other words. But that is just the first step; these women also have to be more sure of their rightness than the world is that they are crazy. They need to shout sometimes, and play the trickster to the big guy's "I'm daddy, do this." I've met plenty of men who can stand against that guy, but women that tough mesmerize me. How do they keep their opposing vision?

My heart needs soft men, too, an antidote to the scary fathers who spanked, the betraying teachers who groped, the one-up boys everywhere. Nurturing, nursiness, soft shoulders, graceful hands, passion and poetics: Walt Whitman. He and Allen Ginsberg (1956, 34), "putting . . . queer shoulder[s] to the wheel" of the world, show me a way to live my own gay life. I'm raising my son on this mythos: Men contain multitudes, so follow the gentle leader.

I'm wary, though, of glib, gifted people, charmers and politicians. Activist Jack Greenberg said, "If someone tells you they know what to do, don't believe them." That sounds right. I saw

Jim Jones, immaculate and beguiling in his Oakland church, lead old black ladies waiting for a tumor removal and a chance to buy a Jesus/Jim Jones medallion right into oblivion. It's a deep-edge example, but I've followed some charismatic, ultimately abusive "leaders" myself, and "the more gifted, the more corrupt" could be a maxim. There's a conundrum: I'm looking for teachers who are burning with their vision, their calling. Their seductive truth will not be mine. Will I always need to step back from full trust?

Learning is transformation. I am not now what I was before I realized my anger, desire, and mistrust, the signatures of my survival. Heart shy, open, I keep looking for the routes to discernment. Singular: a teacher. Plural: a community.

TEACHER

When I dare to be powerful—to use my strength in the service of my vision, then it becomes less and less important whether I am afraid.
Audre Lorde 1984, 112

My definition too: A person working to make a just world needs to have a passion for, or a "calling" to the work of seeking justice. They should be able to dream that world, and think it's possible in real time. They need to manifest bravery.

The nail that sticks up highest gets pounded the hardest.
Chinese wisdom

They will probably have been reviled, or at least unpopular.

Never trust anyone who isn't angry.
John Trudell

They will be angry.

WHAT I'M LEARNING

I owe the basic white person's debt of culture and conscience to black America, plus one: my clearest understanding of justice was shaped by the black family my mother gave birth to after parking me with my grandparents. At eight I declared my visiting black brother "just tan" to my best friend. I was trying to avoid the stigma of blackness by association. Later, I lived with my denied siblings, and loving them pushed me toward defiant affiliation. My song was "Say it loud, he's black and I'm proud" all through the sixties and seventies. During this time I was learning some lessons while watching my brothers live them.

I disliked shopping at the local Chinese-owned grocery with our food stamps. I hated the owners for their high prices and roach-infested goods. The Chinese lady heaped special scorn on my baby brothers, though. They, so brown in a white-trash neighborhood, were whispered about and trailed through the store.

My fundamentalist aunt thought I was anointed and should speak in tongues. We went down to the lake together, and all my sins were washed away. My brother's stains proved more indelible; she didn't flinch when her Hitler-loving son pronounced my brothers "slaves" in his war games. No amount of washing could clear that original sin of arrival. Only problem . . . the wrong people were called out dirty.

I grew to understand that "'white' stood for and stands for not so much a degree of pigmentation as a set of attitudes that takes privilege as an exclusive right" (Eakins 1995). My skin was, is always a protective layer, unasked for but undeniable. What I got, my brothers did not.

But there was something else. In being defined, my brothers gained groupness. They weren't part of the all-faced/faceless dominant mass. Instead they were specifically "ethnic" and in community. I started looking for my locus, my "karass" of Vonnegutian like-minders. High school, "ethnic studies," 1972. It was really about black pride, but I brought Gertrude Stein in for show and tell. Does she count? She's a lesbian. Jewish. Whither thou goest, Gertrude, there also will I go. Is that ethnic enough? The teacher, Elmo Slider, didn't see what I was up to, he laughed at my "women's libber . . . Someone had to change her diapers." The man wanted to change his world but didn't see that mine needed to change also.

Twenty years later I met Hazel Johnson while doing research for a children's museum exhibit about garbage and recycling. I talked with her several times, toured the landfills around her home turf with her, and photographed her. Visiting Ms. Johnson was going to real school. She spent a lot of time patiently doing these things with me, and I wasn't able to give her much back. The museum I worked for censored her message: most of

Chicago's garbage dumps are in the neighborhoods of poor black and brown people, who are getting sick as a result. Her facts were right, but environmental racism can't be addressed when Chicago's Department of the Environment is paying the bills.

Ecoactivism for middle-class white folks often stays at the safe edges of urban areas. Whales and dolphins aren't generally our neighbors. Rain forests are comfortably remote. Ms. Johnson points out that some people's yards are full of shit, so that others' can be free of it. Her message, "We don't want landfills in our backyards, but we don't want them in anyone else's either," isn't vindictive, but it sure isn't popular.

I hadn't had much interest in environmental issues before talking to Hazel Johnson; I recycled cans with my children once after a trip home to California. I was not too concerned about the kind of tuna I used for my noodle casseroles, and honestly, I still avoid those discussions. But if you've got a calling, come see me . . . This woman said, "I've definitely been chosen by a higher power to do this work." Passion really is a powerful magnet. I move in that direction. Audre Lorde (1984) explained that "The master's tools will never dismantle the master's house." I went to Hazel to hear her preaching and learn what tools she's using to change the world. And I returned to her to make good on some of my moral debt to black America.

A COMMUNITY'S TEACHER

Hazel Johnson is a tall round woman, full-cheeked and brown-skinned, with soft grey and black hair worn natural. She carries herself large and graceful. Her voice is soft. She reminds me that poverty is always about teeth; Hazel flashes quick smiles to hide her mouth's empty spaces. She often sounds like she is being interviewed by a television reporter as she reels off demographics and death tolls, selling the urgent facts about life in a circle of fifty-two landfills. Her message is practiced—she's been delivering it for thirteen years. She was sixty a month ago, and told me, while pulling apart a chicken wing with delicate opal-polish-tipped fingers, that she is bone tired. Tired of hunting for funding, running an office, and overhearing whispers that her head's gotten too big. Her body feels it. She has diabetes and high blood pressure, and says she is going home to Louisiana to rest.

A widow for thirty years, she raised seven children, four sons and three daughters, alone. She has been working and helping her neighbors since her high school days in Compton, California. After coming to Chicago from Louisiana in the 1950s, she worked as a receptionist, a typist, a mail clerk, and an employment discrimination tester, applying for jobs with a white partner to see which of them would be hired. Guess who was? She worked for the Chicago Housing Authority (CHA) for a while, and has been mobilizing and organizing people for as long as anyone in her office can remember. Her daughter Cheryl said, "Every time she wanted to give it up, it seemed like she got more energy from somewhere. It came from her heart."

Born in New Orleans in 1935, Hazel was the first of her mother's four children, and the only one who lived past age two. One brother was born dead, another died at nine months, and her baby sister died at two of pneumonia. Hazel was separated from her mother for four years, living in a Catholic boarding school while her mother, ill with the tuberculosis that eventually killed her, stayed in a sanitarium. Reflecting on this later, Ms. Johnson said: "I had to know why I survived. I meditated on that, and I had a vision that showed me I was on the right track [when I started working on environmental issues]. I'm on a mission" (1995). Today Hazel's birth home is called "cancer alley," and her home in Altgeld Gardens has the highest rates of cancer in Chicago (*Chicago Tribune* 1995). In the United States, black people have a shorter life expectancy than whites. According to some reports, the life span of black men is actually decreasing. Hazel Johnson's work shows that some of the reasons for this are environmental.

Hazel Johnson has been living and working in the Altgeld Gardens community for three decades. When she first moved to the Gardens, she says, it was nice, and the place lived up to its name. Every family had a patch of flowers growing. There were tap lessons and basketball games, art classes and after-school programs, block clubs and parties, often sponsored by the CHA. She said, "I vowed if I ever got into Chicago Housing, I'd stay till my kids grew up."

Altgeld Gardens was built in 1940 for WWII veterans and their families, on a garbage pile, it turns out, an early dump site for the Pullman Company. From then until now the Gardens has been surrounded by chemical incinerators, water and sewage treatment plants, paint factories and old steel mills, scrap yards, abandoned lagoons, old and new "sanitary" landfills, at least fourteen illegal dump sites—and all of these places circled by a net of expressways and industrial service roads. Altgeld Gardens is an island, isolated by geography, poverty, and 140 square miles of pollution.

It was hot the day I first drove into the Gardens and followed the road's curve into the small strip mall housing People for Community Recovery (PCR), the organization Ms. Johnson and a friend started in a church in the 1970s. The mall is private property, owned by Sam Jabar, "an Arab," Ms. Johnson told me, plunked down in the middle of public housing. The virtues of strip malls are at best debatable, but this one isn't shiny with affluence or possibility, like something with a Starbucks in Lincoln Park, or even the beauty supplies and bakeries on working-class Lincoln Avenue. Milk costs $2.89 a half gallon at the Garden Food Plaza and there's no competition from a nearby Jewel or Dominick's, or even the kind of bare-lightbulb warehouse stores that are opened in the poorest neighborhoods.

Jabar's high prices, leaky ceilings, and steel-shuttered doors and windows fuel resentments that explode into interethnic tensions: he's "an Arab," people say, and that outsiderness becomes significant. I remember my own discomfort in the Chinese grocery near my Sacramento home. The owner interrogated me one day, "Are these your stamps? Where you get them?" She finally accepted them, but refused to give cash change. My pockets filled with her scribbled scrap paper vouchers, pieces of dollars that stood in for change. I worried them with nervous fingers into the original pulp, before they could collectively amount to anything. Embarrassed, I called that store "the Chink's" in my head.

Ten thousand people live in Altgeld, and there isn't a laundromat closer than a twenty-minute bus ride. Except for a liquor store and a greasy fast-food place run by cousins of the owner, and the PCR office, the storefronts are empty and metal-shuttered. They send a stark notice of few options. Jabar and family must see more profit in "suds" than wash: forty-ounce bottles are scattered near the liquor store and brown-papered in old men's hands. Cheryl says liquor is the "sedative of the people" when I ask her if she's thought about trying to have the store closed down. There's too much pain here, and it needs some numbing, she thinks. I haven't asked Hazel this question: Is alcohol less a toxin than the stuff oozing from the landfills? Would you have more PCR Rangers, youth volunteers, if you closed that place down, and Altgeld got angry? Environmental racism takes many forms.

Rents for everyone outside Mr. Jabar's family are high. PCR wants to expand its offices to make space for more volunteers, computers, files, and curious visitors like me. But the Jabar family is asking $1,200 a month for one of the empty, run-down offices—too steep for this group, struggling from donation to grant deadline. Big bucks don't flow freely to those who seek to stop business as usual. When Hazel started PCR, it was a women's thing, meeting in women's spaces, churches, and kitchens. Now, PCR is internationally known: Hazel went to Brazil in 1993 for the Earth Summit. The group has grown, but it is rooted in Altgeld Gardens and needs a space that reflects both its seriousness and its commitment to this community.

The boundaries between the driving, the walking, and the parking areas are unclear; cracked sidewalks blur into glass-plastered asphalt. Following Caretta's directions, I drive my car right up and park on what would have been a place to walk at another mall, in another part of Chicago. Sitting on a ragged couch and old milk crates, small groups of men and women talk, some sipping from their bagged bottles. Families emerge from the mildewy depths of the food store with small shopping bags. Altgeld is as segregated as the rest of Chicago: the area is over 97 percent black (Chicago Department of Planning and Development 1994), and this crowd is 100 percent black. I feel conspicuous.

What am I bringing to this meeting? I admire Hazel. I want to understand how she leads, how she repeatedly survived, through mothering and widowhood and into activism. "I want," though, is the problem. Hazel's office is often full of young white people, students, asking for something. My black friends were bitter dissecting the "Slim's Table Syndrome," after the book written about Hyde Park's Valois Cafeteria and some of its long-time customers by a University of Chicago student. Privileged white students write their "master works" on the backs of black "informants." Does that resonate for you? William (Upski) Wimsatt (1994) said, "By learning more from [black people] than I give back, I am still accruing a deficit every year on top of the towering debt I still owe." I know who gets paid and who gets the grade, and that knowledge is uncomfortable.

As I walk up to the PCR doorway, a young man asks me, "You the police?" Inside, Luther croons softly on the radio, and another young man steps in to ask for "some little safeties." Hazel excuses herself from our conversation, and with full attention hands over a bag of condoms and lube. I keep my back turned; does he need a private transaction? Or is that solely my need? Later, Hazel tells me that when PCR started, they just tried to get the CHA to deal with Altgeld's maintenance problems, like fixing roofs and pipes and keeping the place clean. Then they took the CHA to court and won a settlement assuring that the CHA will not rent any apartment they can't guarantee is lead free. Now they try to do anything and everything the residents need, from job training to court advocacy to HIV prevention.

Ms. Johnson told me about her trip up from Louisiana to Chicago as a young woman. She and her husband settled into the Gardens and started growing a family. Poverty kills, though; in her husband's home state of Mississippi, black men worked at what they could, often in dangerous and deadly situations. He could have been putting in asbestos, or maybe he was ripping it out. In any case, he wasn't wearing safety gear, and when the cancer showed up, his lungs were thick with it, and he quickly slid to death. After she raised her head from grieving, Hazel noticed that more of her friends were sick. Too many people dying, too many poor people living in unsafe places. That's exactly when she started shifting the focus of PCR from Altgeld's "body" to the bodies of the people living there.

Hazel went to a meeting sponsored by the Illinois Environmental Protection Agency, and after she spoke up about some of the problems in Altgeld, like the pounding headaches caused by the stink of methane and the asbestos "angel hair" insulation that the city was stalling on removing, an official sent her twelve copies of a health evaluation form to have her neighbors fill out. "Like you give a titty to a baby, that's what they were doing to us." She had her daughters make a thousand more copies at work and organized people to canvass every apartment in the Altgeld complex. She mailed these back, with even more detailed information, to the Environmental Protection Agency, which waited two weeks before telling her that the data was no good because the collection "wasn't professionally done." Hazel said, "They probably threw it into the garbage."

Altgeld's physical decline started in the 1970s, around the

time federal funds were being diverted from cities to suburban areas. The longtime alderman, a white "machine politician," told the community that if they voted him out, they could say good-bye to their city services. The white population in the ward had declined, and he wasn't providing much service anyway, so a black politician named Robert Shaw was elected alderman of the 9th Ward, which encompasses Altgeld Gardens. According to longtime Altgeld residents, everything declined after that election. Shaw didn't have the clout, or maybe the commitment, to keep the community clean.

Caretta, who started as a volunteer and now is a paid staffer at PCR, and Cheryl, Hazel's daughter and ally in the struggle for justice, reminisced about Altgeld's past. The 1970s were good for teens, which they were then. There were art and dance programs, clubs, and lots of city and state offices to help them find jobs or get medical care. These thirtyish women, with children now themselves, remembered parties where they "bum rushed" each other's blocks, shattering pop bottles on door stoops until one block won, and the other blocks were buried under glass shards. The losers had to sweep up before the weekend was over. It was good—the kids looked out for each other, and they were proud of Altgeld. The Altgeld Parade and Family Reunion was famous then; on one hot August Sunday every year, Altgeld's patch of 'Sippi up North had plenty of visiting cousins and grandparents from down South.

Altgeld is a garden of growing children—80 percent of its residents are under the age of eighteen. These days children are reaping as well as growing, fighting, and shooting. Hazel says, "Not at anybody, just to show they have a gun . . ." Then she says, "The children out here might be gang-banging, but they are respectful to the elders." Twenty-five teens and young adults work at PCR, all from Altgeld, keeping up the office, learning to be lead-abatement inspectors, and helping with the public meetings that Hazel and Cheryl run. There are still some programs here for kids to attend after school and on weekends. Caretta has a son who goes to Boy Scouts, or as she says, "I take him to Scouts, 'cause you don't see him unless you see me." But most programs are pay per session, and even cheap is too much for many families.

PASSING IT ON: PLAY IS PRICELESS

In African American communities "other mothers" pass on the traditions and information that their daughters need (Collins 1991). Hazel had them, and is a play mother to many. It's a black thing: I had to ask, to understand. Although white women and girls certainly nourish each other, I can't think of any equivalently defined relationship. Caretta explained, "A play mother is someone that's there when your mother isn't. You could speak more freely [with her], sit back and talk." PCR is an organization of powerhouse play mothers, teaching by word and example that change is demandable and doable. They are passing on the will to fight and the ways to fight. Black people connected and defining the fight together, "fictive" family, "play-kin" (Collins 1991). It's about action and connection, and reminds me of Freire's (1994) admonition that the "naming of the world . . . is not possible if it is not infused with love."

Like Dewey, Hazel and Cheryl see opportunity in inexperience. Dewey said simply, "The primary condition of growth is immaturity" (1916, 1944). Cheryl describes the growth to activism as "a grooming process." About her own evolution:

"I'll be honest with you, I went to college because my mother could get Social Security support for me [as long as I stayed in school]. When I graduated I started at Argonne. They went back twenty years in my history, and I was only twenty-one, to get the government clearance. I resigned when my mother could give me a part-time job. It took me seven years to learn to talk about environmental issues. I was always making trouble. Now I challenge the opposition. [I] don't have to be a rocket scientist [to do that]."

Increasingly, economic parity is Cheryl's goal for Altgeld. Individually, folks are poor; collectively, a lot of money moves through their hands. Her example: Altgeld's liquor store profits are $1.5 million a year. She says there are 1,800 currency exchanges in Illinois, and all of them are owned by three families who manage to keep all independent operators locked out. They successfully lobbied for a law that forces all potential new currency exchanges to be approved by all neighboring exchange owners. She notes, "That makes it very hard to crack the system." The exchanges are notorious for charging high check-cashing fees, and they also collect money from the state to hold welfare checks until they get picked up, a perfect double-dipping routine. She hopes a community credit union in New York will serve as a model for one at Altgeld Gardens. The plan is for Altgeld residents to run the credit union, keeping the profits in community hands.

Cheryl says, and Hazel's face shows, that it can be hard to see possibility with no one to seize it:

"Dealing with my own community frustrates me more than dealing with the assholes [who caused these problems]. It's frustrating that I can't get my own community more involved. Poor people don't follow through. Fear stops them."

Paulo Freire (1994) described it this way: "A 'fear of freedom' . . . afflicts the oppressed, . . . who have adapted to the structure of domination in which they are immersed . . . [and] are inhibited from waging the struggle for freedom so long as they feel incapable of running the risks it requires."

Revisioning the poor person's condition, Cheryl advises: ". . . when you go to get your food stamps, remember that [the caseworkers] wouldn't have their little jobs if it weren't for you. No caseworker would be working if there was no public aid. . . ."

A good reminder of our connectedness and how we owe each other our livelihoods and respect.

Cheryl remembers that when community jobs were unpaid, people did the work because they believed in the goals. When some of those jobs started paying, "it went to people's heads." Activists fell to jealousy, greed, and power struggles. Folks with some authority, like Shaw, who could have done something to help this community, seemed more interested in keeping their jobs than in gaining people's trust. I imagine these leaders marching ahead, stumbling and looking back, seeing followers in full force and so continuing. Looking back less often.

A TEACHING COMMUNITY

Repression Breeds Resistance:
Chicano-Mexicano, Puerto Rican, Black, Native American
Slogan, Dr. Pedro Albizu Campos Puerto Rican High School

Mother Teresa once said that Chicago's West Side holds a poverty more dense, more soul-bleaching than Calcutta's. But the West Side is also rich with people, home to a majority of Chicago's

Boricuas—Puerto Ricans. When Spain claimed *La Isla*—surprise, surprise—there were already people living there. The original people called themselves *Taino*, and their island *Boriken*. Hence, Boricua—the people of Boriken. Spain enslaved the Taino and renamed the fertile land the "rich port"—Puerto Rico: the paradigm-shifting name of the plunderer. Then, in 1898, the United States colonized the island. Reclaiming Boricua signals the resistance of colonized people, another transformation.

I'm simultaneously adoring my city's thick culture and tracing my own steps as a student as I trek into West Town, a Chicano/Boricuan neighborhood. There is an alternative school here—a place, I hear, where kids can learn true stories and try on new names. I think all schools are communities, for better or worse. But some are also of community, catalyzed by specific needs and dreams. Just so for Dr. Pedro Albizu Campos High School. I have a bias: I attended a "free" school in the early seventies, and it was a more than disillusioning experience. It was optimistically named Desiderata, a "desirable and needed" place (*American Heritage* 1982). Political-dreamer teachers opened the school, and the place quickly filled with student drifters, fey gay kids, black-jeaned biker girls, and other factory school rejects. We needed many things, but safety is always primary. Terrible opportunists, feigning revolutionary teacher attitudes, followed. One said to me at our school retreat, "I'll know you better if I touch your breasts." At first year's end, three more were having sex with way-under-eighteen-year-olds. Their gluttonous desire land-mined any student solidarity. We had no good community, and we learned ugly lessons.

Maya Angelou has said, "It is almost impossible to grow up. Most people just get older." Desiderata's teachers, for instance. It takes rigor and courage to challenge funk, and how can you, if you're mired in it? Dr. Pedro Albizu Campos High School, named for a Puerto Rican independence leader, hits much closer to the mark. It's brimming with politics and dreams, and its teachers chart a disciplined course, the essential balance for a school. This is a place where young people grow up and out, from the home base of ideas to the world of action.

Bicultural and bilingual, this is the first officially Spanglish-speaking school, and proud of it. The brick building wears a vivid explosion of portraits and words, inside and outside, reminders of activists, poets, and political prisoners, many painted by students.

Words are important here, but the focus is on movement, toward change. Marvin Garcia, the school director, is tall, teen lean, and in motion:

"I grew up in a working-class Chicago neighborhood, poor people, and I knew there was a problem there, but I thought the problem was us, the Puerto Rican people. When I graduated from the university, I wanted to come back into this community to make a change. I thought education could do that. At this school, we want the students to move from theory to practice, from critique to action. Our philosophy is that education has to be a process of liberation."

The school is vitally connected to the neighborhood; students work and intern at Boricuan Bakery, sell their school-learned desktop publishing skills to small businesses, and work on the yearly Puerto Rican People's Parade, *Fiesta Boricua*. And the involvement doesn't end (or even start) with entrepreneurship. Students volunteer with VIDA/SIDA, an HIV-prevention program, and work at the day care center housed in the school building. The walls are plastered with "Wear your condom" posters, and gay papers can be picked up at the door. The school also has a family life program, which lets student parents finish high school and care for their children on site. Marvin said, "I have a vision of a school that's just a stopping place on the way back to the community, and to the work we can do." A school that is the world, with a checkpoint.

Connection is powerful. These kids are graduating at a rate of 85 to 90 percent, when the Latino dropout rate in Chicago is from 65 to 75 percent. Many head straight to college. But the school is not self-satisfied. Insurgence is the goal, and the focus is broad. "Each one, teach one" to change the world, starting close to home. Folks at Albizu Campos have strong ties to Roberto Clemente, the sprawling neighborhood public high school, and they are changing structures there, through school reform work with the local school council. One of Albizu Campos's twelve full- and part-time teachers, Lourdes Lugo, graduated from the alternative school, got her teaching certificate, worked at Clemente for a while, and then returned here to teach. She explained:

At this school, students are safe from . . . violence and racism . . . These kids are colonial subjects; they can't be fully human, they have to be survivors. We want to create a place where students feel they can learn their history, share their lives and get support. But we are not a social service agency. That's about creating dependency, crying on shoulders, therapy. This school is about empowerment.

As we walk through the halls, Marvin greets everyone. The place is bustling, getting ready for a trip. A tall girl asks for a hug and Marvin gives her a big one. The place feels safe. The hug looks right. The teaching feels sure. The messages are everywhere: no ideas are too threatening to contemplate, the truth can be discovered, and a better world can be built.

But Marvin is "a frustrated teacher" with little real time to teach. "We do everything from teaching to grant writing, from janitorial to counseling. We have to be good paper pushers to keep this place going." And new challenges emerge. The neighborhood is changing: the school is trying to stave off the creeping gentrification that threatens to uproot many families. West Town is a new "rich port," and some people's homes, old brick and greystone, are the wealth leaving the hands of the community. More work, more meetings, deeper commitment.

The broader my experience, and the wider my lens, the more circular and connected all these issues and places seem to me. Part of the same package. One side: Hazel's isolated home, Marvin's encroached school. Flip side: Two communities acting. Defining terms. For a moment, the world shifts. Possibilities emerge, midwifed by plain people, through love in action. And yet another side: my responsibility. I am answering the call of my father-mentor and putting my queer shoulder to the wheel, too, next to his. I am still searching and learning, continuing my life-long journey of desire, discovery, and passion, following in the footsteps of my first tough mother, and all the other tough mothers I can find. I hope to honor the work of these dauntless teachers by giving voice to truth, and justice my full attention.

REFERENCES

Allison, D. 1994. Survival is the least of my desires. *Skin: Talking about Sex, Class and Literature.* New York: Firebrand Books.

American Heritage Dictionary. 1982–1985. Boston: Houghton Mifflin Company.

Chicago Tribune. Jan. 15, 1995. WOMANEWS.

Collins, P. H. 1991. The meaning of motherhood in black culture and black mother–daughter relationships. In Double-Stitch: Black Women Write

About Mothers & Daughters. Ed. Patricia Bell-Scott, et. al. New York: Harper Perennial.

Department of Planning and Development. 1994. *Demographic Characteristics of Chicago's Population.*

Dewey, J. 1916, 1944. *Democracy and Education.* New York: The Free Press.

Eakins, P. 1995. Manifesto of a dead daughter. *Race Traitor,* Winter, no. 4.

Garcia, M., and L. Lugo. November 1995. Conversation with Therese Quinn.

Freire, P. 1968–1970. *Pedagogy of the Oppressed.* New York: Seabury.

Ginsberg, A. 1956, 1959, 1974. America. *Howl and Other Poems.* San Francisco: City Lights Books.

Johnson, C., and C. McCarter. 1995. Conversation with Therese Quinn.

Johnson, H. July 1992; March/April 1995. Conversation with Therese Quinn.

Lorde, A. 1984. The master's tools will never dismantle the master's house. *Sister Outsider.* Freedom, CA: The Crossing Press.

McIntosh, P. 1988. White privilege: unpacking the invisible knapsack. Wellesley, MA: Wellesley College Center for Research on Women.

Wimsatt, W. U. 1994. *Bomb the Suburbs.* Rev. 2d Ed. Chicago: The Subway and Elevated Press.

10—A Dream That Keeps on Growing—Myles Horton and Highlander

William Ayers

Myles Horton believed in sticking to something once he started it. He was, he said, a person for the long haul. He founded the Highlander Folk School in 1932 as an adult education center focused on social change, and he was still at it when he died at Highlander at the age of eighty-four in 1990. Early on he decided to set out on a life's work that was large enough to contain his considerable energy, vision, and experience. Once started, he said, he didn't want to have to stop and start over. Highlander was his dream come to life: a place where students and teachers could live, work, and study together, developing through their own experiences a sense of how to participate in a changing world.

In the 1930s Highlander was the education arm of the Congress of Industrial Organizations (CIO) in the South. Myles realized that labor would never be emancipated as long as racial segregation remained intact, turning workers against one another based on race privilege, and he began organizing workshops designed to destroy the racist structures. Martin Luther King, Jr. attended Highlander, as did Julian Bond, Ralph Abernathy, and Stokely Carmichael. Septima Clark was education director at Highlander, and one of her students was Rosa Parks—the summer before that fateful day in Montgomery. Highlander has been the center of social action and change in the South for over sixty years, responding to the needs and demands of several generations of social activists. It is a dream that keeps on growing.

Myles Horton thought that teaching was at its heart an ethical and intellectual activity, that curriculum could be linked in critical ways to social context, and that education was the key to transforming lives and changing worlds. In collaboration with Judith Kohl and Herbert Kohl, two educators who share his vision and commitments and who have made their own unique contributions to a more humane education in the service of a more just world, he produced a moving and inspiring autobiography called *The Long Haul*, published just before his death.

Myles Horton was an American original. Born in Savannah, Tennessee, in 1905, he grew up working on farms and, later, with other displaced farmers in mills and factories and around the mines. His outlook was shaped by these experiences, and by the Christian teachings of his youth. "I always liked the idea of Christianity," he would say later, "only problem was I never saw anyone practice it."[1] His mother taught him that most of what they heard in church was just "preachers' talk" and that the important thing to hold on to was the idea of loving other people. "She had a very simple belief," he said. "God is love, and therefore you love your neighbors." Horton's interpretation of that tenet developed another level of understanding: "If you believe people are of worth, you can't treat anybody inhumanely, and that means you not only have to love and respect people, but you have to think in terms of building a society that people can profit most from, and that kind of society has to work on the principal of equality." And he insisted that while operating on principles of love and equality is difficult, "the principle itself isn't complicated, it's the application that's complicated."

Myles Horton read widely, and he was deeply influenced by the writings of social critics and Marxists. He felt that he could learn from many sources, but that in the end he was responsible to himself and his own ideals. "I have to be the final arbiter of my beliefs and my actions," he said, "and I can't fall back and justify it by saying, I'm a Marxist, I'm a Christian, I'm a technological expert, I'm an educator." Perhaps this kind of stubborn individualism helps explain why he worked with a wide range of people who shared a broad vision of what they thought would be a better world, and yet he never joined a party: "I understood the need for organizations, but I was always afraid of what they did to people . . . [O]rganizations . . . end up in structures and structures become permanent and most of them outlive their usefulness."

---

1. Unless otherwise noted, quotes are from *The Long Haul*.

*   *   *

Myles Horton attended Cumberland University, The University of Chicago, and the Union Theological Seminary. He sought out particular teachers, who in many cases became lifelong friends and supporters: Robert Park at Chicago, George Counts at Columbia Teachers College, Reinhold Niebuhr at Union, John Dewey, Jane Addams, Sherwood Eddy, Norman Thomas. Horton was the kind of student who would attract his mentors and draw them to him: he was engaged, authentic, and idealistic. He wanted to do something worthwhile in his life, and he approached each encounter with a compelling intensity.

As a student in Chicago he heard about the Danish folk school movement, a populist education experiment that had developed in opposition to the lifelessness of traditional schools and the detachment of academic schooling in Denmark. The Danish folk schools were places where people broadened themselves by analyzing important questions and problems and then actively participating in practical solutions. Horton resolved to go see for himself.

In Denmark, Horton's idealism and energy became focused on a specific project: a school for life; a place where students and teachers could live together to pose and solve problems; an informal setting infused with culture where experience would be the main teacher; a site for activists, organizers, and teachers for social change. In his diary Horton wrote,

> The school will be for young men and women of the mountains and workers from the factories. Negroes would be among the students who will live in close personal contact with teachers. Out of their experiential learning through living, working, and studying together could come an understanding of how to take their place intelligently in the changing world.

Horton worried that he could go on preparing to build his school forever and continue to feel inadequate to the task; he decided that the only way he could learn how to embody his vision was to go ahead and get started.

At the Highlander Folk School the purpose of education was to make people more powerful and more capable in their work and their lives. Myles Horton had what he called a two-eye approach to teaching: with one eye he tried to look at people as they are, while with the other he looked at what they might become. He thought that people had a lot of tacit power, and that his job was to capitalize on people's strengths in order to mobilize that power.

The Highlander Folk School was a free space in a decidedly oppressive environment. It was a place where labor organizers, civil rights activists, antipoverty workers, and others assembled, posed problems, and worked to develop their own solutions. Myles claimed that his job was "to provide opportunities for people to grow, not to make them grow because no one can do that . . . My job as a gardener or as an educator is to know that the potential is there and that it will unfold. People have a potential for growth; it's inside, it's in the seed . . ."

For many years Highlander was the only place in the South where white and African American citizens lived and worked together, something that was illegal in that strictly segregated society. Highlander, Myles once claimed, held the record for sustained civil disobedience, breaking the Tennessee Jim Crow laws every day for over forty years, until the segregation laws were finally repealed.

The list of students at Highlander over the years is a roll call of social activists: Rosa Parks, Eleanor Roosevelt, Pete Seeger, Woody Guthrie, Martin Luther King, Jr., Andrew Young, Fannie Lou Hamer. People gathered at Highlander with a purpose: to define their problems; to name the obstacles to their hopes and dreams; to gather the necessary conceptual, human, and material resources to continue; and to return home with a plan for forward progress. The school, of course, was under constant attack from white supremacists, antilabor groups, and the government.

Myles Horton believed that the people with the problems are also the people with the solutions. He knew that this was a hard doctrine, because people often don't know that they have the solutions and often act in ways that are contrary to solving their own problems. The alternative, he thought, was patronization or worse. He had a holistic view of education. "The universe is one," he said, and he resisted chopping life into discrete bits of information, subject matter, or courses. It was all one. He had an intense belief in the innate goodness and potential wisdom of ordinary people. He believed that people need opportunities to make the decisions that affect their lives. Horton built a learning environment where people could explore, share, risk, make decisions, and construct answers—a place where people could become stronger and more capable. It was a school where experience counted most, a place that opposed passivity and obedience and valued imagination and initiative. But experience, imagination, and initiative were the raw materials of learning, and reflection was also necessary for growth. "An experience you don't learn from," Horton wrote, "is just a happening." In this environment teachers became guides and coaches—and also learners themselves, alongside their students. "Education," Horton said, "is what happens to the other person, not what comes out of the mouth of the educator."

Workshops at Highlander followed a common rhythm. In order to hold a workshop, organizations and individuals had to struggle with a few fundamental questions: What problems are we facing that require our focused attention? What do we need to know? What are we trying to solve? After several days of work, sessions would end with an action plan: What are we going to do when we get home?

Traveling the mountains of eastern Tennessee is a trip into an indefinite time. The road cuts deep into the green hills, swings up past a white frame house where an ancient woman sits sewing in a rocker on the porch. Nearby, a farmer and a boy work a field. Down a steep grade and around another sharp bend looms a prodigious automobile graveyard, hulk on hulk of rusting bodies in a strange monument to modern times. Beyond this, a larger-than-life, smiling Dolly Parton points south to Dollywood. And everywhere the characteristic haze rising from hill and hollow, giving this place its name: the Smokey Mountains. We are here to remember Myles, to honor the work of Highlander, and to share our activist hopes and our concrete plans.

Maxine Waller said, "Myles taught me to say, 'Hell, no. I don't like the world the way it is and I'm going to change it.' I hope I can get a lot of people to spend a lot of sleepless nights. I haven't slept well myself.

"Myles started out in the church, and he found out that that's where God's work wasn't being done. Highlander's been called a lot of things, but I call it God's work. Myles Horton was a man of God and he did God's work. All my life I've slept with the Bible. Now I sleep with the Bible and *The Long Haul*, Myles's story.

"Myles taught that all people are smart and all people can do anything if they apply themselves correctly. But you've got to do the work, and you're responsible for it. Highlander ain't perfect. Highlander's life, and life is never perfect."

Bernard Lafayette, "We came to Highlander in the early 1960s on a retreat from the nonviolent battles in Nashville. It was a place to get away, to think, and to connect with ourselves.

"We had become convicts: convicted and jailed by the courts, and convicted by our principles. Our convictions drove us, and they were inescapable.

"In one workshop I attended, Myles asked, 'Why shouldn't white folks have a right to eat by themselves?' We were flabbergasted, and I got up and had a fuss with him. I had never heard the concept of a devil's advocate. Myles caused me to think critically about why I was doing what I was doing. He taught me that you must doubt your first impression, to think about what you think.

"Where do we go from here? What we must do is to give birth to Highlanders all over the country. We must transplant Highlander."

Rosa Parks stood, and in her quiet, dignified voice, said:

"Myles was asked once how he managed to get black and white people to eat together in the strictly segregated South. His response was simple and straightforward: 'All I did was put the food on the table and ring the bell.' I miss Myles very much."

Myles taught through stories. I remember a college classroom Myles was visiting shortly before his death. One student began wrestling with the question of objectivity in social matters and wondered about problems of interpretation and meaning. Myles brought out a picture to show to the class—in it a young Martin Luther King, Jr. is seated among a large group of people at a Highlander workshop. The caption is in bold letters: MARTIN LUTHER KING AT COMMUNIST TRAINING SCHOOL. Myles explained that this was a photograph of a billboard that was posted throughout the South during the 1960s, paid for by the White Citizens Councils, political arm of the KKK, and designed to discredit King and the civil rights movement. Myles then described driving into Birmingham in a van with a group of black youngsters and passing first one and then another of the notorious billboards. As a third sign loomed ahead, one of the kids turned to Myles and said, "That's the dumbest advertisement I've ever seen. It doesn't even give you an address or a phone number. How do you know where to go?"

As the class session wound down, one student, somewhat awed, asked Myles how he managed to avoid burnout, to go on, and to keep his vision alive over so many years. Myles responded: "There are two things that keep me going. First, I think of all the people I've known, ordinary people who've done extraordinary things, people like Rosa Parks, Esau Jenkins, Bernice Robinson, and Septima Clark. I think of how very important those people are, and how very important the work of Highlander has been. Second, I live in the Smokey Mountains, and sometimes I like to walk along the ridge near my home at night and look up at the Milky Way. Whenever I do that I'm reminded of how tiny we are, and that each of us is just a little speck of dust in the cosmos. I work against being insignificant and absurd. It helps keep me going."

A liberating education pointed toward a society of hope and justice: it's a dream that keeps on growing.

REFERENCE

Horton, Myles with Judith Kohl and Herbert Kohl. *The Long Haul: An Autobiography*. New York: Teachers College Press. 1998.

11—The Good Fight—Bill Gandall

Susan Huddleston Edgerton

> *Dear Susan—*
> *Your colleague gave me your address when I called to congratulate all of you and the students for the marvelous reaction to an attempt at censorship. It is even more significant to have taken place in Shreveport—no mecca of freedom or tolerance. . . .*
>
> w/love, Bill G

From 1984 to 1988, I taught at a private high school in Shreveport, Louisiana, a city often described as the most conservative of its size in the country. The school was intended to be college preparatory, and it served children of some of the wealthiest people in town. Not a "white flight" school as are so many private schools in that area, it was nevertheless a product of its place. I was in the high school science department and I taught a course in cultural anthropology in which the focus was on contemporary United States (looking into "ourselves"). My orientation was a thinly veiled neo–Marxism and my agenda was to open some privileged eyes to the workings and costs of that privilege, though I was only beginning to understand much of this for myself. Lynn, a colleague, who taught Spanish, was something of a miracle to me in that time and place. Her perspective was similar to mine with the addition that she had a great deal more experience in the world than did I.

Lynn had lived for a time in Mexico and was passionate about causes connected to Mexico, Central, and South America. She somehow learned that an eighty-year-old man who had fought with the U.S. Marines in Nicaragua in the 1920s was going to be in town speaking to a few local groups. He had been described as "walking history" with regard to a story rarely told in this country. He was on a speaking tour to urge folks to pressure elected officials not to approve Reagan's proposed $3.6 million in military aid to the Nicaraguan Contras. Lynn decided to invite him to speak to her students, and asked if I would like to have my anthropology class join them. I agreed and plans were set.

Shortly before Bill Gandall was to speak at our school, an

article appeared in the local newspaper describing him as a retired labor union organizer and an active critic of Reagan administration policies in Nicaragua: a frequent picketer with various
anti–Contra groups in the United States, Gandall said he realizes
he may find few supporters in the Shreveport area because of its
predominantly conservative and pro-military voters. The area's
congressman, Buddy Roemer (D–Bossier City), has played a pivotal role in backing Reagan's requests for Central American aid
on Capitol Hill (*The Shreveport Times,* Feb. 1, 1988.)

The article also mentioned that Gandall was scheduled to
speak at our school. Several parents were on the phone to the
headmaster that night, livid about the "lack of balance" such a
speaker would lend to the issue, and fearful about what their
children might hear from such a "kook." It was suggested that he
would be acceptable as a speaker only if there were another
speaker present to offer "the other side." Of course, given the
context of this time and place, "the other side" was virtually all
anyone in the area ever heard.

The headmaster relayed these concerns to Lynn and ordered
her to uninvite Gandall. She refused, so the headmaster revised
his "ultimatum" to one of censorship: Gandall was not to speak of
anything other than his personal experiences in Nicaragua in the
1920s, and especially not about the current situation there. Lynn
protested that many other speakers had been at the school, such
as a candidate for governor with none of his opponents (Buddy
Roemer, no less!) and members of the John Birch Society, without
a squeak for "balance." The headmaster countered that Gandall
was just someone "off the streets" who "lacked credentials." We
were both angry, but Lynn conveyed the message to Gandall. Bill
reluctantly agreed to come anyway.

Meanwhile, our students were well aware of what was going on
(it was a small school) and had passed the story around the
school. Not only did our two sets of classes show up in the library
for Bill, but so did the entire student body. Within minutes the
students managed to work out a kind of code with Bill through
which they were able to ask any questions they wanted and he was
able to answer without uttering any of the forbidden terms. He so
engaged the students that every one of them stayed to listen and
dialogue with him for almost an hour beyond the allotted time,
relinquishing their lunch period.

Students did not let the issue die with Bill's departure. They organized meetings with the headmaster to discuss policy at the school. One shy young man, who usually stuttered on the rare occasions he spoke, offered passionate, stutter-free testimony to the degree of insult he felt from the attempted censorship. A lively exchange over the incident appeared in letters to the editors of two local papers. It was agreed that a meeting would be held in the evening (in order to accommodate working parents) to which interested parents, students, and staff would be invited.

The meeting convened with very few of the complaining parents present. Some students shared brief speeches and then opened the floor to dialogue. After several rounds, the parents who were present expressed appreciation for the depth of student and staff remarks, for their own inclusion in the discussion, and for the impressive maturity of the students. That said, the students demanded of the headmaster a written policy that would preclude any such censorship in the future. They won!

The event provided a powerful lesson in participatory democracy. Beyond that, Bill Gandall's message about truth seeking and risk taking made a lasting impression on many of us. One student and I maintained correspondence with him for a time. Within the few years after this event, several encounters with former students convince me that something significant was accomplished by all of us that year, this event being pivotal. I met one former student on the state capitol steps in Baton Rouge during a protest against the inauguration of David Duke as state representative; another phoned to tell me that, because of her experiences with anthropology class, she was better prepared to hear challenges to old beliefs in her Princeton classrooms; another informed me that he had decided to teach high school in Appalachia; and another phoned from Brown University, grateful, to tell me that without his experiences in my classroom he would not have known to attend a performance by Maya Angelou. My own political awareness turned a new corner through the Gandall experience as well, not only affecting my teaching but also setting me on a path I continue to follow. From Bill, Lynn, and my students I learned that teaching about social justice is thin without the living example of working for social justice.

Bill's own story is itself testimony to the power of teaching for social justice. When he spoke to us in Shreveport we learned that he entered the U.S. Marine Corps in the 1920s as, in his words, "a nineteen-year-old high school dropout who was deeply ignorant, arrogant, and only out for a good time." He told us of atrocities in which he participated, including rape, torture, and murder of innocent civilians, destruction of sacred property, and election rigging. When he left Nicaragua and the marines he decided to finish high school. It was through the efforts of his high school history teacher that he was brought to a new political awareness and initiated in work for social justice. Among other things, she shared with him books about Nicaragua's history, and he began to feel deep remorse for past deeds. That remorse drove him to endless reading and activism, including his volunteering to fight with the Abraham Lincoln Brigade against fascism in Spain. He remained so dedicated throughout his remaining life, having endured over one hundred arrests for various acts of civil disobedience. Such were his "credentials." Did he atone for his sins in Nicaragua? Though he was "hailed as a hero upon his 1986 return" to Nicaragua by Sandinista President Daniel Ortega (*Shreveport Times*, Feb. 1, 1988), his actions in the 1920s can never be forgiven. But perhaps the second lesson Bill Gandall taught us was that one need not have his humanity frozen by the worst thing he has ever done, and that teaching for social justice can make that difference. That is a lesson about undying hope.

Though this event took place ten years ago, I continue to meet the name of Bill Gandall and his Nicaragua story in a variety of contexts, from traveling in Costa Rica to political work in Chicago and now in Kalamazoo. I've been told that Bill passed away a few years ago. He lives, however, as a mentor to me for teaching with and about social justice. Bill's humanity bestows a spiritual gift—a lasting lesson on the poverty of cynicism and the possibility in responsibility.

12—History of My Subversive Teaching

Rachel Koch

When I was teaching in public schools, I used to have a recurring nightmare. It involved the school administration somehow finding out something about me, something damning, something teachers weren't supposed to do or be. These suspect qualities included, but were not limited to, having definite political views and acting on them, having a social life, being sexual, drinking occasionally or smoking pot. The nightmare usually involved the discovery of the latter, and, as a result, the dream would involve some larger repercussion for all the staff. In one variation on this dream, a teacher said to me angrily, "Now we all have to get drug tested, because of *you!*" I always lived in fear that the real me, once revealed to the grown-ups, would scare them into firing me. It's not that I am this incredibly wild partier or that I am secretly working to overthrow the government (well actually . . .). In fact, my recreational activities are (probably) not any more outrageous than your average Microsoft employee. It's just that I'm stuck behind this centuries-old stereotype of the sexless, stern, blue-haired old lady. Teachers are held up as bland transmitters of knowledge, devoid of any bias or life. But the kids . . . they wanted to see the real me. They liked it when a real person peeked out from behind The Desk. And in this was the true subversion: I allowed myself to be honest with my students about who I was.

I entered graduate school at the University of Chicago for their Master's program in teaching secondary English. Fresh from Madison, I was filled with idealistic notions of changing the entire high school curriculum to reflect more accurately the student population, of bringing feminism into the classroom, and of creating my own urban Summerhill. I didn't really have any friends at the U of C. My professor viewed me as an annoyance for the first two quarters; he was loathe to call on me, and I can't really blame him. I was spewing rhetoric every chance I got. The other students were fresh from Nebraska, Iowa, and Virginia and were terrified to get on the El. Consequently, they were trapped on the island of Hyde Park, living in fear of the surrounding black communities. When student teaching time came around, we were asked to design our own thematic units. I chose—surprise!—gender roles in literature.

These units were to include reading selections throughout the eight weeks and were to culminate in a central work—an entire novel, play, or other work. I chose *Their Eyes Were Watching God,* a powerful novel by Zora Neale Hurston. The teacher whose class I taught, Vera, was endlessly supportive and turned her class over to me with grace and confidence. Unfortunately, the English Department head, Betty, was not as enthused. This high school, one-third African American, had an African American literature collection that began with *Black Boy* and ended three books later with *Best Black Short Stories,* published in 1968. I had spoken with Betty two months before my term began, and she had agreed to purchase a class set of *Their Eyes.* I was determined to get this book to these students, even if I had to apply for grants or loans or whatever.

Student teaching time rolled around, and little did I know, there had been a battle brewing between mostly African American teachers, who wanted more Afrocentric literature and history included in the curriculum, and mostly white teachers, who felt the curriculum was just fine the way it was. One week before I was to begin, Betty informed me that she was unable to purchase the book because of budgeting problems. By this time, Vera had read the book and loved it. When I told her about the "budgeting problems," she said that it was horse shit. The English Department managed to buy 100 new copies of *The Canterbury Tales.* It was too late to apply for grants and I didn't have an extra $500 for sixty books. Vera suggested we just have the book copied, a few chapters a week, at the school copy center.

The next week, Vera and I both received notes stating that the copy center would not be able to complete the copy request because of copyright law (this was before the Kinko's lawsuit). I looked up the exact law in the library, which had an exception for educational institutions. I discussed this with the teachers facing similar vague resistance from the administration; we all smoked and took our lunch at the Greek restaurant across the street. They tried not to laugh at my naïveté and determination, but instead provided me with a first-hand look at the level of institutional racism in the Chicago area schools.

With Betty still stalling on the copying and the unit rapidly

drawing to a close, Vera took the book to Kinko's and paid for
sixty copies of chapter one.

I confronted Betty with the library copy of the exact copyright
law, and she finally let us use the book, unimpeded. The novel was
an enormous success, as was my unit. The students loved the
novel's honest talk about racism, sexism, sexuality, and society.
They gave me flowers, balloons, and a statue of the Virgin Mary
on my last day.

I entered the Cibola County school system in New Mexico in
January after a short but illustrious waitressing career. I was to
replace, I found out later, a gay man who was driven out by male
staff after being given all the crappy work and essentially made to
feel so uncomfortable that he quit.

After six months at Laguna-Acoma High School on the Laguna Pueblo, a shake-up occurred, as will happen in public school
systems: untenured teachers and new teachers get laid off, crusty
old teachers remain, and superintendents give outgoing teachers
a phony pep talk and give themselves a raise. I was taken aside by
this dirty old man who reeked of yesterday's Scotch and was told,
at a distance a little too close for my comfort level, that because of
my "special background" (i.e., I was white and had graduated
from that bastion of whiteness, the University of Chicago), I
would remain employed by the county.

That fall, I was called into the principal's office at Grants High
School for a meeting of the "curriculum committee," a group of
teachers who needed something extra for their resumé. No, actually we were supposed to keep the principal in touch with the
actual goings-on of the school. Our somewhat young, semi-hip
principal told the eight of us his concerns about students. "Let's
talk about sex, drugs, and rock-and-roll," he said. Well count me
in, I thought. He went on to enumerate his concerns: six girls had
already come in for pregnancy tests, and we'd only been in school
for eight weeks. A number of kids had also been busted for smoking pot. He said it was a priority for us to address these issues, that
maybe we should put the textbooks and the formal curriculum
aside and really talk to the students. Some of the teachers looked
panic-stricken. Others needed clarification.

The next day I talked to the health teacher, the epitome of
coolness in Grants because he was tan, blond, and wore short
shorts showing off his runner's legs. He was one of the few at the
school under fifty, and who could comfortably say the words

"penis" and "vagina" in a room full of teenagers. I bounced my idea off of him: to do a three-day health seminar, separating the sexes to create safety and comfort for both genders, and address some issues particular to each. He responded as I'd thought: "Uh . . . that sounds cool."

I dug up all my Women's Studies 101 health stuff, *Our Bodies, Ourselves*, articles on images of women in advertising, eating disorders, sterilization abuse, birth control, and other important issues you rarely discuss in school, for fear you might actually be getting at something real to kids today, something that affects their lives a little more directly than diagramming sentences. I pored through this material to find a few key women's health articles that were appropriate for teenagers.

I arrived at class excited to be providing good health information for these girls. I wrote on the board possible topics for discussion: menstruation, pregnancy, birth control, nutrition, eating disorders, body image, sexuality, rape, incest, sexual harassment. I passed out a few slips of paper to each girl and gave a brief introduction. Each was to write a question anonymously, any health-related question, not necessarily relating to the topics on the board. I collected the questions, shuffled amidst nervous giggles, and began answering. "What is anorexia?" "If a girl is a virgin, can she still get pregnant the first time?" "Can you get AIDS if you're on the pill?" "Do girls masturbate?"

The last one seemed simple. "Yes, girls masturbate. Almost everyone does, even children in some form, stimulate themselves. Boys talk about it more, so it seems like girls don't do it too, but they do. It's very normal." One girl shyly responded, "Do you?" This one I had to think about for a minute: I knew she meant, "I do, and I need to know that you do too because you're an adult and you're talking about this embarrassing stuff."

"Well, yes, I mean, everybody does. It's perfectly normal, girls and boys do this and so do grown men and women."

And I moved on.

Well, I have to concede my naïveté here about the chemical combination of a fourteen-year-old maturity level and a piece of information such as the teacher admitting that she masturbates. Naturally *"Ms. Koch plays with herself"* went flying around school for the next few days. I wasn't too upset though. I figured if that girl went home relieved that she wasn't sick or perverted, then I didn't care.

But then I got called into the principal's office. In the five years I taught, every time I heard "Ms. Koch, please come to the office," my heart pounded. Uh-oh, what did they find out about me? What did I do? And my entire six years in college and graduate school flashed before my eyes, complete with all the events that could later be used against me in a court of law.

"So . . . what did you talk about when you did your . . . health . . . thing last week?" the principal said, shifting nervously in his chair. I gave him a brief review. "Because, uh, one of the other teachers said that, uh, some of the students were, uh, saying things, and uh . . ." I spared him the embarrassment, and told him the truth. "Well, I guess I would just caution you to, uh, use judgment about, uh, these things."

"But I thought you wanted us to talk about this stuff with them. None of the other teachers did anything, like we'd talked about."

"Yes, but, well just use your judgment."

It was clear to me that we would not be practicing putting on condoms. The seminar was not extended, nor was any other information disseminated.

When I taught at Laguna I met another English teacher who had taught night classes through New Mexico State University. She had a few basic composition classes and said it brought in good extra money, essential when you're living on a New Mexico teacher's salary ($19,500 for master's degree, no experience. I'm not joking.) I called the personnel director at NMSU, and he called me back at school a month later, asking if I would be interested in teaching a women's studies class at the women's prison. I said I would be thrilled to teach the class.

After almost a year of planning, the first class snuck up on me. I copied my syllabus, descriptions of journaling, and other pertinent readings. I'd wanted to have a nicely bound reader for each woman to keep. Unfortunately, a month before the class was to begin, I was informed that because of the Kinko's lawsuit, I had to write each of the thirty-odd publishers of the material I'd chosen to ask copyright permission. Some were unbelievably gracious, such as Aunt Lute Press, publisher of *La Frontera* by Gloria Anzaldúa. They gave me free rights to copy plus ten free books, which I donated to the prison library. Susan Faludi's publisher was not as generous. They actually charged me to copy a portion of *Backlash*. At one point, with my full load of high school classes, this time-consuming snag, and a surprisingly up-to-date copier at school, I decided that one public institution should really help out another. Other teachers wondered how I was fitting the Red Stockings Manifesto and other radical feminist material into the ninth-grade curriculum, so I tried to confine my copying hours to late in the afternoon.

The first day I was struck by how young and ill-prepared I was to stand before a group of incarcerated women, with my middle-class upbringing and twenty-six years of limited experience, and talk about women's lives with any sort of authority. I managed this insecurity through the graciousness of the women, who were so hungry for education and pertinent literature, and whose usual college-level offerings were calculus or geography.

I showed "Thelma and Louise" on the first day.

This may seem like an odd choice, but I wanted to work backwards historically through the last century of feminism and women's resistance to oppression, beginning now. And what better way to illustrate women's anger in 1993 than with "Thelma and Louise." I'd seen this film countless times, but I discovered you haven't really seen this film until you've seen it in a women's prison. At first I was nervous that all the hooting and hollering and yelling at the rapist, the cops, the husband, and the other mainly one-dimensional objects of the women's anger would lead to some kind of Bacchic gutting of one of the sneering, mustachioed guards. These guards were quite confused when on entering through massive steel doors, I'd announced I was there to teach "Women's Studies."

My fear subsided as I soaked in the energy of the feelings of these women, so palpable in the room. It was so different and somehow so immediate to watch women on the run from the law *with* women who've actually been on the run from the law. It felt less cathartic symbolically and more biographical, a thought women later echoed in their journals.

I'd made a decision to use the journals as a way they could communicate their ideas to me privately, as well as record their own thoughts and reactions to readings and films. This was the only time I've read students' journals. I always stress the safety and utility of privacy for writing. But I knew in this setting discussions wouldn't always be as open as I'd like. Reading their journals provided a window into another world.

I remember Michelle, seventeen, mother of two, her spirit not yet broken. She was no sympathy case: she was into crack, dealing and doing, neglected her kids, and wound up in Grants. Michelle was just starting to come into feminism and was also developing a relationship with another woman in prison. She felt very positive about both of these new developments and wanted more information, particularly by African-American lesbians, as she wanted to see her own experiences reflected. She was incredibly lively and open in discussions, which really added to the class. For many women, fear had already settled into their pores, fear of doing everything our reading materials and discussions and films were telling them to do, starting with questioning *everything* and thinking for themselves. I gave her Audre Lourde's *My Name Is Zami*. She read it in three days.

Regrettably, Michelle was not a part of our class for long. She was put in "segregation"—a box-like room away from human contact—for "homosecting." Yes, they actually called it that. She'd written in her journal about her lover, and how everything seemed to fit into place for her in opening to her lesbianism. She didn't think to be ashamed.

Another woman, Roberta, stands out in my mind. A fiftyish Mexican American from Texas with a loving demeanor, Roberta was a recorder. She'd been in the system long enough to keep her mouth shut, her emotions contained, and her truths kept beneath the surface. But in her journal, truths flowed with meticulous documentation. She recorded the abuses by guards, the horrific conditions in the kitchen that would make Upton Sinclair shudder, the chasm of inequality between women and men in the penal system touching everything from sentencing to recreation available in prison (gyms, libraries, classes), to parole. There was simply so much to tell.

I provided as much as I could for those women. We read Susan Faludi, Gloria Anzaldúa, Angela Davis, Rigoberta Menchú, Zora Neale Hurston, and Mary Wollstonecraft, among others. We talked about rage, prostitution, abortion, law, theory, what constitutes gender roles, how we play into them, inequality, class, race, religion, sexuality. We watched "A Question of Silence," a very radical, weird Dutch film about three unrelated women, all at an epicenter of sexism in their lives, who kill a shopkeeper and remain silent afterwards (another wise choice in prison). I couldn't give them enough.

Now I'm on the five-year sabbatical, which I think should be compulsory for all teachers. I'm writing a lot and trying to determine if I should go for another five years. The necessarily subversive element in teaching both attracts and repels me. I love being able to "mess with people," to quote Utah Phillips, and to encourage them to do the same, to think and question. I love Socrates' notion of being a midwife to ideas. And yet I resent the secretiveness, the paranoia that accompanies all the exciting stuff, like an annoying relative who might tell on you. I don't know how to eradicate this problem, or many others for that matter. What becomes quietly calamitous is when teachers give up fighting and pushing for the issues that stir passion. Without this passion, teachers become automatons. Rather, we need to ask ourselves, are there issues we're willing to fight for? Do we find ourselves shuddering when we see thirteen-year-olds in public? Do we understand the meaning of the words our students use in the halls? If you answered no, yes, and no, you qualify for the mandatory sabbatical, and believe me, we'll all be better off. I don't mean to sound flip or light (though a sense of humor would do wonders for the boards of education), but I do feel, at least for me, a year off can do wonders. Perhaps then I can restock my reserves for subversive honesty, so I am able to jump back in for another round.

> . . . In the realm of the imagination all people and their ambitions and interest could meet.
>
> Ralph Ellison

13—The Fourth R[1]

Maureen Reddy

One year to the day after the Simi Valley jury ignited the uprising in Los Angeles by acquitting the police who beat Rodney King, my son Sean[2] reported that an older white child on his school bus had called him "nigger." The jury verdict and the name calling were business as usual in this country, with both emanating from precisely the same source. There having been no revolution in racial attitudes in our lifetimes, Doug and I had assumed Sean would at some stage be called nigger and therefore we were not surprised. Nevertheless, we were angry, and we expected the school's administration to act to demonstrate both to Sean and to the name caller that using "nigger" was definitely a major offense.

What happened in the aftermath of this name calling could be a case study in how schools perpetuate racism, and the roles of teachers, administrators, students, and parents in creating an environment in which racism is the norm. This norm, however, is seldom examined, usually denied, and when confronted, treated as an aberration.

Our expectation that Sean's school would take decisive action in itself may appear to be a step forward; however, it is an appearance that actually masks a lack of racial progress. A friend told us that Sean's reporting the "nigger" incident with the clear expectation of some official redress and our perception that the school would not endorse racial taunting showed that we have all come a long way in thirty years. He said when he was name-called in school and on the school bus, he told his parents without for a moment expecting that the name callers would be punished or even that his parents would inform the school. He knew for a certainty that the school was on the side of the name callers, and that he and his family could not expect the school to defend or to protect them. His parents' response reaffirmed this knowledge: "You're better than those kids who call you names. They're

---

1. This essay is a selection from Chapter 5 of *Crossing the Color Line.*
2. Sean is not my son's real name; I use a pseudonym for him to give him some measure of privacy.

ignorant. They're just trying to make you mad enough to hit them so that you'll get into trouble. Just ignore them."

While it is true that black children who were called "nigger" by whites thirty years ago had no reason to expect institutional support and that at least some black children today have quite a different view, the older generation's understanding that the schools are on the side of those who yell "nigger" reflects a reality that has not changed. What has changed is the surface only: Now schools take a public position—racism is not tolerated—that contradicts their actual relationship to racism, and confuses children and their parents. When overtly racist things happen, children usually get no support from authorities; even when the racism is acknowledged, it's often treated as being of the same order of seriousness as any "interpersonal" problem, like name calling about clothing or appearance.

My friend Joanna told me that her son was called "nigger" by another third grader in his school outside Dallas, where he is one of only two blacks in the class. Jim's response—"I am black and I'm proud of it! So you can kiss my butt!"—seemed appropriate to me and to Joanna, but not to the school's principal. The principal called Joanna, not to let her know about the racism, but to inform her about Jim's use of "bad language." When Joanna inquired further, it developed that the principal had not planned to notify the name caller's parents at all, a decision she justified by saying something like, "We all know they have a problem." Jim's lesson from this episode, then, was that it's okay to use racist language in school when you come from a racist white family, but not to use minor vulgarity when you are black.

The morning after the "nigger" incident, I reported it to the vice-principal of Sean's school, who is in charge of discipline, stressing that I expected him to act swiftly and to keep me informed about what happened. Mindful of Joanna's experience, I was not sanguine about the school's probable response, but felt I had to take a stand. During our conversation, Mr. Walsh said, "Sean is such a nice little boy. It's a shame that he has to put up with this kind of name calling." I replied, "Mr. Walsh, you're unclear on the point here: Sean does not have to 'put up with' this kind of name calling, and it's your job to make sure all the students know that no black child has to 'put up with' being called 'nigger.'"

While apparently indicating real concern about Sean, Walsh's comment also expressed his unreflecting belief that something unchangeable about Sean—his color—caused him to be the target of racial taunting. He surely would not have said about a victim of physical aggression, "It's a shame he has to put up with hitting." This belief is a serious error, as it is actually something changeable about society—its racism—that causes racial insults. While Mr. Walsh and I were having our phone conversation, a poem on "black" was being posted outside a classroom in the school. A line in this poem, which was written by fifth graders, reflects the same perceptual error I pointed out to Mr. Walsh. "Black," a white child wrote, "is why Rodney King got beat up." Well, no: *white* is why Rodney King got beaten.

After we spoke, Mr. Walsh pulled Sean out of his classroom to ask what had happened on the bus. Sean told him, and Mr. Walsh asked, "Did anyone else hear this?" Yes, another child had overheard the whole exchange. Mr. Walsh went to that child next, instead of approaching the name caller directly. When the witness confirmed Sean's account, Mr. Walsh called the accused boy's mother, whom he later described to me as "aghast" and quite worried about what would happen to her son. Then, he finally confronted the name caller and gave him a lecture about the seriousness of his transgression. "This boy is new to the school, and has had a few other problems here," Mr. Walsh confided to me later. "He's trying too hard to fit in." What a terrible comment on the school! "Doesn't it worry you, Mr. Walsh, that this boy evidently believes that name calling a black child is a way to 'fit in' to your school? Have you thought about where he might have got this idea?" I asked. Much verbal dancing around my question ensued.

The next day, Mr. Walsh again took Sean out of his classroom, this time to ask him to think about what might be an appropriate punishment. Sean came home and talked to Doug and me, giving us a very long list of things he thought should happen. After we discussed the list together, Sean narrowed it down to three chief points: (1) the child should apologize directly to Sean; (2) he should be suspended for a day (the usual consequence of fighting); and (3) while he was suspended, he should do some research and write a report on what is wrong with saying "nigger." Doug and I told Sean we were proud of him, because his list was a constructive attempt at education instead of a vengeful punishment.

Sean went off to school, ready to give the list to Mr. Walsh. However, Mr. Walsh did not inquire about Sean's thoughts and the list remained unread. Instead, he gathered Sean, the name caller, and the witness together, gave a shorter version of his earlier lecture to all three of them, required the name caller to apologize, and indicated that he expected Sean to forgive the name caller. Sean told me later, "I accepted his apology, but I don't forgive him, and I won't forget it, either. Once you've said something, you can't unsay it and you can't undo the hurt, so why should I say it's okay?" Sean was bitterly disappointed that so little had happened, and felt the name caller had not really learned anything. "Next time something like this happens, Mom," he said, "I'm just going to punch the kid in the face. At least that way he'll think twice about saying 'nigger' again. I'll probably be suspended, but I just don't care."

Both Sean and the name caller did learn some lessons from this episode, but I doubt they are the lessons Mr. Walsh consciously intended to convey. Both children learned that it is still okay for white children to call black children "niggers." The name caller apparently viewed racist language as one avenue to "fitting in," and his experience did nothing to disabuse him of this notion. The vice-principal's rhetoric aside, racist taunting was treated as an "interpersonal" problem, not as an assault by one child on another. The burden ultimately fell not on the name caller or on the school, but on Sean, who was expected to "make up" with the name caller and in that way to heal a breach he had not caused. From this Sean learned that officialdom is unlikely to defend him, despite its claims about concern for him, and therefore he must defend himself—with fists, if necessary. Further, Sean's testimony alone was not enough to galvanize Mr. Walsh into even the mild actions he took: a witness was needed. Actually, I believe that a white, disinterested witness was needed. Had the child who overheard the name calling been black, or even been a white friend of Sean's, I think the outcome would have been even less satisfactory.

None of the lessons of the name-calling episode were new to me, nor do I think most parents of black children would find the other conclusions I drew from the episode surprising. Mr. Walsh was quick to blame the parents, asserting that the child must have learned racist language at home, while the parents were just as quick to blame others, specifically black people. After talking to the child's mother, Mr. Walsh remarked to me that some black people call each other "nigger," and I later learned that the name caller initially claimed that Sean had called him "nigger" first.[1] The child's mother expressed concern, but not concern about Sean: she was worried only about what would happen to her son. The name caller's parents never expressed dismay or regret to Doug or me—a telling omission, I think—which leads me to believe that there were no consequences for this child at home.

Mr. Walsh categorically denied that the school bore any responsibility beyond reprimanding the child. He refused even to consider that the school itself was culpable in that it had created an environment that supported racism, with black students in an isolated minority. He did acknowledge that it seemed the child had learned the actual word "nigger" in school, during a school play about Langston Hughes. The teacher may have had only the best intentions in putting on this play. Unfortunately, the contemporary school environment is not distinctly different from the environment the play was meant to critique, and so at least one student got the wrong message from the play.

My son attended a private school with an excellent academic reputation, impressive resources, committed teachers, and involved parents. In addition to the basics of reading, writing, social studies, science, and math, Sean had computer class, music, art, gym, and industrial technology (aka shop). He had daily access to a terrific school library and went on a number of interesting field trips each year, to plays, concerts, museums, and historic sites. His classmates were the children of legislators, professors, lawyers, and managers; many were wealthy, very few were poor. Yet even in this privileged environment, racism thrived. What Sean's experiences—and the experiences of other black children I know—suggest is that even when black and white children attend the same school, sit next to each other in class, read the same books, and do the same lessons, the educations they receive have quite different effects.

I first suspected this divergence might be widespread when Sean was in kindergarten. His kindergarten was part of his day care center, whose population of teachers and students was

---

1. Black use of this word is debated among blacks. For a good précis of the controversy see Darrell Dawsey, "Nigger," *Emerge* (June 1993): 35–36.

largely black and Hispanic. This center reflected our city's school-age population, which is about 70 percent "minority." Little did we know then that within just a few years this day care center would come to represent a lost racial paradise. We had chosen our neighborhood in part because the local public elementary school was well-integrated and reputed to be the best in the city. But as we began asking acquaintances with older children their opinions of this school, we discovered a distressing pattern: the majority of white parents we asked were pleased with the school and lavishly praised the principal, while not one parent of a black child was pleased and many bitterly criticized the same principal. Both white and black parents mentioned that very few black children were enrolled in the school's gifted program, but most of the white parents explained this fact in various ingenious ways, whereas the black parents cited it as a concrete example of institutional bias. Black and white descriptions of the school diverged so radically that these two groups of children may as well have been in separate schools. And so, in November of Sean's kindergarten year, we found ourselves betraying our philosophic commitment to public education and researching private school options.

After narrowing the possibilities down to four, we began visiting schools. At every school we were enthusiastically welcomed and, indeed, pursued; I felt like the mother of a high school football star dealing with college coaches. We interpreted this interest in Sean as signifying a real, as opposed to merely rhetorical, commitment to racial and cultural diversity within these schools. As the weeks passed, we talked with other parents of children at Sean's day care center and encouraged them to apply to the places where we were applying. We had a selfish interest here—hoping that Sean would not be in a tiny minority and that he would have a friend or two beginning first grade with him—but also more altruistic reasons: we feel that all black children deserve the best education available, and we then believed that, even if Sean were not admitted to the schools of our choice, perhaps some other black children would be. In the end, Sean was, they weren't. Why? I can't be sure, but I believe that this disparity was about race, color, and money/class. The children who applied with Sean were all intelligent (they tested into gifted programs, for instance) and were evaluated similarly by their kindergarten teacher. The difference among them was that Sean was the "right" kind of black child, I think, in the eyes of admissions officers. He has a white mother, for one thing, with whom white administrators probably felt more comfortable than they did with black parents. He is light-skinned, he is middle-class in every way, his parents have comparatively high incomes. His friends who applied were darker skinned, were of lower-middle-class or working-class origins, their parents had lower incomes than we did, and they probably would have qualified for financial aid. In other words, I believe these schools wanted Sean because he wasn't "too black" and he would not cost them money. He would "fit in" while at the same time improving their racial balance.

The school-search process went on for months, and in June we still did not know what we were going to do with Sean when September rolled around. We finally decided we would take our chances with the public elementary school, where at least there were a lot of black children, rather than send Sean to a school where he would be one of very few black children. We explained to admissions officers that we were not sending Sean to their schools because they had not admitted adequate numbers of black children.

A week before the academic year began, I received a phone call from the new principal of a fifth private school, which had not contacted me after I sent in Sean's application eight months earlier. She had just been hired, and had discovered that the school had six empty slots in a first-grade class. She was calling parents of children on a waiting list to check on interest. I was interested, but wary: how many black children would be in this class? I recalled that there had been no way to self-identify as minority on this school's application, and I was concerned that this absence meant the school had no commitment at all to affirmative action. The new principal said she would happily fill all the slots with black children if she could discover which of the applicants were black and if their parents remained interested. "I've only been here a few days," she confided, "but from what I can see, not much attention has been given to racial diversity. I'd like to change that." Huzzah! We sent Sean to her school, and several of his friends enrolled there too.

This principal was indeed committed to racial diversity and to a multicultural curriculum. Further, she saw the interdependence of the two—without substantial numbers of so-called minority children, no curricular changes will make much difference, and without a multicultural curriculum, minority children will be marginalized and alienated—and worked very hard during her tenure at the school to institute both. From the beginning, however, she was embattled, with the forces of (white) tradition among faculty and parents alike allied against her. Parents of "minority" children formed an organization to support each other and the principal. In the end we lost the principal, who was forced to resign two years after she began.

Sean had his first unmistakable encounter with overt racism at the end of first grade. A white boy in his class with whom Sean often played at school told his friends that his mother had said he could invite three children to a party celebrating the end of the school year. Sean was one of the favored three, and supposedly the boy's mother would call me to make arrangements. Each morning Sean asked me if she had called the night before, and the answer was always negative. Finally, two days before school ended, he asked me to call her. After I explained why that wasn't a good idea, from the position of etiquette, Sean decided to ask Bob if the party was still on. He came home from school forlorn. Yes, the party was on, but Bob had told him that his mother now said he could only have two boys and that Sean could not come.

Sean couldn't understand why Bob's mother so disliked him: "She only met me *once*, Mom, and I was nice to her!" I was present the one time this woman met Sean—at a school function—and from her look of surprise when she saw Doug, me, and Sean, it was clear that Bob had neglected to mention Sean's race. I suspected that racism was at the root of her decision to limit the party to two guests when Sean's name turned up on the list. As Sean wondered aloud about why he was excluded, Doug and I had a silent dialogue over the top of his head: should we tell him our guess?

We began by asking Sean if he remembered what prejudice was. Yes, he did, and he had a good definition: "When people treat other people unfairly because of their race or something else like that." We explained that this mother might be prejudiced against black people—a racist, in short—and this might explain why Bob wasn't able to have him to his house. Sean felt less devastated, as he no longer worried what about him was so awful that he couldn't go to Bob's party, and he turned his attention to what was so awful about Bob's mother. We then explained that he and Bob could still be friends at school, and that he shouldn't blame Bob for his mother's ideas—also, we reminded Sean, this was just a guess by us, not a fact. We came up with an alternate celebration for the last day of school, and things seemed okay.

Three years later, I still wonder if we did the right thing. Later experiences with Bob's mother have affirmed the correctness of our guess, and Bob and Sean are no longer friends, in large part because Bob started saying openly racist things to Sean the next year. On the way to a black history month program, Bob shoved Sean in the hall and said, "I'm sick of black history month! When are we going to have white history month?" Sean, already fairly clear about curricular biases from discussions at home about my teaching and about schools generally, said he answered, "Every other month is white history month, and I'm pretty tired of that!" My doubt about our handling of the end-of-first-grade episode does not stem from any sense that I may have misjudged the mother of this child, but from the effect on Sean. Doug and I have tried not to label every injustice racism, because there is enough overt racism to fight without our having to seek it out. We share the caution later sounded by Comer and Poussaint (1992), who say that "calling all injustice racism can make your child feel that he is drowning in a sea of ill-feeling with no allies or potential allies anywhere. It can cause black children to be fearful and uncomfortable."[2] Knowing what racism is in the abstract does not help one to understand what it is in the flesh, and I really didn't want my son to lose his innocence at age six. But he did.

I did mention all this to his first-grade teacher, whose response was disbelief—"I've known that family for years. I really doubt they are racist." Later I wished I had said something more to the teacher or to school administrators, as when Sean next encountered racism from a peer, we were met with the same disbelief. My naïveté about white teachers surely came from my own whiteness; despite my experiences as an adult, I retained remnants of the belief that most people are basically good and that nonracists would become antiracists when presented with evidence of racism. Darlene and Derek Hopson (1990) warn that "non-Black school officials seldom appreciate or even acknowledge how prevalent racial discrimination, even racial attack, is in their

---

2. Comer and Poussaint, *Raising*, 240–241.

schools, and how deeply such discrimination can affect the victims."[3]

In third grade, Sean again had an experience that he couldn't quite understand on his own. A new boy (white) entered the class mid-year and was assigned to Sean's table for lunch, where previously Sean and two white boys, all good friends, had sat together. A few days after the new boy joined the group, he asked the children at the table what they planned to be when they grew up. Sean, the first to answer, said he wanted to be a paleontologist and an archaeologist. The next boy, evidently at a loss—this was not normal lunchtime chat, I gathered from Sean—said, "Me too." The new boy, Noah, turned to the white "me-tooer" and said, "You will probably be successful." Turning to Sean, he said, "You won't. Everyone knows that you won't get into college, and if you do, you'll flunk out." Now, Sean is a very bright child who does quite well in school—why would Noah come up with this particular analysis? After Doug and I discussed it, we agreed that the episode might well have been racially motivated, and Doug said he'd mention it to the teacher—whether racial or not, Noah and Sean obviously had some sort of problem that needed to be resolved, as this was not the first time Noah had made a cutting remark to Sean.

The teacher's instantaneous response was the usual, "I'm sure it was not racial!" She went on to say that Noah habitually made critical remarks about other children's intelligence, always claiming to be smarter than they. "Well, then," Doug replied, "you really do have quite a problem, which I hope you'll do something about." We heard nothing from the teacher, but Sean reported that she had gathered all four children who had been at lunch together to ask what had happened—beginning this conference with "Sean's father says that . . ."—and basically encouraging Noah to agree that his remark had nothing to do with race.

Later I approached Noah's mother when we were both at school for a class event, hoping to discuss Sean's and Noah's mutual difficulties. At first I did not mention race. Noah's mother had a totally dismissive attitude: "They couldn't have a big problem, because I never heard of it, and Noah gets along with every-

---

3. Hopson and Hopson, *Different and Wonderful*, 152.

one." This provoked me to blurt out, "Well, he doesn't get along with Sean, and I suspect it may be racial."

"It's NOT racial!" she hissed furiously. "Noah doesn't notice race! Until this minute I didn't know if Sean was green or blue or what! He's probably one of these bully boys who uses his fists, and doesn't know how to use words to solve his problems!" Noah's mother saw "black boy" and thought "slow, inarticulate, violent." She did not, and could not, see Sean.

When I told this story to other parents, response split along racial lines. All the black parents saw it as a racial episode and all but two of the white parents said it did not sound at all racial to them. Noah's mother's remarks, especially the "green or blue" stuff (people don't come in green or blue, colors popular with white folks when they want to claim race doesn't matter) and her assumption that Sean had trouble with words and was given to physical violence (which accords with white stereotypes of black males), suggest to blacks that she has a race problem, while many whites don't hear them that way.

Maybe it was not racial—although it's interesting that Noah chose the one black child at the table as the target of a disparaging remark about future success and that his comments echoed racist views of black intelligence and achievement—but the unwillingness of most whites even to consider that it might have been racial exemplifies the problems parents of black children face in dealing with issues at school, and that black people in general face in their dealings with any predominantly white institution.

A white parent once agreed with me that racism was a serious problem in Sean's school and went on to say that it was part of a widespread lack of good manners. It turns out her daughter is sometimes mocked for her fatness. Well, I'm sure that hurts, but I don't think that sort of teasing is exactly the same as racism, nor do I think racism is a "manners" issue. Douglas Bates (1993) reports a similar response from a school administrator, who warned him not to be too sensitive about the racial harassment his daughter was enduring because "all children experience razzing at some point in their lives . . . whether it's for being fat or skinny or having freckles or curly hair."[4] Bates rejected this

---

4. D. Bates, *Gift*, 118–119.

attempt to put racial insults into the same category as common childhood teasing, but was not able to convince the principal to rethink his views. Russell, Wilson, and Hall (1992) note that "taunts about color may seem the same as calling a child with glasses 'four eyes' or a fat child 'tubby'—part of the inevitable cruelties of childhood. Yet children can never outgrow skin color as they do other childhood traits."[5] This analysis misses the point, as the key issue is not mutability but power.

One teacher at Sean's school told another, who then told me, that I take racism "too seriously." After all, she went on to say, she was sometimes teased for being Italian in a predominantly Irish neighborhood as a child. Again, I'm sure this hurt—I was often teased for being tall as a child, and it did hurt—but it does not have the same implications or effects as racism. This seems self-evident to me, and to every black and antiracist white person I know, yet is a major area of contention among whites generally.

There is a crucial distinction between prejudicial attitudes or biases on the one hand, and racism on the other, particularly institutional or systemic racism. We all have biases or prejudices, ranging from the harmless (I can't bear heavy metal music, for instance) to the hurtful (mocking someone's ethnicity or appearance). Racism differs substantially from these biases in its power to affect its targets' life chances—where one lives, where one works, what sort of job one has, where (or if) one goes to school, what one thinks of oneself and of one's group. Biases against rock music or Italians are not encoded into every social institution, after all, while racism is. School is the first place where children experience systemic racism first hand, with the lessons coming from the curriculum, the faculty, and the student body.[6] Describing institutional racism, Andrew Hacker (1992) asserts that most organizational cultures in the United States—from the FBI to private industry—are "inherently white."[7]

> American institutions begin with an initial bias against black applicants, because the presumption is that most blacks cannot or will not meet the standards the organization has set. Historically, virtually all of the people associated with Yale

---

5. Russell, Wilson, and Hall, *The Color Complex*, 101.
6. Hopson and Hopson make a similar point, in *Different and Wonderful*, 141.
7. Hacker, *Two Nations*, 22.

University, United Airlines, and the Omaha police force (to give an arbitrary selection of illustrations) have been white, which has in turn created both the image of these institutions and the way they operate. In this sense, they are "white" organizations, from which it follows that their members are expected to think and act in white ways. This is not as difficult for white people, although some have to make an extra effort if they wish to master class-based aspects of manner and style. However, for blacks the situation is qualitatively different, because they see themselves as being judged by more coercive criteria which call on them to deny large parts of themselves.[8]

Institutions are made up of human beings, in a symbiotic relation: the institution conveys its values to individuals, individuals further reinforce (or, less usually, challenge) these values, the institution reflects these attitudes back, and so on. A lifetime of experiences with institutional racism explains why many black parents immediately assume that their children's school difficulties are rooted in racism and treat schools as inherently antagonistic to their children, attitudes that apparently baffle white teachers and administrators.[9] Some schools and businesses are now trying to overcome their institutionalized racism with the help of diversity consultants, but to do so they must battle not only that racism but also the cynical mockery of those who think systemic racism is a chimera.[10]

Systemic racism is no chimera: when Noah told Sean he would not go to college, Noah was expressing an institutional bias that he had already internalized at age eight; when my acquaintance's daughter was called "fatty" by a classmate, the classmate was expressing a prejudice, but not one backed up by the full force of social institutions. And that, I think, is the crucial difference— one that is understood by virtually all black people, but few whites.

When whites encounter black biases against whites, they tend to label these attitudes "racist" or "reverse racist," but in reality

---

8. Ibid., 22–23.
9. See Comer and Poussaint, *Raising*, 190–191.
10. An example of this dismissive attitude is a recent cover article by Heather MacDonald for *The New Republic*, "The Diversity Industry" (5 July 1993) 22–25, in which the author mocks efforts at cross-cultural communication.

they are nothing of the kind. Black people do not control social institutions, do not have the power to encode their biases into legal and social strictures as whites do. So, although such prejudice is reprehensible and even hurtful to individual white people, it does not have the force of racism. Racism is more than individually held biases. As Andrew Hacker (1992) comments, "Racism takes its full form only when it has an impact on the real world. . . . The significance of racism lies in the way it consigns certain human beings to the margins of society, if not painful lives and early deaths. In the United States, racism takes its highest toll on blacks. No white person can claim to have suffered in such ways because of ideas that may be held about them by some black citizens."[11]

The cumulative effects of dealing with subtle racism include both exhaustion and paranoia. As my friend Elizabeth recently told me, she used to be committed to integration and to raising her children in as integrated an area as possible, but:

"I've come full circle now to the point where I wish to God, with all my heart, that there was an all-black school with an all-black faculty that I could send my children to. . . . So, I'd know that if they [the school faculty] called me about something, that would be what was going on: it's her academics, it's her behavior, whatever. I don't want any hidden agendas. . . . I want my child safe, I'm tired of her being hurt and of worrying about the possibility of her being hurt."

For me, the really heartbreaking aspect of Elizabeth's comment is not that she's given up on integration, but that her vision of an all-black institution, free of racism, is purely fantasy. There are, of course, all-black institutions, but I doubt that any are free of racism. Where would these black faculty, administrators, and staff come from? From this society, where they would most certainly have come into contact with some nonblack institutions and would in all likelihood have internalized at least some of the institutional racism they encountered. Alice Walker's depiction in *Meridian* of "Saxon College," a black institution that is dedicated to teaching black women to be white ladies and that fences out most of the black community, is illustrative here. In other words, there is no safe place, no pure person: we have all, black or not,

_____

11. Hacker, *Two Nations*, 29.

been indoctrinated into our society's racist values long before we reach adulthood.

In contrast to my friend Elizabeth's fervent desire for an all-black environment for her child stands my sister-in-law Beverly's advice to Doug and me. When we told her we were planning to move Sean to a school with more black students, Beverly expressed concern. A school principal herself, Beverly felt that the academic preparation Sean received at his first school was truly excellent and wanted to be sure we based our decision on academic as well as racial factors. I realized that we had spoken only about race, as if numbers were the only issue, and reassured her that the new school was, if anything, more academically rigorous than Sean's former school. Beverly still thought we might be making a mistake. The truth is that Sean has to survive in a racist society. Trying to protect him from racism now could backfire later when he has to deal with racist whites and lacks the tools to do that. "I know you want him to be safe, but keeping him safe now could just increase the danger for him later." Beverly's view—that racism is an intrinsic part of our society and that black children are best served by learning to deal with it early—would be alien to the mass of whites.

White people, perhaps trying to demonstrate their own lack of racism, frequently assert that children do not notice race.[12] At the same time, the old saw that you have to be taught to hate seems to have been updated and simplified to mean that your parents have to teach you to hate. This readiness to locate the learning of racism in the home mirrors our society's bourgeois individualism, but it also bespeaks both an unwillingness to acknowledge the social nature of racism and a flight from collective responsibility. If racism is as much a part of our culture as baseball, as much a part of the school curriculum as reading, and therefore parents need not teach their children racist ideas, then no one can escape it—we are all implicated. Most white people try to avoid this guilty knowledge.

What would it mean for white people to acknowledge the social nature of racism? Most obviously, it would mean needing to

---

12. They are proved wrong by a recent study by Patricia G. Ramsey that suggests that even very young children do grasp the social ramifications of racial differences. "The Salience of Race in Young Children Growing Up in an All-White Community," *Journal of Educational Psychology* (1991): 31–33.

do something or to fall victim to a useless, guilt-induced paralysis. And this doing is daunting. Black people tend to identify with other black people victimized in bias incidents—they can see themselves as vulnerable to that harassment, and many have endured similar kinds of harassment. White people—except gays and lesbians—tend to stand outside, identifying neither with the harassed nor with the harassers. This outsider stance speaks powerfully to the effects of white supremacism, as even women, working- or lower-class, first-generation college attenders, the children or grandchildren of immigrants, single mothers, Jews, and feminists share the single privilege of skin color. Most white people have been indoctrinated into identification with the upper-class white elites who oppress them too. As bell hooks has pointed out, in our society all whites are bonded together through white supremacy.[13]

I am not saying that an antiracist society is unachievable, nor am I saying that it is hopeless for individual whites to try to change themselves and the wider society. What I am saying is that it is hard, very hard. Further, individual change is not enough—to combat institutional racism, we need cooperative efforts. And this, I think, is the sticking point. The fact is that for white people to fight institutional racism and its concomitant white-skin privilege, we will have to give something up: we will have to refuse the unearned privileges accorded us for our white skins. Apart from the initial problem of raising consciousness enough to recognize these privileges, we will run into the problem of not wanting to lose our privileges, especially our (white) children's privileges.

When my son's former school was working on its admissions policy, the multicultural parents' group offered advice to the principal on allocating the limited number of places open each year. To meet the school's affirmative action goals, all open places should be earmarked for minority students, which is what our group at first advocated. It soon became clear, however, that white parents' younger children would not be admitted to the school under such a policy, and our coalition fell apart. Most of the white parents—all of whom thought of themselves as extremely liberal, if not downright radical—wanted to retain the old "sibling

13. bell hooks, *Feminist Theory From Margin to Center* (Boston: South Press, 1984), 54.

policy," by which siblings of enrolled children got preference for admissions. This policy favored white children, as the vast majority of children already enrolled were white and therefore their younger siblings, who got preference under this arrangement, were also white. The white parents did not see this as preferential treatment or as favoritism toward whites—which it blatantly was—but did see an affirmative action policy as preferential treatment and favoritism toward blacks. During our meeting with the principal, it became clear that these white parents—who were a tiny minority of white parents in the school and who had worked hard in other ways for more diversity—only supported social justice if their own children did not have to forgo their inherited privileges. Further, they did not want any white children to lose these privileges, a wish they disguised under concern for the "public relations" of our group: we need to go slowly so as not to alienate other parents.

I believe this episode is a microcosmic example of wider social attitudes. Most white liberals are willing to "add in" blacks, but many are not willing to step aside in order to stand next to blacks, and are not willing to give up any portion of their own advantages in order to redistribute resources and power more equitably.

REFERENCES

Bates, Douglas. *Gift Children: A Story of Race, Family, and Adoption in a Divided America.* New York: Ticknor and Fields, 1993.

Comer, James P., and Alvin F. Poussaint. *Black Child Care.* New York: Simon and Schuster, 1976.

———. *Raising Black Children.* New York: Plume, 1992.

Dawsey, Darrell. "Nigger." *Emerge* (June 1993): 35–36.

Hacker, Andrew. *Two Nations.* New York: Scribners, 1992.

hooks, bell. *Feminist Theory From Margin to Center.* Boston: South End Press, 1984.

Hopson, Darlene Powell, and Derek Hopson. *Different and Wonderful: Raising Black Children in a Race-Conscious Society.* New York: Prentice-Hall, 1990.

MacDonald, Heather. "The Diversity Industry." *The New Republic* (5 July 1993) 22–25.

Ramsey, Patricia. "The Salience of Race in Young Children Growing Up in an All-White Community." *Journal of Educational Psychology* 83 (1991): 28–34.

Russell, Kathy, Midge Wilson, and Ronald Hall. *The Color Complex.* New York: Harcourt Brace Jovanovich, 1992.

An Activist Forum III: Counter Tales

Rashid Khalidi

Rashid Khalidi, courtesy of University of Chicago Office of News and Information

Much of what I do involves teaching for justice, because the very terms I teach about are subversive of so many categories of public knowledge. This is because teaching about the modern Middle East in the United States means confronting a great deal of resistance, notably where the subject of Palestine is concerned.

Because the very term Palestine is considered controversial in some circles—and indeed is considered a provocation by some in and of itself, as is evidenced by hate mail whenever I publish an op-ed article on Palestinian affairs—teaching about Palestinian history can often be quite difficult. For while most teachers can usually at least strongly influence what happens inside our classrooms, all of us engaged in teaching for justice spend much of the time in less controllable situations outside the classroom. Whether this involves public speaking at universities, community groups, think tanks, or churches, synagogues, and mosques, or whether it involves radio talk show call-ins or interviews or articles for newspapers, this is a large and important part of our work. We naturally welcome the opportunity to speak out in such circumstances because it gives us an audience beyond the classroom for some of the same ideas we try to propound inside it.

Beyond generalized prejudices and often not-so-veiled racism against Arabs, Muslims, and Middle Easterners, the main problem comes when I have to confront firmly held and profoundly wrong ideas, particularly ones which are widespread in our culture. This is a common occurrence, because much of my work explains how national (and other political) identities are constructed and relatively changeable, rather than fixed, immutable, and eternal. Where the Middle East is concerned, however, many people prefer to believe in the immutable nature of certain identities, whether "unchanging aspects" of the Islamic world or the rootedness of modern Israel in the ancient Israelite kingdom. Although they are prepared to believe that Palestinian and some other identities are fairly recent constructs, albeit ones based on much older forms of identity, they are less prepared to believe that the same is true of modern Islamic or Israeli identities.

Things get harder when such misunderstandings, which at times are honest and innocent, are combined with the "idiot wind" which blows whenever government policy is discussed, and the lemmings in the media and the inside-the-beltway chorus echo whatever those in power are saying. It is nevertheless vitally important to try to talk sense about such things, whether about the Gulf war back in 1991 or about the "peace process" today, which has so far given us a lot of process and very little peace. And for all those who cling to received notions and fixed ideas, there are many more in the classroom and outside who come up afterwards, or write or call or e-mail later, to say that they have always thought something was wrong with the official version, and they were glad to hear another one. I suppose that is what makes it all worthwhile in the end.

William Watkins

William Watkins, courtesy of Therese Quinn

The cause of social and political justice has been the moving force in my life. Having worked in dingy sweatshops and being regularly confronted by the Los Angeles Police Department as a youth, I found out early about the master plan to contain, exploit, and oppress people in the interest of profits and control.

It was only through education, especially higher education, that my instincts and hunches could be given support, clarity, and theory. I found out about the power of ideas. Ideas make a difference. When grasped by people, ideas can become a powerful even transformative force. Ideas can excite and shape the passions of people. I knew then that teaching and teaching for social justice was my calling in life.

We ask, what knowledge is of most worth? What kind of teaching must we have? It certainly must be the examination of the human condition. How can it be in a world of plenty there is such want? What are the social, political, economic, racial, gender, and historical forces which shape events? Who makes history? Can we the propertyless and powerless influence anything? These are but a few of the organizing questions central to my teaching.

Rejecting idealism and romanticism, I strive to a curriculum of reconstructionism. I want my students to become critical social scientists. I want them to question the arrangements of power, authority, wealth, and control. I want them to believe that we little people can make a difference. We can create a new society without prejudice and want but only if we are armed with the knowledge and ideas to do so.

Jennifer Dohrn

Jennifer Dohrn

When I first opened the childbearing center, a woman who was pregnant with her sixth child registered for care. She had passed our center each morning as she walked her children to school. Even though she was only two months with child, she often stopped by to "just ask a question." One early morning I saw her waiting for me outside the center. Perhaps I looked puzzled as to why she was there so often, having gone through this experience many times before. She answered my silent question by sharing with me that she had questions from five other pregnancies that no one had ever taken the time to answer.

Teaching and learning are the heartbeats of my daily work and life. As a midwife and one who bears witness to birth, I both formally teach midwifery students and also share information with women and their families preparing for new life. And as I do this in a community that has minimal health services and where life for most is a daily struggle for survival, the challenge is how to translate this knowledge into cultural and social contexts that maximize respect and allow others to bloom.

As a teacher, I am in essence a guide. Once basic information and skills are shared, the larger task is one of unlocking the special and unique ways a new midwife can serve women. I work to create an environment in which a new student can draw on her own rich life experiences and mix her new midwifery knowledge to discover the midwife that she is to be. And as she travels this path of self-discovery, I learn and change with her.

Ultimately, I learn from the women and families I serve. Each culture has its own rituals and mysteries for the rite of passage of birth. Urging a woman to learn and reclaim the ways of her ancestors allows her strength in her own identity and contributes to strengthening her family. And again, as she makes her own discoveries and teaches me, I learn the depth of the commonness of all as well as our uniqueness. Helping each child be welcomed, even to an unjust and often unwelcoming world, is a humbling and awesome event that can transform a woman and family, as well as those of us who guide them along this path. I am daily honored.

Noel Ignatiev

Noel Ignatiev, courtesy of
Tom Webb

I am a political person. I spent decades in workers' rights and community struggles and the antiwar movement, and in attempting to build small revolutionary organizations. Several years ago I helped start *Race Traitor: Journal of the New Abolitionism.* I speak widely on political topics, and take part as I can in developing organizations and activity.

For ten years I have been employed as an instructor at Harvard University. I started as a section leader in lecture courses. For the last eight years I have conducted, alone and with various partners, a seminar in the history and literature of America, which I designed and have adapted for students at various levels. In addition, I have supervised individual study and honors essays in the history and literature of America. In my capacity as a teacher I have interacted with hundreds of students, from first-year to graduate degree candidates in the extension school.

It is my contention that my work as a teacher, however rewarding it has been for me and even ultimately beneficial it may prove for some of my students, is of no political significance whatever, if "political" means "directly related to the struggle over power." The example of one student, a young woman from a small New England town, brought this point home to me with particular force. One of only two students I have ever written recommendations for without being asked, she showed appreciation for and insight into the great works of U.S. history and literature from Melville and Twain to Du Bois and Ellison. We stayed in touch after the class ended, and when my son was born, she gave me a gift of a children's book about the Underground Railroad with the following inscription: "Because you will teach your child the same things that you taught me . . . Thank you for opening my mind . . ."

A year later I ran into her and she told me she had just been hired as a proctor for the high school students who attended Harvard in the summer. She reported that many of them had expressed hostility toward people who have sex with members of their own sex and that she had organized "sensitivity" meetings to counter those attitudes. "I am applying what I learned from you," she said.

Now, however commendable her effort to promote tolerance, it did not represent my teachings. What a pass things have come to, I thought. I preach class war and my most promising student responds with diversity training.

There have been other cases of students translating my teachings into social work. The result cannot be attributed to administrative limitations on what I can teach; I have enjoyed a remarkable degree of academic freedom, which I have used to introduce students to a variety of revolutionary thinkers, among others. Nor can it be blamed on the social composition of my classes: Harvard students, while they tend to come from affluent and privileged strata, have as much heart and are as open to radical *ideas* as students anywhere. Nor is the lack of political meaning due to my pedagogic methods: I encourage students to draw on their own experiences in thinking and writing, and to collaborate in their studies; most evaluate my classes favorably.

I explain the lack of political consequence by the weakness of the movement outside the classroom. In other circumstances the student I spoke of earlier would have been out occupying administration buildings and destroying draft files. But except in rare cases those things are not happening now, and as a result her activism, and that of others like her, takes the form of sensitivity sessions, tutoring inner-city children, and "walks for hunger." The predicament I describe is not restricted to the university, although the ebb in struggle may manifest itself differently in the army or the automobile factory from the way it does on campus. Movement creates consciousness, not the other way around.

Ironically, one of the most instructive expressions of political struggle I witnessed was directed against me. In one class my teaching partner and I had loaded the reading list for several weeks with declarations from prisoners and laborers of the eighteenth and nineteenth centuries. Although the students at first took to the material, it became evident that the tone was beginning to wear on them. Finally, at the beginning of one class a student stood up and announced, on behalf of all, that they were tired of that material and wanted to read the great works of American literature. "Noel told us," she said, "that if we wanted power, we would have to take it, so that's what we're doing." I bowed to their demand and revised the reading list accordingly. I also expressed the hope that they carry the spirit of rebellion into their other classes. Sad to say, that might have been the most valuable political experience that some of them had in their university career.

For me, teaching at a university has been an agreeable way to earn my living: it has provided me with the leisure to read and take part in political activity, and allowed me to establish political connections with a number of students and others. Some of the people I have met through the university have become close collaborators in political work, and my actions and arguments may have influenced them. But, with the possible exception of the participants in the Great Syllabus Rebellion described earlier, not a single one was politicized as a result of what went on in my classroom. And that is perhaps as it should be: after all, for an office worker, running a computer is not a political act—although refusing to run one might be. Why should it be any different for a teacher, whose function in the capitalist system is about the same as that of a clerk in the welfare department? When my students ask me for advice about careers that will permit them to earn a living while "working for social change," I always reply that no official agency will ever pay them to overturn the system, and that to seek to do well by doing good is to set themselves up, either to suffer disappointment or forsake their goals.

Luis J. Rodriguez

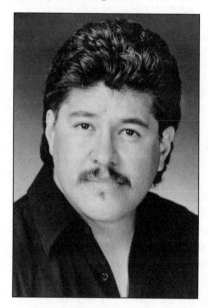

Luis Rodriguez

There are messages in the classroom, overt and implied, that say more than all the lesson plans in the world. As a child, the messages I received amounted to this: I had little or no value in the larger scheme of things, except perhaps as a future factory worker, janitor, or prison inmate. If questioned, any teacher would probably deny this. But the net result would be the same.

My imagination and natural desire for learning were squashed into a single concept. As a working-class son of Mexican immigrants following the known historical path of such sons, it would be difficult for me to overcome what was expected of me.

History is a powerful force. It's a history, I'm quite aware, of having been conquered, of coming from a poor developing nation, of having dark Indian skin that—at the very core of this land—signifies inferiority (none of which, of course, is accurate).

I was expected to fail; moreover, this was my lot.

Sure there are exceptions. I know many Chicano college graduates; I have a brother-in-law who is a California state assemblyman. But they are usually considered special, different, unlike the rest of us.

I don't blame all teachers. It's never that easy. I had great teacher/mentors who helped me realize the powers I possessed for knowledge, for strategy, for speaking and, later, for writing.

And I understand things have changed since I was a child—although not by much.

Recently, my wife and I removed my eight-year-old son Ruben from the neighborhood school in our largely Latino community. In kindergarten, Ruben had forty-one classmates. The school was so overcrowded, children were forced to sit in cloakrooms. His teacher was a caring person; she was simply overwhelmed. The next two years weren't much better. In second grade, Ruben's teacher had placed his desk in a corner of the room, facing the wall, for four months! He had apparently misbehaved. But the teacher's reasoning for keeping him there was that "Ruben liked it." In fact, he was being socialized to remove himself, not to participate, eventually to fail. Whatever mistake he made had begun to be woven into an almost inescapable web.

After consulting the school manual, we discovered that such discipline could not be done without the parent's knowledge. Also, these measures had to be instructive, not punitive. In our mind, there were clear violations. However, the principal spent most of the time at our joint meeting justifying the teacher's action. The teacher was not our main concern here. Yet our son's well-being seemed to be the least critical aspect as we adults worked out a convenient compromise.

I won't get into the other problems at the school (including preschool kids receiving bug bites from sitting in unclean bungalows, and teachers who called children out of their names, including one who had a habit of throwing keys at unruly students). To challenge the inequities, my wife along with other parents and concerned teachers contacted the media and later published a bilingual newsletter called "High Expectations." But with things worsening for our boy, we finally enrolled him at another school (with a focus on Native American culture). So far, he has done better.

The problem is this: The United States has long instituted multitiered schooling. Those families with money, in private schools or in public schools with high property tax rates, have for the most part the best teachers, resources, and "messages" that say you can and will succeed (which has its own problems). Working-class families, particularly in depressed urban and rural communities, have to endure lower levels of education that in the past ran the gamut of slave schools, segregated schools (including Indian boarding schools), and tracking.

This can be overcome, but we must do it for all the children, not only the exceptional few. I ask of teachers and administrators: What messages are prevailing in your classrooms? For any child, the proper and consistent nurturing of their capacities for greatness makes all the difference in the world.

To me, this is the social justice issue in education for the new millennium.

POSSIBILITIES-
JOINING HANDS

What a privilege it is to be a small part of a great and just struggle, to affiliate with people naming the obstacles to our full humanity, and then aiming with passion and conviction toward democracy, toward freedom. In the face of unjustified suffering and unnecessary pain, purpose and integrity are found in joining hands with others moving to the common rhythms of resistance and repair, connecting to the grand tradition of rebellion toward liberty. Of course, no tradition is simply inherited—the tradition is evoked and then attained through labor.

We live divided lives in a shattered community—a society torn by glaring and brutal privileges and oppressions, a world of unprecedented bestiality and barbarity, a culture rent by the evil of racism. While none of us chose the world we have been thrust into, the meaning of each of our lives is measured by how we choose to deal with the evil, the barbarity, the oppression we find all around us.

Every story of evil begins with cries and groans. The American story is at least in part a lament standing next to an ideal, a hope, a promise. The hope of democracy forces us to reflect on the most disadvantaged, the most despised, the most oppressed. In the margins the spark of freedom begins.

In this section—Possibilities—we see people joining together to revitalize public life and lay claim to a wider public space. We see kindness and care, tenderness and imagination leading toward social movements to redress grievances and create a community of compassion and concern. We see a sense of solidarity with people in need replacing the stance of the beneficent benefactor dispensing services. We see people working for small changes that point toward larger reconstructions, rethinking and recommitting in the name of justice. It may look from this or that vantage point merely like a flickering candle in the darkness, but it has aspirations to become a flare for freedom.

14—"Do You Know Where You Are?"—A Memoir of Becoming a South Sider

Jamie Kalven

Of all the memberships we identify ourselves by (racial, ethnic, sexual, national, class, age, religious, occupational), the one that is most forgotten and that has the greatest potential for healing, is place. We must learn to know, love, and join our place even more than we love our own ideas. People who can agree that they share a commitment to the landscape/cityscape—even if they are otherwise locked in struggle with each other—have at least one deep thing to share. Community values (which include the value of the nonhuman neighbors in the "hood") come from deliberately, knowledgeably, and affectionately "living in place."

Gary Synder

I drive a blue 1979 Volvo station wagon with Vermont license plates. The rear seat is folded down and the back is filled to capacity with shovels, picks, axes, hoes, mattocks, pruning saws, hoses, and packets of seeds; there is often a red wheelbarrow upside down on the roof rack. These are the tools my colleagues and I use in a community-organizing initiative on the South Side of Chicago called Turn-A-Lot-Around. Most of the projects I am involved in are concentrated in and around the high-rise public housing developments—the Robert Taylor Homes and Stateway Gardens—that line South State Street from 54th to 35th streets. Often described as the largest concentration of poverty in the United States, this area of the city is notorious for patterns of violence that have claimed many lives.

One day this spring, as I waited for a stop light to change at an intersection near the Robert Taylor Homes, a good samaritan in the next lane, seeing a white motorist who didn't look like a plainclothes policeman, stuck his head out of the window and gestured to draw my attention.

"Do you know where you are?" he asked.

I assured him that I did and thanked him for his concern.

What, I wondered later, had he imagined? That a Vermont

farmer had struck out for the territories with his tools and wheel-barrow and ended up in the innermost "inner city," surveying the vast acreage of open land left by demolition with thoughts of homesteading?

Do you know where you are? It's a good question. A few years ago, before I became engaged in this work, I would have answered it with confidence. No longer. Now, as I pass daily back and forth across borders and between worlds, I am awash in fresh perception and suspended between shifting perspectives. It's a condition rather like that of a traveler who returns home after a long journey and sees with heightened lucidity the strange in the familiar.

The Vermont license plates are an accident of marriage. (My wife grew up outside Burlington; we spend part of the summer there, hence the plates.) I was born and raised in Hyde Park–Kenwood. My father taught at the university. I am a product of the tensions and contending influences native to this place. To this day, when I exit from the highway and enter the neighborhood—from the north via 47th Street, from the south via Stony Island Avenue—I have the sensation I used to have as a child in the back seat of my parents' car, a feeling at once comforting and exciting, of being enveloped by the real.

The area of Kenwood where I grew up was a middle-class white neighborhood, with academic families living, sometimes beyond their means, in the mansions of a bygone era. And it was an elite black neighborhood—the preferred address of African-American businessmen and professionals, politicians and entertainers, who had the means but didn't have a wide range of neighborhoods to choose from. It made for a singular mix.

When I was born, my parents were renting the third-floor apartment in the home at 49th and Greenwood of Professor Harold Urey, who some years earlier had won the Nobel Prize in chemistry. That house was later purchased by Sonny Liston, the boxer, and then Amhal Jahmal, the jazz pianist. (How delicious it would be to know the biographies of various Kenwood houses.) We later rented at 48th and Kimbark, then purchased a house on the 4900 block of Woodlawn. In the course of my growing up, three heavyweight boxing champions owned houses within two blocks of my parents' house: Liston, Joe Louis, and Muhammad Ali. The Honorable Elijah Muhammad lived up the street. (Unbeknownst to us, Malcolm X on his visits to Chicago stayed in the coach house behind Elijah's.) I sometimes played basketball with

Elijah's grandchildren. At night, walking the dog, we exchanged greetings with members of the Fruit of Islam standing guard on the corner.

To the north, 47th Street marked the edge of our world. When I was a child, it was still the main commercial street on the South Side. My enduring impressions of urban vitality and excitement were formed by that street. (I didn't realize it was dying.) We did some of our shopping there—at Kamberos's Grocery, Frank's Hardware Store, Gill's Liquors—but we didn't go north of 47th Street. It was another world—threatening and uncharted. *The ghetto.* The division between worlds, the border along which I grew up, was drawn with double strokes of race and class.

The streets I walked as a child were contested. To be streetwise meant being able to distinguish your middle-class black neighbors from the tough kids from outside the neighborhood who might hurt you. We didn't venture north of 47th Street, but the inhabitants of that world made regular forays into ours. They knocked us off our bicycles and pedaled away on them; they stole our baseball mitts. They roughed us up, administering ritual humiliations that seem, in retrospect, in light of today's styles of adolescent violence, to have been governed by an etiquette of considerable delicacy. And sometimes—in the playground and vacant lots that were common ground—we played together.

Growing up, I was keenly aware of boundaries and was practiced in making class-based distinctions. Yet I also had a strong sense of living in *one big place.* I'm not sure what I would have called it, not sure I knew a name for it, but I knew it was home.

"By a trick of fate (and our racial problems notwithstanding)," Ralph Ellison has written, "the human imagination is integrative—and the same is true of the centrifugal force that inspirits the democratic process." There is no stronger evidence for this proposition than the way children exercise their imaginations in an effort to make sense of the world into which they were born.

A former U of C faculty member who shall remain nameless (hint: he sits on the Supreme Court), once told me, with a note of concern, a story about one of his sons, then in a nursery school class that contained a number of black children. One day the boy had come home from school and asked his father about something that had been puzzling him.

"When," he asked, "do I turn black?"

By adolescence, a white child growing up in Hyde Park can no longer make the world cohere by imagining that blackness is a developmental phase. Yet the integrative effort continues in other ways. In my experience, Hyde Park adolescents are almost invariably more robustly cosmopolitan than their parents—seeking to make connections, to explore their place, animated by appetite for their world to be *interesting*.

In my case, once in high school, it was primarily through athletics and music that I participated in the South Side beyond Hyde Park–Kenwood. I competed against runners from public schools throughout the area and trained with the University of Chicago Track Club. Many years later I heard a black community activist describe the UCTC as the part of the university most hospitable to the wider neighborhood. It was the most genuinely democratic institution I have ever been associated with. Young and old, black and white, male and female, Olympians and beginners, all trained and competed together, on an equal footing, under the benign yet demanding direction of Coach Ted Haydon.

And then there was music. At 47th and South Park (now Dr. Martin Luther King Drive), the Regal Theater presented regular rhythm and blues shows. A friend and I would slip into the balcony and take in the shows. They would build by way of lesser acts (e.g., Mary Wells, Major Lance, the raunchy comedy routines of Red Foxx, Pigmeat Markham, and Moms Mabley) toward the main event. The only whites in an audience of blacks, we were aware of stepping over a threshold. What we didn't yet know was that many of the headlined performers we saw—Smokey Robinson and the Miracles, the Four Tops, the Temptations, the Supremes, Marvin Gaye, Dionne Warwick, Wilson Pickett, Otis Redding—were also just then at the threshold of crossover success and would soon command large white audiences.

The medium of rich cultural confusion I moved through as an adolescent remains for me the particular quality of home. I grew, inhaling in the same breath the intellectual ethos of the university and the turbulent vitality of the South Side. I couldn't sort it out; I didn't feel a need to. It was, simply, the given. It was the world as I found it: an intense intellectual milieu, with a strong Central European flavor, situated in the capital of black America. Only years later did I realize that people could live in the same place and inhabit different worlds.

The decade after high school was full of movement. College of

Wesleyan University in Connecticut during the political and cultural turbulence of the 1960s. Mountaineering on three continents. A motorcycle journey from Paris to New Delhi. A year and a half spent impersonating an anthropologist in a village in the foothills of the Himalayas. Then, in the mid-1970s, the trajectory of my life changed. My father died. He had been working on a book about the American tradition of freedom of speech. I returned to Hyde Park–Kenwood and undertook the task of preparing his manuscript for publication. Having lived in an Indian village, the image that shaped that decade-long effort for me was the prosaic and universal one of a son returning home to assume responsibility for the family field.

Held in place by my circumstances, I rediscovered Hyde Park–Kenwood. When I first returned, I felt isolated by my grief and my task. I found the neighborhood claustrophobic as only the place where one grew up can be, but over time that changed, and I recovered an almost primitive sense of place. The streets of my childhood were a maze of memories and associations. To move through them was to move through my history, to retrace the map of my identity.

Returning to this place with wider experience of the world, I saw things I had not seen as a child. I was helped in this by my traveling companion, soon to be my wife, Patricia Evans. For Patsy, it was not home. A photographer, she explored it like a foreign city. Through her eyes, I saw how *strange* it was—this racially-integrated, middle-class enclave with its strongly drawn borders, at once imaginary and real, in relation to the wider South Side.

Not only had my perspective changed, but the South Side had changed. I had grown up among working people. I remember the sickly sweet smell of the stockyard on the wind, the blaze of the steel mills at full capacity. By the 1980s, the jobs were gone. Disinvestment and demolition had left much of the South Side looking as if the city had waged a war against itself. Streets once full of life were now dead; remnants of the Black Metropolis stood in isolation amid vacant land. In many areas the drug trade was the biggest employer and the streets were dominated by young men with guns.

Growing up, I had a sense of turbulent population movement swirling around the fixed point of our household. My childhood memories include bulldozers and wrecking balls. Yet I was unaware of the construction of the Robert Taylor Homes and State-way Gardens—unaware that South State Street was the destination of many of those being displaced by urban renewal. I was stunned to discover the scale of the phenomenon. Returning from the Loop, I would often drive home to Hyde Park via State Street—fascinated and appalled by what I saw but with no way in. It never occurred to me to stop the car and get out.

I relied on the media to tell me about this place five minutes from my home. And the images I absorbed over years were over-whelmingly images of violence. The net effect of such mediated images, uncorrected by direct experience, was to make South State Street seem akin to Rwanda or Bosnia—a world defined by violence. Remote and beyond my sphere of action. A wholly vio-lent place.

The afterglow of my childhood faded, as I realized that the South Side was divided against itself in ways that could be accu-rately described as apartheid. The rarity of what has been achieved in Hyde Park–Kenwood in terms of racial integration underscores the unfinished business of the society. I took comfort from the thought that I was privileged to live on the front line of the American dilemma—in a place where the defining issues for the democracy register daily on one's nerve ends. It's a privilege I experienced most of the time as an undertow of moral unease.

Our marriage ripened into a family: first, Josh; then, Betsy. As the claims of the domestic intensified, so too did my sense of the dangerous world beyond our nest. There is something poignant about what we do with our geographic imaginations in order to feel safe, in order to feel at home in the world. Consider the maps published by the *Hyde Park Herald* and the *Maroon* each week showing where reported crimes of different sorts were commit-ted. Meant to encourage realism and vigilance, this feature has a curious effect. It collaborates with denial by inviting one to locate danger elsewhere. "I look at the crime maps," a professor once told me, "and because the crime was committed on the next block, not my block, I tell myself my family is safe."

To be the victim of a violent street crime in Hyde Park is to have all imagined boundaries evaporate. One realizes, with the forces of revelation, that it's one big place. That is a frightening perception akin to vertigo. Yet it can be the basis for a remapping process that yields a geography at once more realistic and more encompassing of life's possibilities. For the danger in relying on imaginary boundaries is not only that they do not protect. They also impoverish what they enclose.

The Robert Taylor Homes are visible from the fifth-floor stacks of Regenstein Library. The University of Chicago campus is visible from the upper stories of the Robert Taylor Homes. So close. A world away.

In a blue station wagon full of tools, I daily travel between these worlds, crossing borders that become fainter and fainter with each trip. The area where I work is known as Grand Boulevard. Once the economic and cultural center of the black South Side, it is today a singular mix of vacant land, handsome surviving structures that carry the promise of future renewal, and the public housing projects stretching along South State Street like an armada of urban boat people off shore in turbulent waters. As I move through the area, every perception is a competing perception: waste and possibility, destruction and vitality, grief and hope.

My job description reads "community organizer," but it's a distinctive kind of organizing I do. The Turn-A-Lot-Around program seeks to contribute to democratic renewal by addressing injuries to *place*. At the center of the program is the process of working with neighborhood residents to recover vacant lots for community use—as gardens, play areas for children, convivial open space, or whatever residents desire. On Saturday mornings, work crews composed of neighborhood residents, volunteers from elsewhere, and Turn-A-Lot-Around staff work together at sites around the South Side. We have also established an employment program—a work crew of local men who do grassroots reclamation work. Most afternoons I work as a member of this crew.

The work is strenuous and satisfying. There is an elemental power and shared physical work that we sometimes tap into. Working side by side with others, distinctions of race, class, and gender don't disappear, but they seem to matter less. Such shared neighborly labor—raising the barn, bringing in the harvest—has largely disappeared from our society. On the evidence of our projects, many people don't even recognize they hunger for it until hunger begins to be satisfied. When the process runs true, the work creates a space—at once physical and social—that scarcely exists in our society: a setting where citizens long isolated from one another by urban apartheid have contact on a recurring basis. To inhabit this space feels so natural; it's a relief. It feels like coming home.

What may appear to be a large leap from Hyde Park to South State Street—heroic, reckless, or quixotic, depending on your perspective—has in fact been a series of small steps over time. I can recall how *exposed* I felt when I worked for the first time in the shadow of the Robert Taylor Homes. The image of gangbangers with guns occupied the foreground of my mind. As I came to the area once, twice, a hundred times and met with no harm and much hospitality, my lens widened and I began to see with my own eyes.

This not to say that the young men with guns are not a strong, ubiquitous, disturbing presence; they are. There are terrible realities of violence on the South Side, but there is also a media-induced hallucination of violence superimposed on these realities. What one begins to see, as the hallucination dissipates is *the rest of life*: fellow citizens, isolated and trapped, trying to live full lives under intolerable conditions.

The isolation of the public housing developments on South State Street—an isolation within the larger isolation of the inner city—contributes to unexpected qualities of neighborliness. There is much conviviality on the streets. My colleagues on the crew are constantly encountering people they have known all their lives. Few people pass by one of our work sites without a comment or question. An older man observing one of us swing a sledgehammer: "Make that hammer sing, boy, make that hammer sing." An attractive woman lifts the spirits of the crew: "I *do* like to see black men *working*." A member of the crew, Morris Butler, used to sing with a rhythm and blues group called Windy City. A man walking by salutes him by singing several bars of the group's big hit, *I Still Love You.*

It is a measure of the catastrophe that has struck the South Side that the vast majority of the conversations we have on the street are about a single topic: work. In the course of a day, dozens of men, including hard-core gang members, approach us to ask if we are hiring. Some are stoned, but most are sober and dignified. There is often a delicacy in the way they put the question that testifies to desperation held in check.

I recall in particular a muscular man who approached me while we were working on a project at a drop-in facility for homeless men. I was noncommittal about a job. He worked intensely for several hours swinging a sledgehammer. At the end of the day, he asked me shyly, "What did you think of my resumé?"

Whenever we work in or near public housing, children are drawn to our projects, often in large numbers. They range in age from five to six to early teens—the cusp of gang involvement. Most of them are delicate and wide awake. Their vitality seems especially vivid against the harsh sterility of their surroundings. They have not yet put on hard faces and withdrawn into the sullen solidarity of the gangs. They are full of questions—questions that reflect their isolation as well as their hunger to make sense of the world. After I had worked for weeks with a group of children on a lot across from the Robert Taylor Homes, one of them asked me, "Are you white?"

Roaming barren ground, these children seize on every nutrient they can find to feed their growth. Recently, I came across a scene on the ground of Stateway Gardens that can be observed throughout public housing. In the absence of any play equipment anywhere in the development, a dozen young boys were doing gymnastic routines, landing on a rotting and shredded old bed springs and mattress. The little ones did flips of various sorts over the bar. The older boys gave each a piece of candy after he completed his run.

It was a scene of intricate social order, disciplined energy, and resourcefulness. And yet—every perception is a competing perception—I was left wondering what avenues are open for the energies and capacities of these boys beside those offered by the gangs.

Like the children who come running when they see the station wagon with the red wheelbarrow on top pull up, my colleagues on the work crew are largely invisible to the wider society. That is, they are invisible until they do something destructive at which point they are seen as only destructive. All live in the immediate area; several grew up in the Robert Taylor Homes. A few have done time for violent crimes; some struggle with patterns of substance abuse. They are also survivors—hungry to work and to be productive, full of observations and curiosity about the worlds they move through. We share a sense of belonging to this place. Working side by side, we are trying to figure out what it might mean to be citizens of the South Side.

As we work to reclaim vacant lots, I sometimes feel like we are archeologists digging down through strata on strata of waste and debris, down toward the underlying prairie, in an effort to understand what has happened to this place. It takes a while to begin to absorb the sheer scale of the devastation and what it means in people's lives. "That's where I grew up," one of my coworkers remarks, as we drive by a vacant lot. "That was a club where we used to go to hear music." "That's where my church used to be." "That's where my mother's family lived." On and on. Memories without anchors in the physical world.

The streets I grew up on are largely intact. They are part of me; they are what I think and feel with. I try to imagine what it's like for my friends. Driving past 47th and King, I get a faint hint when I look out at the vacant lot where the Regal Theater used to stand.

Now there is much talk about tearing down the public housing high-rises on South State Street. It took me a long time to recognize that for many of those who live there these developments are *home*—places where strata of memories and associations are embedded. Whatever the merits of various plans for overhauling public housing in Chicago, one of the dangers of invoking South State Street as the symbol of everything deplorable about life in the inner city is that we will forget that simple fact.

The other day I was walking on the grounds of Stateway Gardens with the development manager, R. Olomenji O'Connor. A group of young boys approached us. Seeing a white man with the development manager, one of them asked me, "Do you own Stateway?" I explained that I did not. As we talked, it became clear that they were hoping they had found the single individual who needed to be persuaded not to tear down the place where they live.

Returning to Hyde Park at the end of a day spent working on vacant lots or on the grounds of a public housing development, I am struck by the beauty of the neighborhood. It's so green; there are so many trees. Yet I am also struck by the way it resembles in its isolation the neighborhoods I have just left. These perceptions are sharpened when I am in the company of my colleagues on the work crew for whom Hyde Park is not yet a welcoming or hospitable place. Boundaries that are for me metaphors have for them quasi-legal force; they are often stopped by men in uniform and asked, in effect, for their papers.

These days I think a lot about maps, about what they disclose and what they hide, about whom they make visible and whom they push into invisibility. A friend once described to me an exercise he did with a group of gang members at the Robert Taylor Homes. He asked them to draw maps of their neighborhood. The maps they produced were intricately plotted within a radius of a few blocks, reflecting their vigilant awareness of gang "turf," but the rest of the South Side, the rest of the city, was terra incognito, except in some instances for a line extending out from South State Street to Joliet where a relative or friend was doing time in prison. What, I wonder, would the maps of a representative sample of Hyde Parkers look like? I suspect they would be shaped by a similar interplay between the deep human need to define a place on the earth as home and a geography of fear.

A historian friend once described to me a phenomenon that can be observed in eighteenth-century maps of the North American continent. Prior to westward expansion, these are maps that show in detail Indian populations, French colonies, and so on. Once westward movement begins, the maps show an empty continent waiting to be settled. The parallel with patterns of urban development is exact and disturbing. Whatever else it might mean, in Gary Snyder's words, to live "deliberately, knowledgeably, and affectionately" in place, it surely involves recognizing the others for whom that place is also home and not pushing them into invisibility because it's inconvenient to fit them into the ruling scheme of things.

I am, for the moment, operating without a map. Working on the land with simple tools, I have been dismantling brick by brick a wall of misconceptions and fears, located inside my head, about the realities of life around me. There is much remaining to be done, but this much has been accomplished: I have arrived at the realization—at once destination and point of departure—that I don't know where I am. I am not sure where the path I'm following leads. But I'm sometimes warmed by the thought that I'm headed back, by way of various vacant lots and street corner conversations, to the vision I had as a child—now complicated by an adult's knowledge of how violence and fear distort the world—of the South Side as one big place called home.

15—The Cheney, Goodman, and Schwerner Academy

What follows is an excerpt from a draft proposal to create a New Visions public school in New York City.

At the Cheney, Goodman, and Schwerner Academy, the varied facets of New York City, and the experiences of the students and their families, will serve as an integrated "objective text" for study and problem posing. Students will investigate cultural, social, political, and economic relations: the city's history, peoples, neighborhoods, architecture, infrastructure, trades, industries, and services. Students will work on individual and team projects, creating "artifacts" of New York City: maps, photographs, videotapes, oral histories, and three-dimensional models. The projects will involve both "hands on" work (such as in painting and wiring a wall-sized map of a borough or neighborhood) and problem-solving skills (such as deciding where to locate a new department store that would hire and attract people from the city's diverse racial and ethnic communities). Foreign-language and computer fluency will be integrated throughout the curriculum.

Throughout this learning process, school must also become a place where the students' own experiences—especially painful experiences of devaluation and exclusion—are witnessed and responded to compassionately. Only by breaking the silence about their oppression can students begin to formulate questions they care about, situate themselves and their community historically, and hone their analytic abilities. We know that this kind of approach is more than just up-to-date theory or wishful thinking. People involved in this project have already put these principles into practice.

One of our teachers worked for several years in an all-black and Latino school in the Crown Heights neighborhood where CGSA will be located. He established a seventh–eighth-grade open classroom in which he accepted all the students who hadn't succeeded in other classes, many of them considered to have behavior problems. Several were boys who refused to write but read comic books constantly. He asked them to draw and cajoled them into writing in the course of elaborating the concepts represented in the drawings. He then asked the whole class to produce graphics on race, racism, and history for black history month and saw the students blossom as everyone became actively involved. Students were helped to form work teams in which each person contributed her/his strengths and received help with his/her weaknesses: writing, spelling, and artistic skills; analytical ability; and historical knowledge. Most of the graphics were collective products.

This teacher led students through a structured exploration of race and racism, historically and currently, using videos, primary source materials, diaries, novels, and field observations and interviews in different social milieus in the city (e.g., the homeless in Tompkins Square Park, brokers in Wall Street's financial centers). He encouraged honest discussion of their often hostile feelings about whites, and also of the ways that different people of color (Dominican vs. Puerto Rican, black vs. Latino) stereotype each other and think negatively about themselves. By recognizing their feelings and helping name the different aspects of oppression, rather than preaching prematurely about harmony and togetherness, he led them to broaden their scope and see the connection between racism and other forms of domination, such as sexism and heterosexism.

Finally, because of the hostile relations between Jews and blacks in their Crown Heights neighborhood, the teacher chose the Nazi Holocaust against Jews as a sustained theme, using *The Diary of Anne Frank*, picture books about concentration camps, the PBS video *Genocide*, and other sources. Students wrote essays and created drawings showing the similarities between the concentration camp and the slave ship, and reflecting critically on their own previous anti–Semitism. By the end of this project, students had written several hundred pages each and had edited several pieces for publication. Most of these young people are now successful college students.

At the CGSA, English and social studies will be taught together through a humanities sequence, with themes and projects briefly sketched below. Each student will learn a foreign language—choosing from Spanish, French, Yiddish, Hebrew, Japanese, Italian, and Haitian Creole—beginning in seventh-grade, through conversational immersion as well as projects. For example, students might help community agencies in which lawyers and advocates provide assistance to immigrants who are not English-dominant. In this way, students can both serve the community and draw on its resources to hone their translation skills.

The regular use of computers for word processing, graphic composition, research, calculations, model building, and simulations will be an integral part of CGSA. Resources, both human and material, will be available in each classroom for children with special needs.

Math and science will be integrated into various themes and projects, but we also recognize the need for discrete instruction in these areas. In math, we anticipate using accelerated learning models like the Boston-based Algebra Project, in which students begin learning algebra in the seventh grade instead of the ninth, using urban transportation grids to acquire concepts of positive and negative numbers. Science will be linked to values and to problem solving, will involve emphases on health and ecology in the life sciences, and will examine both conventional scientific method and some critiques and alternatives. We will explore the reflections and research methodologies used by woman scientists like Barbara McClintock and writings by feminist theorists on women's ways of knowing.

Curricular themes might include:

Sixth Grade: Autobiographical Projects. Students explore who they are and how they came here through personal and family history.

Seventh Grade: Community Mapping. In community mapping we can link the academic skills that students will learn in the classrooms to the lives of their communities. Some possible focus questions: What kinds of businesses exist in the neighborhood? What needs do they meet? Who owns them? Is housing stock private homes, privately owned apartment buildings, or projects? What used to be in the building before the pizza parlor, before the bodega? Have buildings been abandoned? How, why, and by whom? Students might interview the oldest people in the community: Where did they come from? What was the neighborhood like then in terms of racial/ethnic composition, housing patterns, jobs, hang-outs, commercial establishments? Did the community move from uni-ethnic to multiethnic, or vice versa?

Through the community mapping theme, students will develop skills in the following areas: charts, graphs, and statistical analysis in mathematics; writing, reading, and editing in English; research question formation, interviewing techniques, and the capacity to analyze social and political relations in social studies.

Eighth Grade: Historical Analysis of the Community.

Ninth Grade: Community Economic Development in the Global Context.

Tenth Grade: Urban Planning and Infrastructure Management—education, health, criminal justice, public administration, social services, political economy of New York City.

Eleventh Grade: Social Movements, Culture, and Urban Arts.

Senior Institute: Students will participate in weekly seminars with guest speakers invited from corporate, small-business, non-profit, and government settings and produce a senior project on a New York City issue.

16—Women of Hope

Following are three brief excerpts from a study guide developed by the Network of Educators on the Americas (NECA), produced by and available through Local 1199, National Health and Human Services Employees Union, Bread and Roses Cultural Project, 330 West 42nd St., New York, NY 10036. The study guides accompany posters of Latinas and African American women. They were written by Noni Mendoza Reis, Irene McGinty, Lynda Tredway, and Diane Yarbro-Swift.

EMPOWERING SCHOOL

Many of the women in the series experienced racism while growing up. Tania Léon tells how she was not allowed to attend a ballet school because the school didn't accept students of color. Antonia Hernández recalls a teacher taking extra time to teach her English because the teacher felt she "was different. You're not like them." The student Pan American Club formed in Helen Rodríguez-Trias's high school was disbanded by the authorities when the members, who were Puerto Rican, Dominican, and Colombian, staged a program for Puerto Rican independence. Also, Dr. Rodríguez was taunted by a chemistry teacher who would sing, "Mañana, mañana, mañana is good enough for me" every time she or her Puerto Rican classmates would walk to the blackboard. Ana Sol Gutiérrez ran for school board to change the common practice of placing many African American and Latino students in lower-track classes while classifying large numbers of white students as "gifted and talented."

In the story "Eleven" (see pages 223–5), Sandra Cisneros writes about a racist incident that happened to her in elementary school.

Activity

Read "Eleven" and have the class do the following:

1. Discuss the story. How did this experience make Rachel feel about school? About herself? Has anyone ever felt like Rachel? How could the teacher have handled the situation differently? Explain that in education, these are called "empowering" and "disempowering" experiences. Brainstorm in pairs: what do these words mean? (It's helpful if the teacher shares some

examples from her own schooling so that students get an idea of the range of disempowering experiences. You can also share some of the examples listed above from "Women of Hope." Once you have done this activity a few times, you will have some students' stories to share.) Then ask the students to reflect through a free write on one disempowering experience they have had in school or that they have witnessed.

2. Have students share their writing with a partner.
3. Ask for volunteers to share with the whole class and for one volunteer to chart the experiences.
4. Ask students, with their partners, to discuss ways to turn around the scenarios that were disempowering. What might the teacher or other school official have done differently? How might she have responded in a more culturally sensitive manner? Or, since some of the examples may be more a reflection of school policy than individual teacher behavior, ask how the policy could be more culturally and racially equitable.
5. Ask students to refer back to their disempowering experiences and brainstorm in pairs what can be done to avoid other students' facing similar problems.
6. List major themes that came up with the empowering experiences. What recommendations do you have for school reform based on these themes? Have students brainstorm ways to make this information public (e.g., school newspaper, newsletter, teacher shares at staff meetings, post in teachers' lounge, etc.).

THE STORY OF MY NAME

Instructions

This lesson, developed by Linda Christensen (English teacher, Portland, Oregon), helps students not only to learn each other's names but also to gain insight into their history and identity.

1. In advance, cut dozens of strips of paper about 2" x 8 1/2".
2. Ask for volunteers to read the sample poems/essays about names (see pages 226–7). If possible, add a couple of poems written by other students or teachers.
3. Ask for a few students to comment on what the readings made them think about in terms of their own name. (Or have them all share in pairs.)
4. Ask everyone to take 10 to 15 minutes to write about their own name, first and/or last name.

It can be a[n] . . . essay, poem or story. Teachers should write too.

5. Distribute enough strips of paper to each participant so they can write comments to each person in the class. (You can distribute these strips at the beginning of class also.) Ask for a volunteer to begin the sharing. Have everyone share the piece they have written. After each person reads, allow time for participants to write the person's name and a comment to them.

6. After everyone has read, get up and personally deliver the comments. Comments should not be left on a chair, nor should students stay seated and pass them around. It is very important that the comments be handed in person to the author. This makes the feedback much more personal.

7. Everyone sits down and takes a few minutes to read the comments.

GROUP POEM [1]

To bring the power and images of the writings of the women featured in this series into the class, create a "group poem" from the text. The short stories, essays, and speeches by many of the women in this series are ideal.

Make copies of the text you select. Ask students to read the text and highlight the words, lines, or phrases that strike them for some reason—perhaps because these seem important to the text, maybe because they like the sound or because they can relate the line to something in their own lives.

Tell the students that they are going to create an oral group poem with words, phrases, or lines they've selected. The teacher can lead by reading one line. Each student can read one of the phrases they have highlighted as an addition to the oral poem. They might want to use some of the devices of poetry and song— repeating a line or word, echoing. Everyone can insert a line more than once—as they are moved to do so. Encourage students to call out lines or words to form the new poem, in what might be described as the literary equivalent of improvisation in music. Students might like to experiment with this call-and-response technique, typically heard in Southern sermons and songs.

---

1. From Christensen, L., "Celebrating the Student's Voice," *Rethinking Schools*, Autumn 1993, vol. 8, no. 1, 9.

Sometimes it takes a few times to get this going. Have patience. It is worth it. As students re-create a poem or any written text in the class, they come to new understandings about the piece.

Listen to the melodic sounds of the group poem. It begins to have the feel of a round, a familiar grade school song technique.

After the re-creation of the text, ask students to write for five to ten minutes on how the group poem made them feel, why they chose the verse or line they did, their reactions to the text, or memories that the text evoked. There are no wrong responses. Then discuss their responses as a group. Some students may wish to read their written comments, while others might want to use their writing as a springboard for their contribution to the class-room dialogue.

GARRET PEOPLE: UNCOVERING COMMUNITY

We know ourselves as social selves, parents and children, members of a people, inheritors of a history and a culture that we must nurture through memory and hope.

Robert Bellah, et al., *Habits of the Heart*

1. Read the following to the class:

Clifton Taulbert's book, *The Last Train North,* talks about the migration from the Mississippi Delta to St. Louis. He talks about country shacks and chinaberry trees and fishing holes and juke joints, but he also talks about the "garret people." Garrets were simply porches where old folks sat—in rocking chairs and gliders—and where children listened and learned. And the garret people were those who passed on history and culture—like emotional attics. "We're not talking about big lessons," said Taulbert. "I'm talking about helpful things they would say to you, or that you would overhear." Or sometimes it would be about dead relatives whose presence was still felt strongly in the family. "Those garret days were important for transmitting culture, for passing on values, for tying young people in both with the day-to-day necessities, and also with a sense of their future . . ."

excerpted from William Raspberry column, *Washington Post,* March 27, 1993

2. Ask the students to write about a garret person in their lives (8 to 10 min.).

This could be explained as someone who lives in their mental attic, who passed on values and attitudes, or who still sits on their shoulders today. The teachers should also write about a garret person.

3. Read aloud the garret writings.

If the group is large, divide into groups of three students each to read to each other. (Instruct participants not to get involved in long introductions or stories, but just read what they have written.) If time permits, four to five people can share with the entire group.

As you read the biographies of the women in this series, ask: Who was the garret person for this woman? Who or what did the heroine count on to help her/support her/teach her?

EVERYONE HAS A STORY TO TELL

Not every writer will be a Toni Morrison or Alice Walker, but everyone can be a writer because everyone has a story to tell—even if it's only in a private journal or diary. Toni Morrison took the tales she heard in her family—their history, their culture, and their stories—and turned them into masterpieces of fiction that we all can read and relate to. She began her writing career by writing about an adolescent in *The Bluest Eye*, her first novel. She felt that the perspective a young person brings to life was a vital one.

A popular form of fiction is the short story, in which a setting, characters, and their conflicts make up the story. Alice Walker has produced numerous short stories that speak about the internal and external dilemmas that people face in their lives. "Everyday Use" is about an intergenerational family conflict.

Morrison and Walker have practiced the art and craft of writing. They no longer think about the steps of writing that are outlined below because they have internalized the process. However, nearly every writer begins by thinking about process and by writing from personal experience, from what they know best. Everyone's life experience offers the setting, the characters, and the conflicts that can make a good short story. Although the characters, dialogue, setting will be autobiographical in many ways, it is a work of fiction because the details are invented or altered to suit the writer. A new book of short stories by Edward P. Jones, *Lost in the City*, gives an accessible example of how to write fiction based on childhood or young-adult experiences and perspectives.

Writing short stories is best done in the context of reading good short stories—no surprise! Choose a number of stories that students can analyze according to the writing process below before starting the process. Another good way to examine setting, character, and conflict is to choose five or six art reproductions for students to examine. Choose some paintings that have conflict and some that do not (landscapes with people but no dramatic tension) so that students determine the difference between setting and characters with and without conflict.

The directions that follow for writing are made directly to the student.

STEP 1: SETTING

Imagine a familiar place—a location that has significance for you. It might be a safe place or it could be a street corner in your neighborhood or a special place in the country with nature around you. You should know it well. Jones's stories occur in specific neighborhoods in Washington, D.C.—often at one corner, like 5th & O Streets, N.W. These places resonate for him (to resonate means it brings lots of pictures and feelings into your head). Toni Morrison's first chapter of *Sula* also provides a good example of the description of a place. What do you see, hear, smell, and feel at the familiar place you have chosen?

In one or two sentences, state where the place is or what it is. It may be easier to put yourself right in the place by using "I" somewhere in the sentence(s).

Examples:

1. At the corner of Brookings Ave. and Highland St., four small stores served the neighborhood. There was Mr. Park's barbershop; a small corner store owned by Korean immigrants; a liquor store where my Uncle Ben spent too much time; and my favorite place, Alice's Carryout.
2. The shelterbelt that ran along the gravel road near the wooden nineteenth-century farmhouse was filled with all sorts of trees that I could identify from looking in a tree book.

Practice your sentences about your familiar place on scratch paper and then put your idea on an index card.

STEP 2: SETTING

Think about what you see, hear, smell, feel, etc., in that place. On a piece of scratch paper, make column lists, using as many descriptive words as possible.

Examples:

- The wild plum tree with the thorny branches.
- The air in Alice's Carryout was thick with the smell of homemade barbecue sauce, a recipe Alice refuses to give to anyone.

Choose the best details from your lists and write about your setting (place) on another 4x6 index card. Save your list. As your story develops, you may edit out the details you chose first and substitute others. Share your description with another student. She can give you feedback. Edit your setting now or wait until your entire story develops.

STEP 3: CHARACTERS

In a good short story, developing more than a few (two to three) characters is difficult. Imagine the people in your story—one of them might be you. Describe each (first on scratch paper). Everything you say has to mean something. It doesn't matter if the character is 5′ 8″ tall, but it does matter that he is wearing a faded chambray shirt with a rip on one side or what his personality is like. Be specific.

Read your description(s) to a classmate. Ask if they can see the person you are writing about. What do you need to add to complete the picture? Listen carefully and take notes on their suggestions. Transfer each completed description to an index card. You can "shuffle" your index cards later with the plot to see when is the best time to introduce each character.

STEP 4: CONFLICT

The central part of a short story is the conflict. The conflict or dilemma may be an internal one faced by a character or an external one between characters or between the character and the environment (setting). This is the essence of dramatic fiction—the problem being faced. The conflict/dilemma produces the suspense and tension and is the driving force behind how the character(s) develop. As you read different short stories, identify the conflicts/dilemma and discuss how they are resolved—did the characters do the right thing? make the right choices?

STEP 5: PLOT

By the time you have completed the setting and the characters, you have probably been thinking about what they are doing—the action. The standard sequence of events in a short story begins with introducing the setting, the characters, beginning the action, building the action throughout the story to a climax (usually about 75 to 90 percent of the way through the story), and then following with a resolution or ending. Usually the plot involves some kind of conflict—either internal in the personalities of the characters or external in what happens.

Plan out the plot in sequence, a very rough draft of what will become your story. You may want to begin the action before you actually introduce the characters or begin the action and then introduce a character. After you get a rough sequence, put each part of the plot on a separate card. Share your plot with a classmate peer editor before you go on.

STEP 6: ROUGH DRAFT

Shuffle the plot with the setting and characters until you get a final sequence. From these cards, write the story—your rough draft. Of course, after you have prepared your rough draft, you need to reread it, checking for how much sense it makes—is it coherent? understandable? believable? Read your story aloud to a peer editor for feedback.

STEP 7: FINAL DRAFT

Using the suggestions of the editor and perhaps your teacher, too, rewrite in final form. It may take a number of drafts before you have a final copy. Check the spelling, punctuation, and grammar.

ELEVEN

What they don't understand about birthdays and what they never tell you is that when you're eleven, you're also ten, and nine, and eight, and seven, and six, and five, and four, and three, and two, and one. And when you wake up on your eleventh birthday you expect to feel eleven, but you don't. You open your eyes and everything's just like yesterday, only it's today. And you don't feel eleven at all. You feel like you're still ten. And you are — underneath the year that makes you eleven.

Like some days you might say something stupid, and that's the part of you that's still ten. Or maybe some days you might need to sit on your mama's lap because you're scared, and that's the part of you that's five. And maybe one day when you're all grown up maybe you will need to cry like if you're three, and that's okay. That's what I tell Mama when she's sad and needs to cry. Maybe she's feeling three.

Because the way you grow old is kind of like an onion or like the rings inside a tree trunk or like my little wooden dolls that fit one inside the other, each year inside the next one. That's how being eleven years old is.

You don't feel eleven. Not right away. It takes a few days, weeks even, sometimes even months before you say Eleven when they ask you. And you don't feel smart eleven, not until you're almost twelve. That's the way it is. Only today I wish I didn't have only eleven years rattling inside me like pennies in a tin Band-Aid box. Today I wish I was one hundred and two instead of eleven because if I was one hundred and two I'd have known what to say when Mrs. Price put the red sweater on my desk. I would've known how to tell her it wasn't mine instead of just sitting there with that look on my face and nothing coming out of my mouth.

"Whose is this?" Mrs. Price says, and she holds the red sweater up in the air for all the class to see. "Whose? It's been sitting in the coatroom for a month."

"Not mine," says everybody. "Not me."

"It has to belong to somebody," Mrs. Price keeps saying, but nobody can remember. It's an ugly sweater with red plastic buttons and a collar and sleeves all stretched out like you could use it for a jump rope. It's maybe a thousand years old and even if it belonged to me I wouldn't say so.

Maybe because I'm skinny, maybe because she doesn't like me, that stupid Sylvia Saldóvar says, "I think it belongs to Rachel." An ugly sweater like that, all raggedy and old, but Mrs. Price believes her. Mrs. Price takes the sweater and puts it right on my desk, but when I open my mouth nothing comes out.

"That's not, I don't, you're not . . . Not mine," I finally say in a little voice that was maybe me when I was four.

"Of course it's yours," Mrs. Price says. "I remember you wearing it once." Because she's older and the teacher, she's right and I'm not.

Not mine, not mine, not mine, but Mrs. Price is already turning to page thirty-two, and math problem number four. I don't know why but all of a sudden I'm feeling sick inside, like the part of me that's three wants to come out of my eyes, only I squeeze them shut tight and bite down on my teeth real hard and try to remember today I am eleven, eleven. Mama is making a cake for me for tonight, and when Papa comes home everybody will sing Happy birthday, happy birthday to you.

But when the sick feeling goes away and I open my eyes, the red sweater's still sitting there like a big red mountain. I move the red sweater to the corner of my desk with my ruler. I move my pencil and books and eraser as far from it as possible. I even move my chair a little to the right. Not mine, not mine, not mine.

In my head I'm thinking how long till lunchtime, how long till I can take the red sweater and throw it over the schoolyard fence, or leave it hanging on a parking meter, or bunch it up into a little ball and toss it in the alley. Except when math period ends Mrs. Price says loud and in front of everybody, "Now Rachel, that's enough," because she sees I've shoved the red sweater to the tippy-tip corner of my desk and it's hanging all over the edge like a waterfall, but I don't care.

"Rachel," Mrs. Price says. She says it like she's getting mad. "You put that sweater on right now and no more nonsense."

"But it's not — "

"Now!" Mrs. Price says.

This is when I wish I wasn't eleven, because all the years inside of me — ten, nine, eight, seven, six, five, four, three, two, and one — are pushing at the back of my eyes when I put one arm through one sleeve of the sweater that smells like cottage cheese, and then the other arm through the other and stand there with my arms apart like if the sweater hurts me and it does, all itchy and full of germs that aren't even mine.

That's when everything I've been holding in since morning, since when Mrs. Price put the sweater on my desk, finally lets go, and all of a sudden I'm crying in front of everybody. I wish I was invisible but I'm not. I'm eleven and it's my birthday today and I'm crying like I'm three in front of everybody. I put my head down on the desk and bury my face in my stupid clown-sweater arms. My face all hot and spit coming out of my mouth because I can't stop the little animal noises from coming out of me, until there aren't any more tears left in my eyes, and it's just my body shaking like when you have the hiccups, and my whole head hurts like when you drink milk too fast.

But the worst part is right before the bell rings for lunch. That stupid Phyllis López, who is even dumber than Sylvia Saldóvar, says she remembers the red sweater is hers! I take it off right away and give it to her, only Mrs. Price pretends like everything's okay.

Today I'm eleven. There's a cake Mama's making for tonight, and when Papa comes home from work we'll eat it. There'll be candles and presents and everybody will sing Happy birthday, happy birthday to you, Rachel, only it's too late.

I'm eleven today. I'm eleven, ten, nine, eight, seven, six, five, four, three, two, and one, but I wish I was one hundred and two. I wish I was anything but eleven, because I want today to be far away already, far away like a runaway balloon, like a tiny o in the sky, so tiny-tiny you have to close your eyes to see it.

SAMPLE NAME POEMS AND ESSAYS
SEPTIMA

Septima is the Latin word for seventh, and in Haiti it means sufficient. My parents named me Septima, and I wondered why, because I was not the seventh child and neither was I sufficient, because six came after me. But I got that name from an aunt down in Haiti, whose name was Septima Peace. Sufficient Peace. I was supposed to be sufficient peace, but I certainly wasn't sufficient and I don't know about the peace, because I did so many things that weren't peaceful.

Septima Poinsette Clark, *Ready From Within*

Reprinted with permission of the author.

LILY

Lily, Grandma's hand me down.
Lily frog jumps, bee's sting, a flower grows.
I am one of the valley.
Lily, big orange tractors drive over me,
left is Willie or Lillian.
Lily, not the kind of name that rolls or even slides,
but stumbles and falls off your tongue.
Lily when said fast is never understood,
but when slowed is sarcastic.
Lily rewritten still looks the same.
Lily that I love and would not change.

> Lily Palin, Student, Jefferson High School,
> Portland, Oregon

17—Chaos Theory—
A Journal Entry

Rick Ayers

February 20, 1996. On last Friday, I once again courted disaster in my freshman class by having a kind of free time, free writing and time for peer response. And disaster arrived right on schedule. The problem is that I want to have group time, class interaction, free and creative time. And either I don't know how to set it up or the kids are too bouncy to accept the freedom without tweaking out—probably both.

We have just finished reading *Coffee Will Make You Black,* a novel by April Sinclair which is great at grabbing the attention of teenagers. Sinclair describes coming of age in Chicago in the 1960s with great immediacy. The book is explicit about sexual issues (the onset of puberty, first petting) as well as struggles in the black community (those that are timeless and those specific to the era, including the murder of Martin Luther King, the rise of Black Power).

Besides journal writes, there were two writing assignments. One was to interview their parents to find out about the 60s, what they were like, how the times were different from today, etc. That went quite well—they got lively and interesting information and made some good connections with parents. I want to mount some of these on the wall. The second writing project was to advocate for or against the book: Is this an appropriate book to adopt for ninth-grade curriculum?

I have decided this past week to give them four days of writing workshop. Tuesday their first draft is due; we do peer review, just on the level of ideas—not correcting spelling and grammar. Students read aloud to each other and the listener fills out a response sheet on what they like, what they'd like to see developed more.

The next day, Wednesday, draft two is due. Students read each other's with a red pencil in hand, correcting errors and making revisions. Thursday is a day off. Friday the final draft is due. When a student has all drafts done, he or she has free writing time. Those who are behind can now catch up.

But Friday is an example of the chaos. For the most part,

students are fooling around. Some are actually done but do not do creative writing (though they have begged me for creative writing time again and again). Those who are not done still take the freedom as a message to play, sometimes loudly, sometimes with jumping, running, throwing.

Needless to say, I am in there trying to get things focused. I try turning on some music. I try turning off the music. I try talking to the class quietly. I try shouting. I speak to students one on one, nose to nose. I talk to groups and clusters. I promise. I threaten. But chaos reigns.

Part of me thinks: Screw 'em! Give them worksheets! But I have committed to a free-lesson plan for next week: I want to do a speaking workshop, with lots of wide-ranging discussion designed to teach the concept of how persuasion is done (evidence, use of emotion). This is supposed to lead to better writing.

But I'm picturing absolute chaos. Can they do it? Can I? The problem is that they are unsure what to do with freedom. It is similar to when A. S. Neil told young students they were free; they tore up the building for months before they decided to do something else. I am walking into a school system based on order, coverage, alienation, lock step. I can't just declare them free and expect utopia to blossom. So I give little bits of freedom (the rest of the time being complicit with the system—this is where the craziness of teachers comes from) and see what can be done.

This brings up an issue that has been quite vexing during the past year. It is the question of the high school essay, specifically the so-called five-paragraph formal essay. Admittedly, Eastern High is particularly obsessed with this format, but it is a general high school issue. Last year, during my credential program at Mills College, I was skeptical about its usefulness and attempted the radical approaches to cultural discourse advocated by Kurth Spellmeyer of Rutgers as well as such composition teachers as Cynthia Scheinberg at Mills. This year I have run into the harsh realities of the issue. Sometimes I am more resolved in my resistance to the formality, while at other times I am in despair as to whether I am serving my students by not being more of a drill-and-practice teacher in this regard.

After the recent "writing proficiency exams" for ninth graders, I was outraged and disgusted, especially when I saw that the failures had achieved almost perfect apartheid in the classroom: almost all the African American and Chicano/Latino students had failed. A few of the whites who failed were my best writers (in the sense of most creative). I decided that they must have done something awful like stream of consciousness writing. But I was amazed that someone like Sharonne—the black girl who gets all A's and writes carefully and formally—failed. This set me to thinking, and arguing, about the whole issue. How do we properly serve students who are being short-changed by the educational system?

In some ways, you could have predicted the outcome. Writing grades are predetermined by the ethnic and economic status of the kids. The kids who fail the kindergarten proficiency tests fail them in high school. So why go to all the expense and trouble of giving the test? Just check their economic status and assign a grade. Why the charade of teaching?

I worry about being too much of an empathetic teacher, one who is pegged as "easy"—the kiss of death. I don't want to be patronized as a "touchy feely" one who is academically flabby but good in the overall mix of the department. Actually, I believe that the best teaching awakens the passion, ignites the spark, and also shows the wise ways, the savvy ways to talk to different audiences. I believe all writers need to become aware of audience and learn to talk across differences, the many differences in our modern society. The idea is to make writers who have *ideas*, who are confident of their writing, and who can wow the college-admission reader as well as the homies. The problem is, if I attempt this complex task and fail, then my students only have some creative chaos and bad writing.

As a teacher, the task is to find a third path between stern formalist and loose creative type. As John Dewey said, progressive methods require more, not less, rigorous teaching. What is needed is a pedagogical defense of student-centered, idea-centered teaching. It won't be the banking model; it will be a process of education in which knowledge is socially created; it will mean deep engagement and exploration, and even positive action in society. I think about the story in the papers this week about the journalism students at Northwestern whose research project on prisoners ended up freeing three guys who had been wrongly imprisoned for the past eighteen years. Now there's an "I search" paper I'd like to read!

Part of the problem, as I've said, is assessment. If the whole year is summed up in how well your students do on the five-paragraph essay, this greatly impacts what you do during the year. Even if you use more "progressive" methods, they become only sweetening for the real medicine, the five paragraphs. One area to work for change in is the world of assessment, much as I hate it. I've always felt there should be a big struggle with the SAT and AP testing folks. Why don't they give a Chinese T'ang Dynasty poem for the AP instead of another John Donne poem? It would force those grade grubbers at New Trier High School in wealthy Winnetka, Illinois, to scramble for a broader curriculum.

But the problem is not only in the world of academic assessment. What about the real world? Doesn't a child today, going into a world which brings us close to folks from all over the world, need to know how to speak wisely to a Chinese student in Beijing or work in a group with an African student from Biafra? Aren't universities retooling to make people ready to deal with this real world?

The same holds true for expository writing. Composition teachers at universities are howling about the waves of students they receive who write heartless, bloodless prose which mimics a formal style they were drilled in for four years. They complain that students are timid and rigid in their writing. In addition, of course, they are only receiving those students who have gotten to college through the gatekeeper of the formal essay reader. Then there are those thousands more college freshmen who cannot write at all, formally or informally. The formalists will claim that this means more drill is needed. But it may be an indication that the answer is to entertain a new approach.

The problem with the way many teach the "formal essay," the five-paragraph essay, is that it is devoid of content. I don't know how many assignments I've encountered next to the English Department copy machine, outlines that show the opening paragraph ending with a thesis statement, then the following paragraphs, each guided by a topic sentence (and, for some teachers, each requiring two quotations—making for some very long paragraphs) as evidence, then the final paragraph to sum up and restate (but don't restate exactly) the thesis.

My daughter Sonia was humorous about this. She, in fact, passed the proficiency test, but she was cynical and wise about it at the same time. Talking of the essay she wrote about two things she would change in society, Sonia said, "I wrote a helluva boring essay 'cause I knew just what they wanted. It was all about how I wanted to solve the problem of homelessness and end racial tension. It was just kiss-ass, liberal, white-girl writing. And of course they ate it up."

Now that's quite funny, actually, to see how she had learned the way to mimic a thoughtful essay, to touch all the bases and get the "pass" grade. The point here, however, is that Sonia has never been encouraged to pursue and develop her ideas, to take an idea deeper. She gets by with good grades while she is basically numb about school. It is something she has learned to endure but she has no passion for it.

Really, this is what I am concerned about. The issue is that writers have to be engaged at the level of their ideas. Another teacher I know defends the rather stiff format of the five-paragraph essay by using the analogy of a musician—you have to teach the musician some notes, some scales, before he can play a song. He makes the point that without this rather stiff convention, the student has no tools of clear thought and has no control over where he or she is going with a thought, it just wanders.

I thought about that for a while and decided there is another analogy: the child playing baseball. A child can't simply keep doing batting practice, fielding practice, throwing practice, year after year, and only start playing games when he or she reaches age sixteen. Hey, you start games at age five because the game is the thing. And, actually, the best music teachers also start some improvisation in the first months.

It is the same with writing. You have to honor the ideas, what the child is trying to say, from the beginning. If you like working with teenagers and you like the way teenagers think (and plenty of high school teachers don't), then you actually engage their ideas, with enthusiasm. When the child starts wanting to write better to get his or her ideas across, then the form follows.

Too often at Eastern High I have seen student essays just bleeding with red ink, marked all over with the teacher's pen. When I look closer, there is not one response to the point the child is making. Actually, the point is often belabored and stale anyway because the student knows that the point is not the point. So the teacher is harping on this and banging on that. Instead of being a person interacting in a discourse, he or she is a nagging critic. "No title . . . needs clearer thesis statement . . . don't use jargon . . . fragment here . . . this overlaps the previous point." Et cetera, ad nauseum. You can picture the teacher making these marks leaning over the desk, head propped on open palm, eyes at half-staff, trying to stay awake with a stiff cup of coffee. Alienation: the teacher is bored, the kid is bored, school is boring.

There are other issues such as the dominance of different rhetorical conventions in different cultures. I remember being struck by Gerald Wu's writing. He would always resort to extravagant nature imagery; he would persuade by sensual devices—the flowery laying on of emotions—and by metaphor. He never got the hang of linear proof or logical development of evidence, in spite of the fact that he was also a crack mathematician. In fact, most of the Chinese students at Oakland High followed this convention, and some of the images that I thought were uniquely Gerald's turned out to be Chinese clichés.

In Ibo culture, the wise communicator does it through indirection, using proverbs and paradoxical constructions to draw the reader into the ideas he wants to get across. As for young African Americans in our society, is there a rhetorical convention that should be recognized? This goes back to the struggle about "Black English," and of course the answer is yes.

In the West, with its adversarial—and, dare I say it, male— rhetorical conventions, the impersonal and supposedly all-knowing author is supposed to be the best. Now, again I would not argue to avoid this style. It is only that a good writer, one who is wise to the many ways of the world, can cross boundaries and speak to them all. This does not mean necessarily mimicking all styles. It means speaking across boundaries in a way that can be understood.

We all remember high school through a distorted lens. For the most part, we look back with sophistication on a time when we were quite flat in much of our thinking. My older daughter Aisha told a funny story last week. It seems that when she was in social living class in 1987, she was told to write a letter to herself in the future. She was to address it to be mailed to her nine years later. Well, a few weeks ago her letter arrived at her mother's old house and she retrieved it with excitement.

As she opened the envelope, she looked forward to some deep insights about her struggles in high school, about her hopes and dreams at the time. Instead, she was disappointed to find a letter of embarrassing shallowness—all about this boy she had a crush on, about how mad she was at her friend Jessica, about all the petty things that fill a sixteen-year-old's mind. But really the letter is a wonderful reminder: that is the banal crap that fills up most of the high school child's mind. When you are right there, being the teacher to sixteen-year-old Aisha, you have to learn to like her preoccupations as well as show her new and wonderful connections that can enrich her life.

This is the point that Eleanore Duckworth makes in "The Having of Wonderful Ideas." The teacher does no good to demand that the student leap to the next stage. In fact, it is a stupid and futile effort, and one that misconstrues the task of teaching. But it is the teacher's job to create conditions in which students can "have wonderful ideas." And that means the teacher must engage the student, enthusiastically, in the thoughts he or she is having and then—through this interaction—to make both the present an adventure and the future a welcome possibility.

Just knowing my son Max, at age nine, I can see five or six serious ideas he comes up with every day. Yesterday's included: the idea that there is a causal chain between all events, a kind of nondeist determinism; the idea that he and his friends actually possess magical powers that can affect the weather, the behavior of others, and their own luck, but that these powers should not be discussed with adults, including parents; the idea that Jim Carey has created a completely different kind of comedy in *The Cable Guy* by being a sinister, rather evil character instead of the innocent hero he has been in the past; the notion of irony in a poem by Shel Silverstein. But I would only notice these things, or give him any credit for them, or extend them, by being aware of what he is saying and giving him some way to say it. How often has he gone off to school with these great intellectual ideas rumbling in this head and sat through hours of drills?

I love the part where Duckworth says, "I react strongly against the thought that we need to provide children with only a set of intellectual processes—a dry, contentless set of tools that they can go about applying. I believe that the tools cannot help developing once children have something real to think about; and if they don't have anything to think about, they won't be applying tools anyway. That is, there really is no such thing as a contentless intellectual tool."

What is wrong with giving kids a positive experience with literature, being open to their ways of expression, encouraging that critical mass of interest, that take-off point for the chain reaction of enthusiasm? So often high school teachers take credit for the great achievements of the AP students—credit we don't even deserve because the students would probably be doing these wonderful things if they went to any school. At the same time we brush off the "others," the "losers" who we cannot reach or never bothered to reach. If we take to heart the arguments of Lisa Delpit as well as Gloria Ladson-Billings, we would stop approaching African American students as if they were a bundle of deficits. We would honor their perceptions and strengths and build from that.

That's the other thing. I have made the mistake of mulling over and over the moments when things went wrong and ignoring the victories. So I would obsess over the bad day we had and not notice the incredible poems that have gone up on the wall as a result of the work we are doing. I would not notice the small steps toward connection that students are making.

I remember calling Darrel's father and having a long talk about his son's refusal to work. Finally his father came in and we spent an hour talking about school, how it was for us when we were there. He told a tale of struggle, the many moves and changes he has made in life just to get Darrel through school. "And," his father concluded, "these people are not building more colleges for my son. They are building prison cells. I'm not just trying to get him into Cal, I'm trying to save his life."

Darrel's father made me remember that we have to teach the whole student. He is not simply a skills-training project. He is a young man with a history, a future, and the hopes of his family are on his shoulders. After our meeting, Darrel began turning in work. The writing was angry, insulting even. But it was writing and it was his real thoughts on the assignment. Then he wrote a short essay, ironic and angry, but clearly engaged. Then a poem, halting and defiant at the same time. Would he have begun to write if he were only getting "technical training?" How can these bits of writing be carried forward to stronger, longer, more successful composition.

Well, it doesn't happen in one great moment. You won't one day reach a breakthrough and then everything is fine. It is not like in the movies. There are small battles won, small victories, small and large setbacks. But thinking about this, I realize, I am not in any doubt about proceeding with the speaking workshop next week. There will be some chaos. There will be things I need to learn to win their attentiveness. But there is no alternative but to plunge ahead. Even if they are just getting part of it. Even if they partly sabotage it! It has to be done and I also know some great stuff will come out of it.

I am always learning, adjusting, searching for the thing that will make the connection. April Sinclair was one step. I want the writing workshop time to be another, even more radical. Perhaps it will dissolve into madness, but we won't figure out how to make something wonderful if we don't start taking those chances. So, here we go again, into next week.

—An Activist Forum IV: Pledging to the World

Jay Rehak

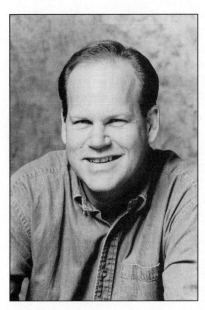

Jay Rehak, courtesy of
Tanya Tucka

I think the hardest part of teaching is recognizing that solutions to large problems occur in small daily increments, and not through any one grandiose action. Achieving social justice in the classroom, I have come to believe, occurs in the same way. That is, solutions to complex problems such as racism, sexism, classism, and other forms of prejudice, are lived and taught in small daily increments, and not through any one grand event. Initially, this is disappointing, especially to someone like myself who wishes to "right the world's wrongs" as quickly as possibly. But ultimately, if one can get over the fact that being a teacher does not mean one has all the immediate answers, there can be cause for celebration and a life of sustained joy. Although this may seem obvious to some, I did not always understand this.

When I first started teaching, I had hopes of modifying children's behavior quickly, decisively and permanently. I'm sure I had been influenced a great deal by my father, who used to tell me that all behavioral problems could be solved with a two by four to the head. Although, of course, I did not believe this, I did hope that I could "metaphorically" tap someone upside the head and change his or her behavior instantly and permanently to the good.

One of my first teaching jobs was as a substitute teacher in the New York City public school system. I was sent to work at Intermediate School 13 in Chelsea on the lower west side of Manhattan. I was "filling in" for a social studies teacher who had been absent since the school year began. The man, I learned, had no intention of ever teaching again, but at the time had yet to resign his position and so the students had a continuous year of revolving substitutes. It was late November when I entered that seventh-grade room. The desks were arranged in a "U.N."-style horseshoe shape, with all of the desks lined up around the perimeter of the room. Of the twenty to twenty-five students in the class, half a dozen had books. The rest of the students had either lost their books or given up on bringing them to class.

When I arrived, I introduced myself and asked the students what chapter they were on. Most of the children sat listlessly, while the rest talked to one another and ignored me completely. Suddenly, and for no apparent reason, the smallest boy in the class jumped up on his desk and began running atop everyone else's in the room. Momentarily stunned, I watched as the boy ran atop a dozen desks, each desk sliding toward the student who sat behind it. A few of the seated students were amused, but most seemed to be in a state of listless annoyance; that is, they seemed not to be enjoying the antics in front of them, but they weren't disturbed enough to look to me for help.

It didn't matter to me. I was offended. I hurriedly ran over to the desk where the boy was standing and quickly grabbed on to his leg.

"Let go of me, faggot," he yelled, as he whipped his leg free.

"Come down here!" I nervously commanded. With that, the boy jumped off the desk and into the hall. I followed him, but was relieved when I saw that the hall was clear.

I returned to the front of the room and asked those who had books to share with those who didn't, and those who weren't near anyone with a book to listen to what was being read. I decided and announced that we would start on chapter 2. I was about to call on someone to read, when the "desk dancer" came back in and jumped back on to the desks.

I didn't hesitate. I ran over to where he was, and grabbed his ankle with both hands.

"Let me go, you wacko!" he yelled as he tried to wriggle himself free.

I squeezed tighter. "Get down here, son!" I bellowed, as I pulled on his leg to come down. With no place to go, and with an obvious desire to be released, the boy came down off the desk and looked at me with both rage and fear in his eyes.

I was not about to be stared down by a seventh grader. I put my hands on his shoulders and squeezed as I talked to him with my own rage barely in check. I was insulted that this boy had the nerve to "front me" like that.

"Don't you ever do that in my classroom again!" I commanded, adding, "Do you hear me?! You're wasting my time, and the time of every student in this class."

"Let me go!" he yelled.

"No, no. You're not listening," I said as I held on to him more firmly. "You will not run on my desks again, do you understand?" I was convinced of my moral rightness and I felt sure he would at some point understand this.

"Let me go! Wacko!"

"No, no, no. We still don't have an agreement yet. Here's how it's going to be. You're going to promise to sit down in your seat and then I'm going to let you go. Got it, son?"

Something burst inside that boy. He started to wail a siren wail that scared me. It was not a cry of physical pain, but of an emotional distress that I could not remedy in that instant. I let go immediately and the boy ran out of the room and down the hall. I never saw him again.

When the boy did not return, my first reaction was, "Wonderful! Glad to be rid of that problem." But by day's end, I was disappointed in myself and frustrated by my inability to make the "desktop dancer" understand that I was interested in teaching him. I'm sure I did not resolve his "problem," whatever it was. I remained conflicted throughout the semester, so much so that each day the New York Teacher's Registry called me in to work, I vacillated to the point that I never worked more than three days in a week. Some days I could do it, other days I didn't have the energy to go in.

After that one semester, I gave up teaching and got a job in construction, where I could see tangible results of my efforts. Interior office spaces in Manhattan were altered, in part, because of me. Walls were demolished and replaced; architectural drawings were actualized. There was a level of satisfaction that I had "done something."

A year and a half later I returned to teaching, the result of a need at a local Catholic school which found itself short a teacher for a sixth-grade class that had run its former teacher out the door. When a friend suggested to me that I take the position (she was familiar with my background as a substitute), I told her that I was no good as a teacher.

"How do you know?" she asked.

"You know I tried subbing for a while. It was the toughest job I ever had. I never made it through an entire week. The issues these kids have to confront every day, well, there's not much I'm going to be able to do about it."

"How do you know?" she asked again.

"Because I've been there and done it. I didn't change a thing."

"How do you know?"

I proceeded to retell her the story of my subbing experience. In the end, she repeated her question. In time I realized I would have to let go of the need to see grandiose change as a result of any single action.

That was twelve years ago. Since then, I have taught at the junior high and high school level. Although my students and I talk and write of the problems that encompass our collective experiences, I do not know how much social justice has been learned in my classes in the intervening years. I do know that, for my part, I have attempted to teach it through as much human tolerance and understanding as I have. Ultimately, I hope my students have learned from me that regardless of the issues they bring into the classroom, I will be there for them the next day.

Chris Carger

Chris Carger, courtesy
Northern Illinois University
Art Photo Department

My first year of teaching was wonderful—warm, shining moments in my memories. I can't believe twenty years have passed already. They seemed to sail by as quickly and inconspicuously as an ordinary autumn leaf floating downstream on a windy autumn day.

My fifth-grade bilingual class of twenty-eight children in a crumbling little city that perched above the Hudson River in upstate New York was a mixture of Puerto Rican, African American, and European American children whose parents voluntarily signed them into a dual-language program. The goal was for the students to learn each other's native language as they progressed academically in their own. Hopes were high.

Somehow, the district had forgotten to order books and supplies for my newly added class, but that did not deter us from having a rich learning experience together that year. My principal took me to the school playground where a wooden trailer, which served as a storage room for discarded books and donated materials, was parked. I chose my class's textbooks from piles strewn on the floor and pulled the bright "discard labels" from their covers so that the children would not feel dejected. A local raincoat factory had donated mounds of navy and black fabric which was also tossed into the trailer. It would later become costumes for fifth-grade plays. My supplies came from Mr. Morales, the school janitor and my close friend's father. For years he had collected leftovers as he cleaned classrooms out in June and stored them in a wire bin at the far end of the school's ancient, dim basement. Lighting the way by flashlight, he proudly led me to his stash and I gratefully selected what I could use. Our art projects that year were restricted to purple, gray, and black construction paper, but that did not hamper our creativity. The purple, gray, and black construction paper which no one wanted turned out to be the perfect colors for the events of that year—it was 1974. The world was exploding, the Vietnam War covered our bulletin boards, along with John F. Kennedy, Martin Luther King, and Bobby Kennedy. Our purple and black and gray paper letters, ironically appropriate in color, accompanied our *Time* magazine images and fittingly conveyed our sense of loss, over and over. In Spanish we extolled Cesar Chavez, and framed his picture with carefully cut purple grapes. Some new words had appeared in our Weekly Readers and newspapers across the country that fall, which we used to title the final bulletin boards— *Our Environment* and *Ecology*. We would work hard that year to save our environment, cleaning garbage from our school neighborhood streets and helping Pete Seeger, a town local, load hundreds of pumpkins onto the Sloop Clearwater to be sold to support his project to clean up the Hudson River. We could walk to the riverfront from our school, and as volunteers for the Clearwater Project we formed a long line of students and parents and passed hundreds of pumpkins onto the Sloop, Pete Seeger smiling and working side by side with us.

In the front of our room, under our American flag and on one of our few real bulletin boards covered with cork, I printed in bright green letters on borrowed yellow paper, the simple "Pledge to the world." It began:

> I pledge allegiance to the world
> And every creature living
> To earth and sea and sky above
> Respect is what I'm giving.

I had found our pledge in a teacher magazine the summer before I began teaching and adopted it as our alternative to the daily pledge of allegiance which came over the classroom intercom. I had decided that I could not, in good conscience, look into the eyes of the children of color in my little classroom world and mindlessly recite the words "with liberty and justice for all."

I had visited many homes of my fifth graders that year; had seen families of six and seven squeezed into tiny two-room apartments with worn but immaculately clean linoleum floors and lovingly placed knickknacks carried from island homelands; had witnessed the children in those families voraciously read the books I found for them, conscientiously care for the environment we learned about; had visited our district's only Mexican immigrants whose son appeared in my room after the school year began. I noticed that he always wore a turtleneck shirt, even in ninety degree weather, carefully washed each day. I learned that he had nothing else. That winter, when I visited his apartment, I found that the landlord was not supplying heat. Mrs. Cordero's five children were shivering and wrapped in bedspreads the music teacher, Edwina, and I had collected for them when we were told by our school administrator that no school or town agency would help them because they were illegal aliens. Our principal was doing them a favor just by accepting them into the bilingual program without a lot of questions, he said. Edwina and I found clothing, some furniture, books, toys, and got the Cordero's a small garden plot from a local church. We helped them through several difficult months until their factory jobs materialized and ignored our principal's "hands-off" policy. I learned, firsthand, the first year teaching, that liberty and justice were still dreams for many. So my class and I quietly waited for he daily opening pledge to end each morning, then with hand on heart, recited our short and sincere global promise.

I never brought attention to my decision not to have my class recite the traditional pledge. I never even realized that in my district and state it was mandated by law until one very conscientious student in my class once commented that he thought we *had* to do "that pledge." I simply told him that we had a great alternative. It was my quiet rebellion.

From time to time I wonder how Enrique and Awilda and Jimmy, Jose and Johnny and Maritza are doing. I wonder if they realize what an exciting and important time in the world their fifth grade was. Once in a while I hear from or about one of them. The "illegal alien" graduated from the Great Lakes Naval Academy not far from my home several years ago and visited me and my family. I spoke to Martitza, a quiet, sweet girl who was living through a sad divorce in her fifth-grade year. Her husband and father of her three young children is dying from several insidious diseases involving his heart and kidneys. "Miss Liska," she told me still using my name of twenty years earlier, "I sit with him in the hospital day after day. My mother watches my kids. I can't finish college or work. I stay with him even though he sleeps a lot. We're waiting to hear about transplants. But you know what saves me,

Miss Liska? I remember your class, I remember how you taught us to love books; I read and read for hours in the hospital. They have a book lady who brings things to read for me and I escape from that hospital room through those books. I can be a million miles away," she said wistfully.

She talked of her memories of that year, her efforts in her own small way, to eat healthy, to care about what was natural, to be a teacher someday. She spoke of her acceptance of the fact that there might not be a transplant and that she needed to help her husband and family to face that reality. It was a phone conversation I will never forget as was that year we all quietly and persistently pledged allegiance to the world.

Jim Carnes

Jim Carnes, courtesy of
Penny Weaver

Because my job consists largely of talking to, reading about, and writing about teachers who are committed to social justice, my vision is a little skewed. At times, this constant contact with "teachers for change" resembles a groundswell—or a tidal wave—which can obscure the vast array of challenges that remain unmet.

One challenge that has recently loomed into view here in Alabama, as in other areas, is the movement in support of prayer in the schools. Thirty-five years after the landmark Supreme Court ruling, a vocal minority of Americans are clamoring to reverse it by means of a Constitutional amendment. One reason, I think, that the decision was widely misunderstood and resented in the first place is that the original case was brought, in part, by atheist members of a statistically tiny minority with a long history of discomforting their peers. The circumstance has subsequently made it easy to cast the whole separation principle as "atheistic."

In a sense, the conservative tide in this country represents a religious revival. The irony is that recent decades have brought a surge not only in right-wing Christianity but also in the open practice of every world religion on U.S. soil. The soundness—and the compassion—of the 1963 decision is proven every time a Baptist child and a Sunni child, or a Jewish child and a Hindu child, or a Roman Catholic child and an atheist child sit side by side as equals in the classroom. Teachers can contribute significantly to the coming debate about their rights and responsibilities by shifting the focus from godliness vs. godlessness to religious tolerance vs. religious tyranny.

Mark Perry

Mark Perry, courtesy of M. Geffner

Teaching for social change is a battle on many fronts. I recently attended a meeting at my sixth-grade daughter's elementary school which has just been granted authority to expand from K-6 to K-8. Committees were set up to determine the new classes' direction and sources of funding. I joined the curriculum subgroup with a dozen other parents and one of the two current sixth-grade teachers. I knew we were off to a rocky start when we were informed that the curriculum is already set by state mandates so all we have to come up with are recommendations for other programs, such as the arts. I volunteered that how a curriculum is implemented is crucial to the success of the students. We set up a plan to visit other programs to see first hand what they were doing and, feeling empowered by the success of my last suggestion, I offered that it would be useful to talk with the current sixth-grade students. They could even do a project where they design their ideal middle school. This was met with a unanimous wave of opposition. Responses ranged from laughter at the very idea to the belief that "they don't know what's good for them." As proof, one parent said her eleven-year-old daughter would eat candy all day if she could get away with it. Partially out of frustration I said, "Why not let her decide. If she eats candy all day and gets sick, I'll bet she decides to ration herself in the future."

What struck me in this meeting was that the content of the curriculum, as prescribed and supported by the parents, is what would generally be named as multicultural and socially relevant. The school has a mission of "purpose-oriented" study and tries to include project-based work for students. So what's wrong with this picture? Why do teachers and parents react so strongly and negatively to student involvement and participation? As parents we are protective of our own children and want the best for them. We want safe and challenging learning environments and ask teachers to help prepare them with the needed knowledge and tools to survive and contribute in the adult world. But, again, what's wrong with this picture? When, as parents and teachers, do we begin to believe in and trust our children?

Teaching for social change is a constant battle. I use the above incident with the parent group only to point out the conservative side of even the most well-meaning parents who are still unwilling to challenge the status quo of schooling. We have accepted schooling as synonymous with learning and in doing so leave out the input of our own children. As a parent, I am empathetic. As a teacher, my harshest critique is reserved for teachers. What are we afraid of? Why are we hesitant to hear and fight for the voices of our students? In teaching undergraduate pre-service teachers, I generally find that their biggest perceived concern, after class management, is job security. When I provide a framework based in student-centered learning, culturally relevant curriculum, and an engaged and democratic pedagogy, there is an audible squirm in the classroom. But if I do that, I'll lose my job, they chant in mantra. But what about your students, I ask. They agree an engaged pedagogy would be more ideal, but even after reading Herb Kohl, Gloria Ladson-Billings, bell hooks, and others, and hearing from experienced teachers who are successful both within and outside public schools, they still wince at the thought of challenging the status quo.

Am I frustrated? Yes. Have I given up hope? Absolutely not. But it makes me think that we need to reframe or rename the questions. Part of my hope lies in teacher education. If this new generation of teachers begins from a point of teaching for social change, schooling has the possibility of accomplishing needed reform and restructuring. Of course, teaching for social change is not easy. In fact, it's harder than "regular" teaching. The hook is that it is profoundly more satisfying.

George Wood

George Wood, courtesy of *Democracy and Education*

I do not believe you can teach for social justice—you must live for social justice. To learn about social justice means to experience it. I believe it is the general lack of social justice in our society that deprives our young people, and us, of knowing just what this all-too-elusive concept means.

For educators, the only response to this is to try to make our schools places where social justice is practiced. If we can create schools where social justice is somewhat a reality—where people are treated decently, humanely, and with honesty—then there is a chance that we will teach our children what social justice means. If just once in their lives they see right triumph over wrong, good over evil, justice over inequity, they will at least know that social justice is possible.

Ultimately, that's what it's all about: giving young people hope that social justice is not simply a slogan or a curriculum package, but something that compels us to treat one another as members of a shared community. Only when our schools are communities where social justice is practiced can we claim to be teaching for that justice.

18—School Projects Investing in Community Development

Following is an excerpt from a document developed at the Chicago Innovations Forum, Center for Urban Affairs, Northwestern University, 2040 Sheridan Road, Evanston, IL 60208. Reprinted by permission.

This list of thirty-one projects is a beginning effort to give concrete examples of how a new partnership between schools and communities might be implemented.

STUDENTS AND TEACHERS

1. Identify the key assets of the community (businesses, associations, clubs, facilities, etc.) and create a guidebook for community development. The local chamber of commerce or service clubs may cooperate in its publication and dissemination. This initial work can educate students and teachers about their community while initiating a cooperative working relationship with community groups.
2. In cooperation with interested community groups, create community history projects that will enhance commitments to the future. These could be done with senior citizens, ethnic associations, historical societies. The completed work could be published in local newspapers.
3. Working with local development groups, research information that will facilitate community planning, i.e., inventory vacant lots, identify land ownership, map capital improvement plans, identify economic development groups, update census data on local demographics.
4. In collaboration with local neighborhood organizations, development groups, or business associations, conduct local attitude and consumer market surveys. These could be conducted door to door or by telephone.
5. Conduct research on the choices involved in community issues and convene community forums in the school to discuss the issues based on the background research prepared and presented by students.
6. Most neighborhood organizations in larger urban

neighborhoods need to learn about developments at the block level and channel information to the block residents. Local students could become "area reporters" for the two or three blocks where they reside, acting as liaison between the neighbors and their associations. This civic information function could be the basis for course work on the nature and practice of democracy.

7. The community development process requires local media to involve residents in planning, notify them of action, and celebrate the local progress. The students, in cooperation with local groups, could create a newspaper serving these functions in areas too small to be served by other media.

8. In cooperation with local government units, students could engage in public service by conducting studies and performing functions with local units of government. They could do air quality monitoring, assist public health officials in surveying toxic sources, conduct traffic control studies, etc.

9. In cooperation with local business associations, students could do studies of consumer attitudes and preferences as well as reports on the proposals and ideas of local business people regarding improving economic opportunity. They could also develop proposals for closer links between the school and local employers.

10. Students could become direct participants in development activities such as housing construction and rehabilitation, where they could develop skills and contribute to the development process.

11. Many churches are involved in running community projects such as tutoring programs, sports, services to the elderly, preschool child care, etc. They usually depend on community volunteers. Students could become volunteer workers, developing skills for future employment in the service sector while building the community's capacity to meet local needs.

12. Many nonprofit organizations involved in the community development process could use the capacities of students. They could work with the office support staff in connection with a curriculum in office management. They could assist in tracking housing in violation of codes and study the process of enforcement.

13. Every community has organizations involving senior citizens. There are innumerable ways for students to cooperate with these groups and their members. All of the projects described earlier could be conducted in cooperation with individual senior citizens or groups. Intergenerational housing develop-

ments could be jointly studied and planned by students and seniors. Students could develop a matching service connecting students and seniors to provide mutual support, i.e., daily phone checks to see that seniors are all right, etc.

14. In cooperation with local artists or an arts council, students could create outdoor murals to beautify the local environment.

15. As major users of the parks, students could study the history of community parks, survey local residents' use and desires, sample students' use and desires, and develop a neighborhood plan for park development and improvement.

16. As part of a curriculum focused on energy issues, students could develop an energy efficiency program for their school, with the savings placed in a fund to capitalize new venture development by students.

17. Students could conduct a study of crime and vandalism in the neighborhood by using data provided by the police force. They could also survey community attitudes toward crime. Based on this information, they could develop a proposal for crime reduction, seek student participation, and seek local governmental and community support.

TEACHERS

18. As specially trained and skilled professionals, teachers have a great deal to contribute to groups involved in community development. They could develop a school inventory of the skills and expertise they have to offer. This inventory of capacities could be made into a teacher skills directory and distributed to local community development groups seeking technical advice and assistance. Subsequent requests for assistance could also be the basis for involving students in apprentice-like learning experiences with their teachers.

19. Most community development groups have boards of directors representing diverse interests in the community. Administrators and teachers could indicate a commitment to serve on the boards, contributing their knowledge and identifying opportunities for school participation in organizational development projects.

COURSES

20. A special course in business accounting could be developed for local small-business people. Similarly, a course on local

community development enrolling both students and local adults could be created.

21. Special courses to help people earn credentials, such as the test on General Educational Development, could assist local residents with their job preparation process.

IN-SCHOOL VENTURES

22. A center created by the school involving teachers, students, and local citizens could experiment with the development, use, and sale of neighborhood technologies to improve the local economy. These technologies could include solar energy systems, greenhouse horticulture, energy-saving activities and materials, waste treatment, and recycling systems.

23. Students could develop commercial ventures for community maintenance and improvement. These could include contracts to maintain and develop railroad and local public transit embankments, maintenance of tot lots for the park authority, tree-planting projects with local block clubs, etc.

24. Using school facilities, develop a student enterprise to prepare and deliver Meals on Wheels to homebound citizens.

25. Students and teachers could develop an enterprise using school equipment, when not in use, to create a computer center providing bookkeeping, word processing, or mailing services for local enterprises.

26. Enterprise "incubators" could be developed in local schools. There, students would plan and develop student-run community enterprises such as growing flowers, auto repair, or a "rent a kid" service.

27. The profits from these ventures could be used to create a scholarship fund or contributed to a community economic development fund.

FACILITIES

28. The school could develop a student-run "latch key" program for the children of working parents (perhaps staffed, in part, by older students).

29. Community facilities needed by both students and citizens could be used by both groups, cutting back on public facilities costs. Thus, the community library, gym, and swimming pool could be in the school, bringing citizens, teachers, and students into more frequent contact with each other.

PURCHASING

30. Local schools could make special efforts to contract for goods and services with local merchants. They could cooperate with local economic development efforts to help create local markets for local ventures. In large school systems, local authority for purchasing could be granted to encourage support of local vendors.

31. Students could conduct a study of their school's purchasing patterns and procedures. This information could then be made available to local merchants and economic development groups.

19—A Story for Social Justice

Jaylynne N. Hutchinson
Rosalie M. Romano

The late scientist for the people Carl Sagan once said, "We make our world significant by the courage of our questions and by the depth of our answers." Those who are concerned about teaching for social justice are seeking to create those kinds of educative experiences that draw out courageous questions and open a space for rich, responsive answers. The commitment to teach for social justice is not a commitment to a particular ideology, but a commitment to assist students as they grapple with the demands of daily moral living. It is a commitment not to shy away from incorporating the whole lives of your students into your teaching, nor to avoid the difficult social issues we and they face in any given society.

Herein lies a significant, but subtle pedagogical problem. As teachers concerned with teaching for understanding, our rhetoric commits our pedagogy to begin with the natural instincts, interests, and life experiences of the child. Yet, one of the great dilemmas of the progressive educator is how to meet the child at this personal and unique place, and from there to teach and expand the child's world. In other words, how do we truly foster growth and educative experiences? John Dewey describes this process:

> The child's own instincts and powers furnish the material and give the starting point for all education. Save as the efforts of the educator connect with some activity which the child is carrying on of his own initiative independent of the educator, education becomes reduced to a pressure from without. It may, indeed, give certain external results, but cannot truly be called educative. (1992, 363)

Teaching for social justice must avoid teaching that is "reduced to a pressure from without," because without connecting to a child's life, teaching loses its moral dimension.

Teaching for social justice can be conceptualized in two different, but complementary ways. One way to understand teaching for social justice is to employ a teaching strategy that fosters and gives students an opportunity to experience and gain practice exercising those attributes and traits that help social justice to flourish. For example, to prepare for democratic living, students need opportunities to learn how to be tolerant, handle conflict, trust one another, and build community, to name a few. A second way to view teaching for social justice is to address specific topics by having students examine their curriculum critically and uncover its intersections with social justice concerns. To illustrate how this might be implemented we can look at a unit focusing on Northwest Native American culture. Traditionally, this type of unit has been presented in classrooms by learning about and celebrating the many wonderful and rich dimensions of this culture as it existed before European contact. Although this is a marvelous unit for children to explore, teaching for social justice would not present the unit as an unconnected body of knowledge. A teacher concerned with social justice might ask students to explore the status of those very same tribes in the world today and ask students to address the connective complexity between indigenous peoples' lives before European influence and indigenous people's lives today. As you can see, both ways of viewing teaching for social justice draw on a more holistic model of teaching.

One strategy we often employ is called storyline. Imagine for a moment that you are a teacher of third graders at the beginning of the winter season. Since the time that school began in the fall many of your students have been bringing in tales of the people who sleep in a nearby park and of whom the children seem fearful. These homeless people are teased by your students, some of whom will throw things at a sleeping person or taunt them with name-calling or scream to wake someone up and then run, run, run to school. Your third graders frequently come into class steaming and disheveled from escaping "those people in the park." A mythology is now being established in your third-grade class about how "brave" a student is by the degree of taunting, the cutting nature of a remark, or the crescendo of a scream that scares a homeless person out of an uneasy sleep.

Though the teacher, Mr. Greg, had spoken to the children individually, in small groups, and as a whole class since this teasing began in September, the children's attitudes toward the homeless people in the park remained negative and fearful. For the children, these homeless people were the embodiment of the "Other," not one of them. Mr. Greg was concerned by the children's ongoing attitude and behavior and knew he had to respond in order to help the children openly discuss their behavior and take responsibility for it. We know as teachers this is easier to define than to do. Like us, Mr. Greg could not simply tell his students to stop. (He did, but they didn't!) If he threatened them with consequences, then he knew from long experience that the behavior would simply continue, but be hidden from his view.

To confront the children's behavior, Mr. Greg would first have to help them become aware of the reasons for their reactions. This meant that he had to find a way that they could honestly express their beliefs about homeless people without a sense of being judged by an adult. You see, the children knew they should not behave in this way toward the homeless people in the park. On many occasions when Mr. Greg talked to them, all had quickly agreed it "wasn't nice to be mean to 'those people.'"

Originating from their real lives, the children had posed a problem that was fraught with ambiguity, yet was rich in potential for discussion, conflict, and understanding. It was a problem that was local, but with larger implications, given the increase in homeless people in the city and in this country. How then to promote open discussion in a safe environment in order that the children could critically examine their ways of behaving, their beliefs, all while teaching the standard curriculum of reading, writing, and arithmetic? Such was the task of uncovering the intersection with social justice. To do this, Mr. Greg chose an instructional methodology recently brought to this country from Scotland called the storyline method.

Storyline is a structured approach to curriculum organization that addresses the need for language, mathematics, and conceptual content development. Academic skills such as reading, writing, computation, and research are taught and woven throughout this integrated approach. In this way, these skills are not taught as contextless skills, but are learned by necessity as a means to an end. What are the primary features of this strategy? First, a teacher chooses a topic of study (in our example, homelessness) by explaining to the class that they will make a story together. In storyline, the teacher creates the place or setting, while the collaborative work of the students is to conceptualize the story onto an artistic frieze or wall mural. Characters are developed who live in this time and place. Additionally, each student creates an individual character for him- or herself. Each individually developed character has personality traits, family and other relational ties, a role in the story, and dreams. As storyline develops, the children's characters interact with other student-created characters in order to respond to key turning-point questions that the teacher poses. This is collaborative story making that will lead the children through a number of episodes in an unfolding narrative determined in large part by their responses to the questions framed by the teacher as the story progresses.

Storyline is a strategy that by its very nature draws on how we make sense of the world through stories. In *Acts of Meaning*, Jerome Bruner (1990) posits that human beings are "fueled by a need to construct meaning" (89). In other words, human beings are born meaning makers. This meaning is created within the context of cultural constructs that are couched within a narrative form. To be meaningful, learning must be incorporated into the narrative of a student's life, rather than being held at bay in a predetermined set of school learnings. Even more so, when the domain is that of social justice, education must, of necessity, incorporate the broader cultural context. Hence, the storyline method, drawing as it does on narrative and context, is a match for meaning-based learning.

Issues of social justice begin with a sense of urgency. They are cloaked by a significance that much of traditional education avoids. Maxine Greene (1995) aptly describes this ambiance as a "weightedness." She states:

> there is always a certain weight in the lived situation—a weight due to the environment, to traumas from the past, or to experience with exclusion or poverty or the impacts of ideology. We achieve freedom through confrontation with and partial surpassing of such weight or determinacy. We seek this freedom, however, only when what presses down (or conditions or limits) is perceived as an obstacle. Where oppression or exploitation or pollution or even pestilence is perceived as natural, as a given, there can be no freedom. Where people cannot name alternatives or imagine a better state of things, they are likely to remain anchored or submerged (50).

A fundamental step in addressing issues of social justice is to learn to name obstacles, see their contingent nature, and imagine alternatives. Storyline facilitates this through constructing a story with the students.

Not only is story a powerful teaching heuristic because it reflects how we make sense in our lives, but story also expands from the private to the public and back again. Consider for a moment the work of Vivian Paley (1990), whose classroom revolves around the stories children tell. She comments on the impact of placing story as a primary vehicle for meaning making. She states:

> Our kind of storytelling is a social phenomenon, intended to flow through all other activities and provide the wisest opportunity for a communal response. Stories are not private affairs; the individual imagination plays host to all the stimulation in the environment and causes ripples of ideas to encircle the listener (20).

Social justice tensions often spring from differences in life stories or how one experiences the world. The "ripples of ideas that encircle the listener" when one engages in story making and telling, facilitates an exploration and understanding of diverse life stories.

Storyline becomes an avenue of teaching for social justice because of the multiple aspects it provides within a holistic learning experience. Consider how each highlighted aspect facilitates teaching for social justice.

Storyline begins with the premise that the world is *complex* and that children have already formed myriad conceptions about the world and their place in it. This reservoir of knowledge and understanding about the world is rarely tapped in the traditional classroom, but unless learning can connect with the daily moral terrain of students' lives, it will not address issues of social justice. As you will see, storyline invites the children to bring forward their assumptions about the world. It is from this vantage point that the class starts its journey.

Because storyline is *conceptual* in nature, the children must draw on their preconceived ideas about the topic being studied through activities. Both the child and his or her character are involved in figuring out solutions to the dilemmas they encounter as the story progresses. Such contextualized experiences promote socially constructed knowledge and understanding of the world. Such collaboration contributes to the students' motivation for learning. Each question that is posed propels them toward deeper thinking, that, in turn, raises more questions. Their original conceptions of the topic are challenged in a way that fosters their own questioning. Children negotiate with one another and with one another's characters in order to make sense of new ideas.

Storyline takes these intrinsically motivated questions and asks students to seek out new knowledge. Students often turn to other rich and varied sources to "check out" their hunches and find out if the answers to their questions do fit the given setting they are creating. When Mr. Greg invited a social worker into his classroom to talk with the children about homelessness after they had been working on their storyline for some time, the utter engagement and sincerity of the children's questions astounded the social worker. She had never had a group of third graders ask such pointed, pragmatic questions of her. The students were serious because her answers to questions such as "What do homeless people do when they get sick?" or "How do homeless people get food?" directly affected their characters and indirectly affected themselves as well. This is pure *inquiry* that is driven by a need to know. The students were not asking questions of the social worker simply to find answers to a unit test or to garner an "A" in class. They were asking because they *needed* to know in order to continue to develop their story. In this regard, storyline creates an intrinsic motivation.

Problem solving is a cornerstone of storyline as it encourages diverse ways of dealing with the dilemmas the students confront in their story, either through their own exploration of connections between characters and unfolding events or through the facilitation of teacher-guided questions. Finding the "right" answer fades in importance as the children explore the dilemmas inherent in storyline. They bring to their story both what they already know from their own lives as well as what they can imagine as possible outcomes. Storyline offers students the experience of being collaborative story makers as they work together to address the teacher's guiding questions.

"What words come to mind when I say 'homeless'?" asks Mr. Greg.

A flurry of hands go up. As Mr. Greg calls out each name, he writes the child's answer on a large sheet of paper. This list will remain in view during the weeks when storyline is going on in the classroom. The students will continue to add to it and use the words in their journals and writing. The third graders call out these responses:

"It means without a home."

"It means to sleep in a shelter."

"No food or money."

"You sleep in alleys, subways, parks, and benches."

"It can mean you stay in a hotel."

"Maybe they have problems like drugs or alcohol."

"It means a hard life."

"They have to deal with others on the street."

There is no clue here as to the students' past behavior and negative attributions toward the homeless people they pass on their way to school. Teachers understand that these answers are protected ones that the children are giving. It is safe and proper to say that homeless means you do not have food or money. Such safe responses might convince some teachers (and parents) that the children *do* understand about the unfortunate circumstances of those who are homeless. Hence, teachers might move on, thinking that understanding has occurred and the children will not engage in name calling and other negative behavior against the homeless. But the consistent cruelty of the children belies their spoken declaration of compassion or empathy with the homeless. "Correct" answers do not necessarily reflect habits of mind or habits of heart.

As responses begin to repeat themselves, Mr. Greg asks the next storyline question. "Well," he says, "why are people homeless, do you think?" More hands are raised and Mr. Greg calls on the students, writing their answers again on another sheet of butcher paper. In storyline, students' responses are publicly displayed to affirm what they know, to provide opportunities for the social construction of knowledge, to allow for others to build on common understandings, and to offer chances to correct and amend assumptions about the world.

"They could have lost all their money."

"Maybe they left their homes."

"I know! Maybe they ran away."

"And their house could have burned down."

"He could have lost his job . . ."

Storyline can create a safe environment where children may take their fears and beliefs and make them public. This safe space for exploration occurs as children work out these varying circumstances through their storyline characters and through the story narrative. Yet, because they are exploring these issues through characters, they do not draw attention directly to themselves, providing a safe space to think about the consequences of both belief and behavior.

Traditionally, storyline has children create an artistic frieze or mural and characters whom the children create and endow with histories and personalities. In this way, storyline draws on *multiple forms of expression*. Children are working with colors, design, glue, markers, crayons, each contributing something to the frieze and their characters in order to make a whole and ever-evolving mural as the story progresses. (While this kind of creative activity is traditionally associated with the early grades, older students are as engaged by this creative work as are younger children.) Students seem to relish using all their senses in this academic setting. Mr. Greg establishes the storyline topic of homelessness and sets a framework by the conceptual questions he poses. Then he turns to the children and tells them they are going to make a homeless character. Because of the nature of this topic, instead of developing and placing the characters on a frieze or mural, these characters will have no frieze because they are homeless. They take any space they can on the blackboard, in itself, a powerful statement that is sent through a visual message. This homeless storyline has the potential to reveal how the children might also feel about school. At times, children themselves feel homeless in school, as if there is no place for them. Not only does this allow them to explore how they perceive homelessness, but allows for glimpses into their own worlds.

The students are already familiar with storyline because in the fall Mr. Greg chose the topic of space and astronauts. The children still talk about many of the characters they created there. Now Mr. Greg points to the construction paper, pens, scissors, and glue that he has set up on the tables. The children begin to create the characters of homeless people according to their own ideas, experiences, and assumptions. They animatedly talk and create the biographies of each of their characters as they cut, paste, and color. The children are engaged in and focused on this activity, talking to one another across their group tables. How to choose the color of paper that will become a homeless person leads to a discussion of skin color and eyes.

"I don't know how to make eyes," says Nino, who has been

using his pencil to sketch out eye shapes on some scratch paper.

"I don't know how to make sad eyes," says Juanita, who has also been sketching eye shapes.

"I like those," says Nino, pointing to the two eyes Juanita has just drawn.

"What would he be looking at then?" asks Juanita.

"Oh, he would be looking at his friends," replies Nino.

And so begins a discussion about who would be friends with a homeless person. Throughout the classroom, third graders are concentrating and talking about each other's characters as the paper and glue become someone's face, someone who is alive, someone who has a history. As the children create their characters, each one imbues his or her character with a distinct biography, the story of a human being who happens to be homeless. And the collaboration of storyline begins. The *collaborative* nature of storyline is crucial and pinpoints an important insight into teaching about social justice: we are intricately connected to one another. In telling her own story, author Eva Hoffman (1989) remarks that "Human beings don't only search for meanings, they are themselves units of meaning; but we can mean something only within the fabric of larger significations" (279). As the children create and interact with their characters, this lesson is not lost on them.

Chase is ready to introduce his homeless character to the class. Mr. Greg calls on him.

"My character's name is Brian, Brian Robbins. He is twenty years old. He has been homeless a long time. His parents were living on the street. People helped Brian when he was young. They didn't help his parents because they were a little druggy looking. His parents were cold and hungry. They got sick and died.

"Brian lived with a family for one year. A family took him in and helped him. He went to school, but if you were bad, they used to hit students with paddles for not following the rules. He did not stay at school for very long. Then they found out he was doing drugs. They said he was a street person and that he wouldn't stop and they kicked him out.

"Brian loves pizza. His favorite movie is 'Hard Target.' He likes to listen to compact disks by the Spin Doctors. He is sorry he could not see them when they were in Seattle, but the tickets were too expensive. He does not have any close friends but he likes to play football. He usually plays football with the other bums. Brian is afraid of guns and the police. He has stolen food, clothes, and other things and he is afraid they might come after him."

Listening closely to Brian's biography, the reference to "bums playing football" is revealing. Such a comment is in contrast with the children's list of opening answers given when Mr. Greg asked what it meant to be homeless. Those answers were reasonable, almost sympathetic. Now as we meet the character of Brian, all of us in the classroom are given another perspective including one that Chase himself may not have deliberately revealed. This gives the class and the teacher an opportunity to discuss issues when they are raised by students in context.

Additionally, storyline draws on the students' field of experience and knowledge by engaging them in creative problem solving about their characters. Chase has to explain about Brian to his peers and then their characters must now interact with his. In so doing, Brian becomes part of the story, as they become part of Brian's. A *community* forms by such small stories shared with each other. Over time, these homeless characters form associations with one another and weave each other into their own stories as they meet the challenges of living on the street. This is not simply a grouping of students, but once characters in the storyline have been created and introduced, they act in character and others must respond to the actions each take. One does not act in isolation. This is a powerful lesson related to social justice that at best is only abstractly addressed in traditional education.

In this regard, storyline is *communal*; the story is created and developed together. A guiding principle of storyline is that no character either dies or is alone. Therefore, to work in a classroom where storyline is going on means more than just being in a cooperative group. You see, once each student creates his or her character, that character also becomes part of the classroom, and often a response to the teacher's questions is from a character. For example, one of the homeless characters, Robert, was created by Sal. Robert, it turns out, knows another homeless character, Courtney, who has met him while he was rummaging in garbage cans for food. Both characters embellish their resourcefulness in finding leftovers behind fast-food restaurants, and they have become friends. At one point, Robert is telling the class about how he is afraid of being caught by the police. Courtney nods her head in agreement.

"But why," asks Mr. Greg, "should Robert be afraid of the police at all?"

"Because of the way he looks," Sal says of his character. "Robert *looks* scary even though he is not."

Here is one indication of imagination at work. Sal had participated in the teasing of the homeless people in the park. Through his character Robert, Sal can explore the idea that people might be afraid of someone because of the way he looks, even though that person may not be scary when you get to know him. Mr. Greg had asked about how much we can tell about a person simply by looking at him or her. Although Mr. Greg could make his point by telling the children outright why such assumptions based on appearance can be faulty, he provides a way for the children to discover this and incorporate it into their understandings themselves.

Discovering and entertaining such personal questions highlights the way storyline draws on *multiple perspectives*. The different characters each bring their own perspective to the story. Not only must students respond to these differing character perspectives, but in asking a student to play the role of a character, one is having that student him- or herself entertain a different perspective. This often brings questions to the fore that would not have come about. For example, where *do* I brush my teeth if I am homeless? and with what? What do I do if it rains? What do I do on my birthday? Each character has a different, but logical response to share with others in the story.

Storyline involves *critical thought*, which includes critical listening and critical questioning. Today Mr. Greg is posing a critical question that will spur critical thought and dialogue. He begins, "Today is the day that your character becomes homeless. Imagine that you can take one bag of possessions. What are the things you will need if you live on the street?" Mr. Greg asks the students each to make a list of the possessions that they think they would take with them as they become homeless. These lists will be shared with the class.

"Well," says Nino, "my character needs milk. And sweatpants and a sweatshirt, some bread and apples, a sleeping bag, a toothbrush, and oh yeah, a TV." As Nino makes his list, he looks up and raises his eyebrows when he gets to the TV. There are some things to be figured out and Nino knows someone or perhaps a character will challenge his decision to take along a TV. After all, this is not such a practical item to haul around when there is nowhere to plug it in.

Challenges such as Nino might face can spur conflict and debate. Besides bringing a television along, other students indicated that they would take items that required refrigeration. The making public of and dialogue about these items allows for critical thinking to occur as students question one another as to the viability of their choices. Conflict, both explicit and implicit, occurs throughout storyline. This becomes evident as children discuss dimensions of a character and their decisions, accuracy of information about a place or idea, the logic of a possession or contradictions within a character's biography. *Conflict* is expected, acknowledged, and used by storyline teachers to help children learn to share their ideas in such a way that others can hear and understand them. In this context, conflict is not the polarizing event that a teacher avoids bringing into the classroom. Instead, conflict provides an opportunity to forge connections in the classroom community. Negotiation is the norm, as are respect and civility, for truly that is the only way to entertain such multiple, diverse viewpoints. Storyline actively facilitates and uses conflict to create critical teaching moments. Dealing with conflict is a preeminent, but most often overlooked aspect of democratic living. We like to hide from it because it makes us feel uncomfortable. At our best, we hide conflict in our efforts to respect others. In this regard, we mistakenly have not been willing to engage with difference for fear of offending. At our worst, we harbor attitudes that actively dismiss the other and that are the antithesis of democratic living. Either way, avoiding conflict prevents us from engaging with issues of social justice. Storyline provides a constructive opportunity to engage with difference and learn how to negotiate conflict constructively.

Storyline is *contextual*, requiring that all participants build and thereby understand the context of their story prior to any action. And because the participants are the ones solely responsible for the direction of the story (through their responses), everyone knows what is happening and everyone belongs with his or her characters. The building of context through story making is the glue of creating a community of learners by fostering and deepening ties of connection between all in the classroom. Storyline teachers have found that children are compelled to want the storyline to make sense to them and be realistic. Therefore, each introduction of a character, every aspect of a character's posses-sions or his biography is scrutinized by the entire community, who (like any community) will not hesitate to chide or correct or make it their business to share how they feel about someone's actions.

Raymond has been absent for over a week and, as is usual, he is far behind in all his class work, including introducing his char-acter, known by the other children only as Redhead, named for the red hood over his head. Though Raymond is a bright, gentle boy, because of his frequent long absences he has fallen behind in his work and is an outsider to his classmates. Because of this, when Raymond is in class, Mr. Greg makes sure that he participates and is made to feel part of the group. It is an important step for Raymond to come up to the front of the room this day, holding his character Kurt, who is the only character that has not been introduced to all the others. Everyone is curious about the char-acter they named Redhead. Raymond begins quietly and slowly.

"Kurt is a man who has been homeless for long time. His house burnt down. He was living with his mother and father, but he lost both parents in the fire. He had no brother and sister." Mr. Greg knows that there was a tragic fire in the community recently that claimed the lives of four firefighters. It had been extensively reported in the daily papers and on the television newscasts. Storyline often creates a place for children to explore their own worries and fears about social issues that impact their own lives.

"What is Kurt best at doing?" prompts Mr. Greg, trying to encourage Raymond into telling us more about his character's personality.

"Looking for food, that is what he is best at."

After a long silence, Mr. Greg asks, "Has Kurt ever worked? Has he ever earned money?"

"Well, Kurt has helped garbage men."

"Does he have any friends?" asks Mr. Greg.

"Oh no, Kurt doesn't have any friends at all because he is homeless."

Another boy who has been listening intently to Raymond blurts out in a sympathetic tone, "Well, they wouldn't be real friends anyway." Is this another window into the children's views of the homeless in the park? Homeless people don't have friends. Homeless means friendless. What a terrifying idea this must be to a third grader: being all alone with no place to call home or to belong. One can feel the wondering that is sparked by such a discussion.

Storyline is *imaginative,* and fosters a sense of wondering that draws on the imagination in a way little else does in school. Imagination is critical to social justice because before we can be part of making the world a more just place, we have to be able to imagine the world as if it could be different. Greene (1988) explains how education that names the world and sparks the imagination can engage young people:

> Without being "onto something," young people feel little pressure, little challenge. There are no mountains they particularly want to climb, so there are few obstacles with which they feel they need to engage. They may take no heed of neighborhood shapes and events once they have become used to them—even the figures of homelessness, the wanderers who are mentally ill, the garbage-strewn lots, the burned-out buildings. It may be that no one communicates the importance of thinking about them or suggests the need to play with hypothetical alternatives. There may be no sense of identification with people sitting on the benches, with children hanging around the street corners after dark. There may be no ability to take it seriously, to take it personally. Visible or invisible, the world may not be problematized; no one aches to break through a horizon, aches in the presence of the question itself. (124)

As teachers we constantly search for ways to weave connections with our students' experiences and with the curriculum we must teach to them. How to engage them in meaning-making is a never-ending task. When we find those teachable moments, those moments when our students connect with an idea, we do not soon forget it, and we seek the next teachable moment in all we do. Storyline cultivates teachable moments, without imposing ideas and concepts from without. Rather, students are pedagogically nurtured so when they are ready, the seed of a new idea or realization is planted. Creating these teachable moments is to reach to the core of students' understandings. Storyline facilitates this as it invites the child to bring the whole of him- or herself to the table of learning; feelings, minds, artistic expressions, bodily movements, all are incorporated. Students not only are given a chance to explore topics of social justice, but most foundationally, they are exercising those aspects of character that will allow them to create and re-create a more just and humane world.

Let us return to Mr. Greg's class. The children have been having an animated discussion this afternoon about guns and other weapons that a character has decided to bring along with him in his bag of possessions. Mr. Greg comments, "We've met some characters who have weapons with them. This seems to bother some of you. Sounds like being on the street is not so simple and there is a lot of potential for violence. You have to watch out for violence, don't you? What kinds of dangers do homeless people face, I wonder."

The intense discussions have subsided as each child turns in his or her chair to listen to Mr. Greg's question. The class becomes very quiet. Without raising her hand, Sue says softly, "Some people are afraid of the homeless, so they threaten them." Sue's comment ripples palpably across the silent room. Are the children thinking about the times they teased or listened enthusiastically to another student's taunting of a homeless person in the park?

Mr. Greg lets the moment hang in the air.

ENDNOTES

The storyline method was developed by a group of experienced teachers in Scotland at the Jordanhill College of Education in Glasgow in the 1960s. In response to a report from the Scottish Education Department, their goal was to design the "curriculum not as a set of separate subjects but as a series of educational experiences that help children see the world as a connected whole." In so doing, they developed a curriculum tool that was a "powerful instrument for learning to make coherent sense of the world around us and our place within it." See Margit E. McGuire, "Storyline: A Strategy for Collaborative Storymaking to Teach Social Studies Concepts," presented at the National Council for the Social Studies Annual Meeting, November 1994.

For more information about the storyline methodology see, Margit E. McGuire, "Conceptual Learning in the Primary Grades: The Storyline Strategy," in *Social Studies and the Young Learner*, January/February 1991,6–8; Ian M. Barr & Margit McGuire, "Social Studies and Effective Stories," in *Social Studies and the Young*

Learner, January/February 1993, 6–11; Kieran Egan, "Teaching as Storytelling: A Nonmechanistic Approach to Planning and Teaching," *Journal of Curriculum Studies*, 17, 397–406.

REFERENCES

Barr, I. and M. McGuire. 1993. Social studies and effective stories. In *Social Studies and the Young Learner* Jan/Feb.

Bruner, J. 1990. *Acts of Meaning*. Cambridge: Harvard University Press.

Dewey, J. 1992. My pedagogic creed. In *Kaleidoscope: Readings in Education*, edited by Ryan and Cooper. New York: Houghton-Mifflin.

Egan, K. 1985. Teaching as storytelling: A non-mechanistic approach to planning and teaching. In *Journal of Curriculum Studies* 17.

Greene, M. 1995. *Releasing the Imagination*. San Francisco: Jossey-Bass.

——— 1988. *The Dialectic of Freedom*. New York: Teachers College Press.

Hoffman, E. 1989. *Lost in Translation*. New York: Penguin Books.

McGuire, M. 1991. Conceptual learning in the primary grades: The story-line strategy. In *Social Studies and the Young Learner* Jan/Feb.

——— 1994. Storyline: A strategy for collaborative story-making to teach social studies concepts. The National Council for the Social Studies Annual Meeting, November.

Paley, V. 1990. *The Boy Who Would Be a Helicopter*. Cambridge: Harvard University Press.

Romano, R. 1996. Forging an educative community. Unpublished dissertation, University of Washington, Seattle.

20—Welfare Workbook

Following is an excerpt from a workbook developed by literacy students at the Adult and Family Learning Center, Stanley Isaacs Neighborhood Center, 415 East 93rd St., New York, NY 10128. Reprinted by permission.

Welfare is not a dirty word. Look it up in the dictionary and you'll see lots of definitions. Two of them are:

1. Health, happiness and general well-being.
2. Public relief.

Look up the word "relief" and it says:

1. Anything that lessens pain or discomfort.
2. "On relief"—Receiving government funds because of need or poverty.

When did welfare become a dirty word to some people? Why do some people feel ashamed to be on welfare? What is your image of a person on welfare? What do the TV news, talk, and newspapers tell us about people on welfare?

Denise, Iris, Pearl, Rebecca, Maribel, and Myriam, six of the pre-GED students at the Adult and Family Learning Center, looked in the mirror and didn't see welfare cheats who were drug addicts and drunks having one baby after another, too lazy to work and too stupid to go to school. What they saw were hard-working, strong, intelligent, serious, loving mothers who needed some "relief" in order to survive.

In order for a person receiving welfare to get the services they need, he or she must fill out many different forms and run around to many offices. A few times a year, students on welfare have to go to the welfare office to meet with a caseworker. This meeting is called a face to face. Each time the student goes to a "face to face," he or she must bring many papers, including a letter from school verifying attendance.

Forms are especially important when a student decides to go back to school and is eligible to receive extra money from welfare for carfare and child care. These special allowances are called

Training Related Expenses (TREs). For a student to get these TREs, he or she is made to go from place to place, collecting letters and handing them in, running from one office to the next.

The first thing students must do is go to their Office of Employment Services (OES) and pick up two forms: one is the Full-Time Enrollment Verification Form and the other is the Child Care Provider Form. The first form must be filled out by the school, and the second form must be filled out by the child care provider.

Both forms then need to be returned to OES for review. If all goes smoothly and the student is approved, he or she will start to receive the extra money within two weeks. TRE money is picked up at the same place where the student picks up their regular Public Assistance grant.

Once a student is approved, he or she must meet attendance requirements in order to keep getting TREs, which means he or she must attend class 75 percent of the time. In real numbers, that means attending class about three out of every four days.

Unfortunately, if, for example, your child gets sick and you need to miss more class time than OES allows, you may not get your TREs that month. If this happens, you receive a letter stating your attendance was unsatisfactory for the thirty-day period and your school or program needs to fill out an Attendance Verification Form all over again. You then have to bring the form to the OES office again for review. They will only reimburse you if you weren't really absent and there was some kind of mistake. They will put you back in the computer as still being in school, and you should start getting your TREs again.

For some students, there is an extra step they have to take. Students who are in Board of Education (BOE) classes that meet at community centers are required to have their attendance verified by the BOE. Their teacher can't do it, and the people who work at the community center can't do it, so they have to travel to the BOE's Regional Office to have the attendance verification letter filled out before going to OES. The way this system is set up now, students sometimes have to spend up to five dollars going from office to office, which means they're spending more money than OES will give them once they hand in their forms!

There are many ways for something to go wrong, and almost always the student is the one to suffer, even if there is a computer error at OES. Many times a student must borrow money to pay for transportation and/or a baby-sitter until all is straightened out. If they can't borrow, they miss class until OES corrects the error. In addition, whenever something needs to be changed or corrected, the student has to spend money to travel to OES and may miss class because business hours are also class time hours. If a student is ever confused or feels they have been treated unfairly, they should ask to speak with a supervisor at the OES office. Sometimes the Allowance Control Unit can help fix a problem, but if not, a student can always move up the chain of command to get what they need to stay in school. Students can also go to the counselor at their school for help dealing with the welfare system.

DENISE'S LETTER ABOUT HER CASEWORKER

Dear Commissioner of the Human Resources Administration:

My name is Denise. I am a recipient of welfare. My complaint is my caseworker. She is not doing her job. She doesn't know how to speak to people on the phone. For example, I called her for help about two important papers. One of the papers is concerning my GED and the other is a letter concerning the gas in my building which has been turned off.

She told me in a very nasty voice that she will not help me with any of my papers. I have been asking for an appointment since April and now we're in May and still no response.

I feel her attitude is uncalled for and her way of speaking needs improvement in all areas.

The supervisor has helped me with some of what has to be done. Every time I speak to my caseworker, she gives me a hard time. I do not sit at home waiting for a check. I go to school for my GED and at the same time I am looking for a job. It is not easy for me. I am a recovering alcoholic. I have four years of sobriety and I'm working hard to keep it.

Sincerely yours,
Denise

WELFARE BILL OF RIGHTS

1. THE RIGHT to be a member of a welfare rights organization.
2. THE RIGHT to fair and equal treatment, free from discrimination based on race, gender, religion, or sexual preference.
3. THE RIGHT to apply for any welfare program in writing.
4. THE RIGHT to have the welfare department make a decision promptly after application for aid.
5. THE RIGHT to be told in writing the specific reason for any denial of aid.
6. THE RIGHT to a hearing before your check can be reduced or cut off and before your medical aid is affected.
7. THE RIGHT to appeal a denial of aid and to be given a fair hearing before an impartial hearing officer.
8. THE RIGHT to get welfare payments without being forced to spend the money as the welfare department wants.
9. THE RIGHT to be treated with respect.
10. THE RIGHT to receive welfare aid without having the welfare department ask you questions about who your social friends are (such as who you are going out with).
11. THE RIGHT to the same constitutional protections that all other persons in the United States have.
12. THE RIGHT to be told and informed by the welfare department of all of your rights, including the way you can best make sure that you can get welfare money.
13. THE RIGHT to have, to get, and to give advice during all contacts with the welfare department, including when applying, when being investigated, and during fair hearings.

Originally published by the National Association of Welfare Rights Organizations (1970).

CAN YOU MAKE ENDS MEET ON WELFARE?

Here is a list of expenses that many people have. Put a check mark next to the expenses you have. Write down any expenses you have that are not on the list.

HOME
rent _____
electric _____
gas _____
water _____
phone _____
_____
_____

FOOD
food shopping _____
restaurants _____
take-out _____
_____
_____

CLOTHING
clothes shopping _____
laundry _____
dry cleaning _____
_____
_____

MEDICAL
doctor _____
dentist _____
prescription drugs _____
hospital _____
_____
_____

TRANSPORTATION
bus _____
subway _____
carfare _____
car maintenance _____
_____
_____

CHILDREN
child care _____
diapers _____
toys _____
_____
_____

SCHOOL
supplies _____
books _____
_____
_____

ENTERTAINMENT
movies _____
videos _____
music _____
sports _____
cable _____
magazines _____
_____

PERSONAL
pocket money _____
allowances _____
cigarettes _____
hair care _____
toiletries _____
_____
_____

OTHER
_____
_____
_____
_____
_____

Now that you've checked off the things you spend money on, estimate how much you need per month for each group of items and write down the amounts in Column B below. When you are finished, add up all the amounts in Column B and write down the total on line 12.

A EXPENSES	B AMOUNT NEEDED PER MONTH
1. HOME	$
2. FOOD	$
3. CLOTHING	$
4. MEDICAL	$
5. TRANSPORTATION	$
6. CHILDREN	$
7. SCHOOL	$
8. ENTERTAINMENT	$
9. PERSONAL	$
10. OTHER	$
11.	$
12. **TOTAL AMOUNT**	$

1. How many people are in your household? _____

2. Look at the chart below. Based on that chart, how much would your household get in public assistance and food stamps each months?

$ _____

3. Look at the amount you need to cover your monthly expenses from line 12. Compare this to how much you would get in welfare from question 2. Which amount is greater?

$ _____

4. What is the difference between the amount you need each month and the amount you would get in welfare payments?

$ _____

Monthly Welfare Grants by Household Size for New York City

	HOUSEHOLD SIZE							
	1	2	3	4	5	6	7	8
PA	$352	$468	$577	$687	$ 800	$ 884	$1010	$1101
FS	$112	$178	$239	$290	$ 332	$ 400	$ 422	$ 483
Total	$464	$646	$816	$977	$1132	$1284	$1432	$1584

PA = Public Assistance Grant
FS = Food Stamps

Questions for Discussion or Writing

1. Some politicians say that people on welfare are taking advantage of the system and using taxpayers' money to live "high on the hog." Do you think this is fair and truthful? What would you say to these politicians if you had the chance? How could you use your answers above to support your argument?

2. If people on welfare really aren't getting enough to meet their needs, why do you think some politicians say that they are getting too much? Why do you think the media (television, newspapers) don't seem to question what the politicians say?

3. What do you think are some things people on welfare do to make ends meet?

Suggested Activities

1. Interview a friend or relative who is on welfare and find out how they make ends meet.

2. Do a research project on making ends meet with food stamps in different neighborhoods. Cut out supermarket ads from different stores and see which neighborhoods have more bargains. Visit stores and compare food prices in poor and wealthy neighborhoods. Which neighborhoods have twenty-four-hour stores? How safe and clean are the stores? Which neighborhoods have stores that accept food stamps? How many stores are in the different neighborhoods?

21—Teaching for Change

Deborah Stern

Eight years ago I started teaching at Prologue Alternative High School in uptown Chicago. Prologue is a last-chance school for teenagers who have been classified as "unteachable" in public school. As my students began to talk and write about their own lives, it became apparent that they were in no way unteachable. Although they were dissatisfied and disaffected by school, they had learned plenty, in school and on the streets.

The problem was that their "street smarts" were important only to my students themselves. Teachers and administrators generally regarded students' expertise—i.e., their experiences negotiating violence, racial stereotyping, and the legal system—as distracting handicaps. My students had been exhorted to rise above their unfortunate circumstances and to attend to the skill deficiencies which were impeding their progress in school. Although it is true that many of my students had poor basic skills, the students who could read and write well also felt disconnected from school. They seemed to have dismissed it as irrelevant to the true business of life: survival.

They lived with poverty, danger, teen motherhood, incarceration, and the certainty that life was not going to get easier as they got older. If I was going to help these teenagers, we would have to focus on both academic and life skills. We needed to create a learning environment where students' experiences mattered, where they could speak freely about their concerns and fears, and where they could begin to unlearn some of the passivity each of them connected with being "a good student." This was my mandate: to wake each student to the possibility of genuine personal change. If they believed they could create a better world in the classroom, they might come to believe that they could create a better world outside it.

We worked toward this goal by "cocreating" a student-centered curriculum. In English classes this meant that we studied themes and issues suggested by students. These units of instruction were supported by student input at every stage of planning and implementation. Students determined which key issues should be addressed in the unit. They brought in materials (usually pop songs and videos) which illustrated these key issues.

Students generated questions for discussion and rubrics by which we could evaluate individual progress and the overall effectiveness of the unit.

How did these lessons change students individually? How might our classroom activities engender social change? First, my students learned new, active roles as they participated in this fully collaborative, democratic process of curriculum creation. Further, in each of our thematic units, students learned what it feels like to practice socially responsible behaviors. By gaining awareness of differing social realities, they saw their own circumstances in context and began to redefine some of their personal goals and values. Through a close examination of life choices, they questioned and took responsibility for one another. Always, they taught each other.

GAINING AWARENESS OF DIFFERING SOCIAL REALITIES

When my students chose to study "Education," they were eager to tell stories and complain about their past experiences. They relished the thought of indicting their former teachers and administrators in journal entries and class discussions. I had other, more political objectives: Could I show students how to look at their own educational experiences critically? Could I help them get some perspective on the fact that the most familiar institution in their lives had classified them as "throwaways"? Could I help students see the relationship between economic status, educational opportunity, and power?

We began the unit by studying phenomena such as "lowered expectations" and "educational bias." We read fiction and nonfiction, and students wrote about their own struggles and successes in the classroom. We ended the unit by conducting video interviews. One class generated a list of interview questions that included the following:

1. Do you think you learn anything in classes? Do you think the teachers care?
2. What's the average number of students in each of your classes?
3. What is the racial makeup of your school?
4. What conditions are the facilities (gym, library, computers) in?

5. How often do you cut classes?
6. Do you want your children to have the same education you have had?
7. Given your education, where do you think you will be in ten years?

Students interviewed each other about their public school experiences, telling stories of sleeping teachers, chaotic classrooms, school libraries with "no good books left"—generally, of being left on their own, to get what they chose to get from school. Few admitted they had learned anything worthwhile. I wanted them to understand why they had been able to skip so many classes. I wanted them to demand more from their future educational endeavors. They needed and deserved to see that not every school experience mirrored their own.

I assigned excerpts from Jonathan Kozol's *Savage Inequalities* (51–74), which detail and compare the various services and resources available to schools in affluent and poor communities. I supplemented the excerpts from Kozol with copies of a school newspaper, a recent annual report, and a calendar from Niles North High School, in Skokie, Illinois, a prosperous suburban community just north of Chicago.

We brought the video camera to Niles North one afternoon and interviewed a few Niles students for our documentary-in-progress. Prologue students gained exposure to a whole other world there. Although they spent some time gawking at the plush facilities, most of their attention was given to the Niles seniors' interview responses. These students were full of excitement about college and were able to reflect fondly on their twelve years in school.

The resources and opportunities students received at Niles contrasted starkly with those offered to my students by their own public schools and by Prologue. Unlike Prologue students (none of whom wanted their children's education to be like their own), each Niles student expressed the hope that their kids could have "everything I had in school."

When we showed the finished video at an all-school assembly, my students led a thoughtful, humorous discussion which touched on opportunity, inequality, achievement, and individual initiative. This unit engaged students in an analysis of their own experiences, showed them how these experiences compared with and related to other social realities, and informed their hopes for themselves and their children.

ANALYZING LIFE CHOICES

One year my students said they wanted to study the following topics: cults, gangs, religious fundamentalism, the KKK, and the military. These were separate suggestions, but I recognized common themes—the subjugation of individual will to a "greater" goal, and the power of indoctrination. How could I help students recognize what these ideologies had in common? I wanted my students to think critically about their own choices and about the choices facing the (mostly disenfranchised) adults in our communities. But I could not preach to them. If I did, I immediately set up that familiar, dysfunctional dynamic: I know, they don't. I'm right, they're wrong.

Instead, I would have to begin by using student life as text. We discussed the different kinds of demands made on all of us by parents, friends, and teachers. Students shared stories of what was expected from them as children. This led to an examination of what society expects from us as teenagers, students, boyfriends, girlfriends, Americans. From there, we moved to sacrifice. What should we be willing to give up, if we are asked? Students were arranged in small groups and told to try to reach consensus on issues such as those presented in the box below.

Students struggled to articulate their values and challenged each other on their responses to statements regarding sacrifice. Upon reflection, students began to question some of the affiliations and expectations they had previously accepted. We continued our examination of the uniquely human search for significance, for answers, for something to give our lives meaning. We read poetry (e.e. cummings, "pity this busy monster"), fiction and nonfiction (Yukio Mishima, "Patriotism" and Luis Rodriguez, *La Vida Loca: Gang Days in L.A.*) and viewed selected videos (*Born on the Fourth of July*).

Our most provocative reading was an interview with an L.A. gangbanger named Racketeer, which had been reprinted in *Harper's* magazine. In this short interview, we learned that Racketeer does not expect or want anything from life but violence; he unsentimentally predicts his own murder within the next ten years.

I divided students into groups and asked them to create questions about Racketeer's attitude. Here are a few of these student-written questions:

1. If you're a Crip or a Blood is that the same as being in a war? Is it the same as being in the army?
2. Is Racketeer very loyal or very stupid?
3. Do you think it's "worth it" for Racketeer to belong to the Crips? If you say he doesn't have a choice, what are you really saying?

These questions and their written responses displayed students' developing critical faculties. Because we read this piece at the end of the unit, they were able to evaluate Racketeer's blind devotion to his gang. One young woman wrote:

"Racketeer is wasting his life. He may think he is really down with his set [devoted to his fellow gang members and to the gang itself], but he is wrong to give all that. What is he getting from it? Nothing but dead, which is a shame. He ought to be able to see that being asked to give up your whole life when your young and just starting to live your whole life is ridiculous. The only thing worth sacrificing your life for is something you love. His sacrifice is self-destructive. And there is no love in killing your brothers, 'cause that's what they are."

Students then wrote in their journals about the systems they'd been offered to explain, rectify, or save them from injustices of the world. Some wrote about religion. Some wrote about drugs. Despite the class's collective rejection of Racketeer, some wrote about the gang as family. All students struggled to understand their choices and were compelled to evaluate them in reference to a larger social context. We ended the unit by generating the following list of key questions about joining an organization:

1. What do you hope you will get?
2. What are you being asked to give up?
3. Who is in it with you? Are they being asked to give up the same thing?
4. How will you know if your sacrifice turns self-destructive?

Students had started this unit (we called it False Gods) with casual curiosity about systems of social control. Not only did they learn how to analyze these systems critically, they made sure that everyone in the class was able to recognize the telltale signs of a restrictive ideology. By ending the unit with this sort of defensive checklist, students affirmed their belief in themselves and their concern for each other.

TEACHING EACH OTHER

Clearly, even disaffected students can be interested in instruction if they determine it is of value to them. As their belief in the relevance of the subject increases, so can their investment in what is taught and how. When my students said they wanted to study AIDS (which they do every year), I knew student leaders would arise within the class. Sometimes students who are the most resistant initially become the most zealous peer educators. One seventeen-year-old boy began by warning me, "No way am I gonna sit and listen to someone who's got it. It ain't my problem. I'll be absent." After a few weeks, this same student wrote, "The youth of the world need to know about this disease!" and braved peer pressure to lead an all-school discussion about AIDS.

We established operational guidelines: respect, honesty, and compassion. After a week or two of teacher-led, mostly informational sessions, my students worked in groups preparing role plays, discussion questions, and original plays to share with their peers in and out of the classroom. Even students who had been reluctant to work in small groups before were eager to collaborate with peers during the AIDS unit. They welcomed the chance to express "the truth" about teens, sex, and drugs. I found students to be most forthright, responsible, and mature when I trusted them—that is, when I kept out of this creative work.

In teams, students planned activities that would highlight the real-life situations that put teens at risk for AIDS. They collected information about sexuality, birth control, HIV testing, substance abuse, counseling, crisis hot lines, and other issues related to AIDS. As students led peer education sessions, they were seen as credible, powerful role models by other Prologue students. Together, all students learned the facts, unlearned their prejudices, and engaged in candid discussions.

Peer educators began with a discussion of myths associated with AIDS. After this brief presentation, they moved on to risk taking in general. Why do people take risks? What kinds of risks do teenagers take? Do boys and girls usually like to take the same types of risks? What kinds of risks do individual students in the class enjoy? What puts teens at risk for HIV?

Students were then divided into small, single-sex groups of four or five. Based on their own experiences, each group wrote out a short, detailed description of a typical social evening for a typical male or female teenager, from pre-party preparations to post-party behavior. When groups finished writing and reading aloud their descriptions, the class identified certain actions or attributes as dangerous (provocative clothing, drug use, or aggressive behavior) and discussed why these put the teenager at risk.

One group of girls wrote the following scenario. They underlined the risks, and then we analyzed them as a class:

"Mercedes got ready by putting on her *leather miniskirt and sheer blouse and red high heels*. She did her hair and makeup and her friend, Denise came to pick her up in her boyfriend mother car. She *didn't have a drivers liesen* [license] but the party was close by and her *boyfriend would take care of both of them*. She handed Mercedes a *half a joint* and they drove to the party at the party the lights were low and this one boy that Mercedes had been liking came up to her with a 40. He looked at her in her hot outfit and they *drinking* out of the same bottle together and *dancing real slow*."

The class concluded that her clothes, the joint, and the alcohol put Mercedes in danger of having unprotected sex and thus being at risk for HIV infection.

In other sessions, students acted out plays they wrote themselves, and then the actors led discussions, asking questions like, "What would you have done in my situation?" Another effective instructional technique is for the teacher to prepare a script, have the class act it out, and then ask the class to discuss what worked, what didn't work, and how they would change the scene to reflect more accurately the reality they knew.

In these activities, Prologue students came to see themselves as powerful, valid sources of knowledge and experience. They worked together to create an exciting learning environment which was grounded in their own realities. They learned to recognize and evaluate the barriers which separate all of us according to class and race, lifestyle and geography.

Here in Chicago, in 1995, no teacher has to tell a teenager that we need drastic social change. The most useful thing we can do is help each student believe in change itself. As a classroom teacher, I cannot really know if or how these lessons and my students will change the world. What I do know is that my students at Prologue took part in creating a new classroom dynamic. They came to know what it's like to be in control of their own educations, and what it feels like to enrich others' learning. They wrestled with the responsibility inherent in this democratic experience. They changed themselves.

REFERENCES

Bing, L. 1988. Confessions of a Gangbanger. *Harpers,* 277(1659): 26. *Born on the Fourth of July.* 1989. UIP/Ixtlan.

cummings, e. e. 1972. pity this busy monster. *Complete Poems 1913–1962.* New York: Harcourt, Brace, Jovanovich.

Kozol, J. 1991. *Savage Inequalities.* New York: Crown Publishers.

Mishima, Y. 1966. Patriotism. *Death in Midsummer and Other Stories.* New York: New Directions.

Rodriguez, L. 1993. *Always Running: Gang Days In LA—La Vida Loca.* Willamantic, Conn.: Curbstone Press.

OPINIONNAIRE: WHAT WILL YOU SACRIFICE?

Complete this partial list of things that we are supposed to be willing to sacrifice in various roles and situations:

1. "**Citizens** should be willing to give up MONEY, _____ , and _____ for their country."

2. "**A friend** should be willing to give up _____ , _____ , and _____ for his or her friend."

3. "**A woman** should be willing to give up _____ , _____ , and _____ for her _____ ."

4. "**A man** should be willing to give up _____ , _____ , and _____ for his _____ ."

—Afterword
Some Reflections on Teaching for Social Justice

Herbert Kohl

The idea that you have to advocate teaching for social justice is a sad statement about the state of moral sensibility in our schools and society. I remember one of my elementary school students who was involved in a civil rights demonstration saying, "You know, Mr. Kohl, you can get arrested for stirring up justice." You can also be fired as a teacher for stirring up ideas and provoking conversations that challenge privilege and try to make issues of democracy and equity work in the everyday life of the classroom. The problem is that many people do not believe that justice is a value worth fighting for. Sadly, this applies as much to children as it does to adults. One cannot simply assume that because an action or sentiment is just, fair, or compassionate that it will be popular or embraced. At this moment in our history, there are many sanctions for the idea that self-interest overrides communal sanity and compassion. The enemy of teaching for social justice is "The Real World," which is characterized as hard, competitive, and unrelenting in its pursuit of personal gain and perpetuation of bias and institutional and economic inequities.

So what are social justice teachers—that is one who cares about nurturing all children and is enraged at the prospects of any of her or his students dying young, being hungry, or living meaningless and despairing lives—to do in the classroom so that they go against the grain and work in the service of their students?

I have several suggestions, some pedagogical and some personal. First of all, don't teach against your conscience or align yourself with texts, people, and rules that hurt children. Resist in as creative a way as you can, through humor, developing and using alternatives, and organizing for social and educational change with others who feel as you do. Don't become isolated or alone in your efforts. Reach out to other teachers, to community leaders, church people, parents. Try to survive, but don't make your survival in a particular job the overriding determinant of what you will or won't do. Find a school where you can do your work, risk getting fired and stand up for the quality of your work. Don't quit in the face of opposition: make people work hard if they intend to fire you for teaching equity and justice.

However, in order to do this you must hone your craft as a teacher. I remember trying to jump into struggles for social justice when I first began teaching. During one of my earliest efforts someone in the community asked: "So, what's going on in your classroom that's different than what you're fighting against? Can your students read and do math?" I had to pause and examine my work, which was full of passion and effort but deficient in craft. I needed the time to learn how to teach well before extending myself with the authority and confidence that might lead to sustained change. This is essential for caring teachers—you have to get it right for your own students before presuming to take on larger systems, no matter how terrible they are. As educators we need to root our struggles for social justice in the work we do on an everyday level in a particular community with a particular group of students.

I believe there is no single way to teach well, no single technique or curriculum that leads to success. Consequently, a third piece of advice I would give teachers is to look around at everything other people say is effective with children. Pick and choose, retool and restructure the best of what you find, make it your own, and most of all watch your students and see what works. Listen to them, observe how they learn, and then, based on your experience and their responses, figure out how to practice social justice in your classroom as you discuss and analyze it.

Teaching is fundamentally a moral craft and makes the same demands on our sensibilities, values, and energies that any moral calling does. That means, in a society where there is too much institutionalized inequity and daily suffering, you have to understand the importance of being part of larger struggles. It is not enough to teach well and create a social justice classroom separate from the larger community. You have to be a community activist as well, a good parent, a decent citizen, an active community member. Is all of this possible? Probably not—certainly it isn't easy and often demands sacrifices. Believing that all children can learn can be a blessing in your own classroom and unleash your creativity. It can transform angry and resistant students into challenging, creative, funny, loving learners. It can also get you in trouble with your supervisors for creating new expectations for other teachers who might be failing or unwilling to put the energy and love into their work that you somehow call up. And at the end of the day it might also make you sad because there is so much more that needs to be done, so many students who don't even have the advantage of a decent classroom and a caring teacher.

This leads to my final suggestion. Protect and nurture yourself, have some fun in your life, learn new things that only obliquely relate to issues of social justice. Walk, play ball or chess, swim, fall in love and give yourself in love with joy and fullness to someone else. Don't forget how to laugh or feel good about the world. Sing with others, tell stories and listen to other people's stories, have fun so that you can work hard and work hard so that you and your students and their parents can have fun without looking over their shoulders. This is not a question of selfishness but one of survival. Don't turn teaching for social justice into a grim responsibility but take it for the moral and social necessity that it is. And don't be afraid to struggle for what you believe.

—An Activist Forum V: Racing Justice

Michele Foster

Michele Foster, courtesy of
Lensart Studio

Prior to emancipation, blacks held in slavery were forbidden to learn to read. Despite prohibitions and severe punishment, blacks valued literacy and many learned to read. Some were taught by sympathetic whites; others learned alongside their master's children. But a significant number were taught by free blacks or by slaves who were literate themselves. Well regarded and respected, these black teachers understood about the power and danger associated with literacy. Leroy Lovelace, a retired high school English teacher, underscores the power of education: "When a people can think critically, they can change things. They are less likely to be taken advantage of and more likely to be able to avoid the traps that others set for us. An uneducated people can be taken advantage of because of their ignorance or naïveté."

Leonard Collins, a young teacher, is even more adamant: "I want kids to examine their world critically, to question everything. As kids get older they automatically accept the American ideology. But I don't want kids to just be the future; I want them to change the future."

Quoting James Baldwin, Edourard Plummer, a New York junior high school teacher who has taught since the early sixties declares: "Teaching black children is a revolutionary act."

"As black teachers we have got to make our presence felt. We owe it to black children to speak up on their behalf and to keep the other teachers honest," says Pamela Ogonu.

Perhaps it was W. E .B. Du Bois, a pragmatist, who although he remained steadfastly committed to a desegregated society throughout his lifetime, best summarized the situation:

> and I know that race prejudice in the United States today is such that most Negroes cannot receive proper education in white institutions . . . If the public schools of Atlanta, Nashville, New Orleans, and Jacksonville were thrown open to all races today, the education that colored children would get in them would be worse than pitiable. And in the same way, there are many public school systems in the North were Negroes are admitted and tolerated, but they are not educated; they are crucified. To sum up this: theoretically, the Negro needs neither separate nor mixed schools. What he needs is Education. What he must remember is that there is no magic either in mixed schools or segregated schools. A mixed school with poor unsympathetic teachers, with hostile public opinion, and no teaching of the truth concerning black folk is bad. A segregated school with ignorant placeholders, inadequate equipment, and poor salaries is equally bad. Other things being equal, the mixed schools is the broader, more natural basis for the education of all youth. It gives wider contacts; it inspires greater self-confidence, and suppresses the inferiority complex. But other things seldom are equal, and in that case, Sympathy, Knowledge, and the Truth outweigh all that the mixed school can offer.
>
> W. E. B. DuBois, "Does the Negro Need Separate Schools?" *Journal of Negro Education*, 4 July 1935, pp. 328–35

Henry Giroux

Henry Giroux, courtesy of *Democracy and Education*

Social justice has always had a profound connection to education. It has inspired theorists as different as John Dewey, Paulo Freire, and Raymond Williams. Moreover, the notion that learning and persuasion must be rooted in eliminating social injustices as well as in creating pedagogical practices that help students to imagine a different and better world has motivated a wide range of social movements. But the relevance of making social justice a necessary part of education in part depends on the nature of the contexts, content, and problems educators address and on their willingness to enter into such challenges less as a journey into sacred theoretical ground than as ongoing critical practice open to humility, compassion, and the willingness to take risks in concert with others in order to make democracy a viable aspect of education as the practice of freedom. If social justice is to become a part of educational work, we need to address some important issues.

First, the issue of struggling to create a viable substantive democracy must be located at the center of any pedagogy of social justice. By addressing radical democracy as a political, social, and ethical referent for rethinking how students can be educated to deal with a world made up of different, multiple, and fractured public cultures, teachers can begin to confront the necessity for constructing a new ethical and political language to map the problems and challenges facing America at the end of the twentieth century. Second, we need a new language to make youth in all its diversity a central focus for addressing how we take up the relationship between social justice and democracy. Youth have increasingly been left out of discussions about democracy, rights, justice, and compassion. As educators, we need to create spaces for youth to speak, represent themselves, and organize. In part, this means progressive educators need to become more sufficiently attentive to connecting the concerns of youth with the language of ethics, agency, power, and identity as part of a wider revitalization of democratic public life. Moreover, as progressive educators we need to become more alert to developing new theoretical frameworks for challenging the way we think about the dynamics and effects of cultural and institutional power. We need to study both texts and institutions. This suggests addressing the issue of radical democracy as part of a wider discourse of rights, political economy, and social policy. In addition, progressive educators must ground their work in social relations tempered by humility, a moral focus on suffering, and the need to produce alternative visions and policies that go beyond a language of critique. Social justice in the curriculum must be rooted in a sense of hope, connected to the future, solidarity with others, and a willingness to fight for what one believes in. Last but not least, social justice can frame our work as educators only to the degree that it connects with the experiences and histories of the students we teach and work with. Crucial here is the ongoing necessity of understanding how youth are being transformed within popular cultural spheres structured by the new technologies of images, sounds, and print. Schools need to connect with popular culture so as to both affirm the cultures that shape everyday life and engage them as an important site for learning.

Gloria Ladson-Billings

Gloria Ladson-Billings, courtesy of
Democracy and Education

No challenge has been more daunting than that of improving the academic achievement of African American students. Burdened with a history that includes the denial of education, separate and unequal education, and relegation to unsafe, substandard inner-city schools, the quest for quality education remains an elusive dream for the African American community. However, it does remain a dream—perhaps the most powerful one for people of African descent in this nation.

Perceived as the most direct avenue to the realization of the dream, education and access to schooling have been cherished privileges among African Americans. Slaves were not allowed to learn to read or be educated, and this has underscored the possibility and power of education for liberation. The chronicle of the civil rights movement in the United States illustrates the centrality of education to the fight of African Americans for equal opportunity and full citizenship. Thus, Central High School in Little Rock, Arkansas; the University of Mississippi; the University of Alabama; the Boston Public Schools; Brownsville, New York, all symbolize the willingness of African Americans to sacrifice all for the sake of education.

Jonathan Kozol

Jonathan Kozol, courtesy of Harvey Wang

It certainly can't be good for American competitiveness to have millions of people who are at very marginal or low literacy levels, because there aren't many jobs left that require only limited literacy. For years now I have done what many other advocates have done in areas of housing, education, health care—essentially to say to business interests in America, "This issue is important because it's costing you money, and that's why you should deal with it."

I still think in the long run that's true. But I think of it as an unworthy argument which debases the one who makes it and the one who hears it, because the reason we should deal with injustice is because it's not just, not because it's expensive. The best reason to give a child a good school with a teacher who is confident enough to be relaxed and pleasant in a cheerful building with a great playing field outside is so that child will have a happy childhood, and not so that it will help IBM in competing with Sony, or GM in competing with Toyota. I think the argument is a legitimate one, but there is something ethically embarrassing about resting a national agenda on the basis of sheer greed. It's more important in the long run, more true to the American character at its best, to lodge the argument in terms of simple justice.

Michael Apple

Michael Apple, courtesy of *Democracy and Education*

This is a time of conservative restoration. What education is for, how it should be carried out, who benefits from it—all of this is in danger of being radically reconstructed as arrogant rightist movements make it ever more difficult for an education worthy of its name actually to go on in schools. Because of this, it seems to me that it is crucial that our teaching focus on situating our educational activities within the larger social context in which they are found. Thus, our colleagues and students need to recognize who is being helped and hurt by the push to privatize education, the pressure to return to an utterly romanticized (and often racist) view of the "Western tradition," the push to redefine education's goals into those defined by corporate America or to reduce all content down to atomistic facts that will supposedly make us "culturally literate."

Although a recognition of this is critically important, this is not enough. We also need to know what is actually going on throughout this country in the many schools where educators, community activists, students, and others are keeping alive the very real possibilities of an education that is pedagogically progressive and socially critical. There are public schools that *now* work to do exactly this, even in economically distressing circumstances. These stories of successful schools, with their progressive and critical curricula and teaching, need to be shared and made public. It is this combination of criticism of the rightist reconstruction we are experiencing and the stories of real folks doing something about it that can make a difference.

—Resources

RESOURCES FOR TEACHING FOR CHANGE

Books

A Different Mirror: A History of Multicultural America, by Ronald Takaki, Little, Brown and Company, 1993.

A People's History of the United States, Abridged Teaching Edition, by Howard Zinn, The New Press, 1997.

Always Running: Gang Days in LA—La Vida Loca, by Luis J. Rodriguez, Curbstone Press, 1993.

An Anthology in the First Person, by Bart Schneider, Crown Trade Paperbacks, 1997.

Beyond Silenced Voices: Class, Race, and Gender in United States Schools ed. by Lois Weis and Michelle Fine. State University of New York Press, 1993.

Black Teachers on Teaching, by Michele Foster, The New Press, 1996.

Bone Black, by bell hooks. Henry Holt and Co. 1996.

Changing The Educational Landscape, by Jane Roland Martin, Routledge New York–London, 1994.

Crazy for Democracy: Women in Grassroots Movements, by Temma Kaplan, Routledge New York–London, 1997.

Critical White Studies: Looking Beyond the Mirror ed. by Richard Delgado and Jean Stefancic. Temple University Press, 1997.

Dead Man Walking, by Sister Helen Prejean, Random House, 1993.

Deculturalization and the Struggle for Equality: A Brief History of the Education of Dominated Cultures in the United States, by Joel Spring, McGraw-Hill, 1994.

Divided Sisters: Bridging the Gap Between Black Women & White Women, by Midge Wilson and Kathy Russell, Anchor Books, 1996.

Dreams From My Father, by Barack Obama, Times Books, 1995.

Education and Power, by M. W. Apple, Routledge, 1985.

Education, Democracy and Public Knowledge, by E. A. Kelly, Crown Publishers Inc., 1994.

Everyday Acts Against Racism, by Maureen T. Reddy, Seal Press, 1996.

Everyday Acts Against Racism: Raisng Children in a Multiracial World, by Maureen T. Reddy, Seal Press Feminist Pub., 1996.

Faces at the Bottom of the Well: The Permanence of Racism, by Derrick Bell, Basic Books Press, 1993.

Facing Racism in Education (Harvard Educational Review Reprint Series, No 21), by Nitza M. Hidalgo, Harvard Educational Press, 1989.

Growing Up Gay/Growing Up Lesbian: A Literary Anthology ed. by Bennett L. Singer. The New Press, 1994.

Homophobia: A Weapon of Sexism, by Suzanne Pharr, Women's Project, 1988.

I Am Who I Am: Speaking Out About Multiracial Identity, by Kathlyn Gay, Franklin Watts Press, 1995.

I Answer with My Life: Life Histories of Women Teachers Working for Social Change, by Kathleen Casey, Routledge, 1993.

"I Won't Learn from You" And Other Thoughts on Creative Maladjustment, by Herbert Kohl, The New Press, 1994.

Incidents in the Life of a Slave Girl, by Harriet A. Jacobs, Harvard University Press, 1987.

Kwanzaa and Me: A Teacher's Story, by Vivian Paley, Harvard University Press, 1995.

Letters to Marcia: A Teacher's Guide to Anti-Racist Education, by Enid Lea, Cross Cultural Communications Center, 1985.

Lies My Teacher Told Me, by James W. Loewen, New Press, 1995.

Long Walk to Freedom, by Nelson Mandela, Little, Brown and Company, 1994.

Making It: Black Youth, Racism and Career Aspirations in a Big City, by Carl E. James, Masaic Press, 1992.

Nixon's Piano, by Kenneth O'Reilly, The Free Press, 1995.

Off White: Readings on Race, Power, and Society, by Michele Fine, Lois Weis, Linda C. Powell, L. Mun Wong, Routledge, 1997.

One Teacher in 10: Gay and Lesbian Educators Tell Their Stories, by Kevin Jennings, 1st edition, Alyson Publications, 1994.

Poisoned Ivy: Lesbian and Gay Academics Confronting Homophobia, by Toni H. McNaron, Temple University Press, 1997.

Race: An Anthology in the First Person, ed. by Bart Schneider. Random House, 1997.

Race Matters, by Cornel West, Beacon Press, 1993.

Rethinking Schools: An Agenda for Change, eds. David Levine, Robert Lowe, Bob Peterson, and Rita Tenorio, The New Press, 1995.

School Girls, by Peggy Orenstein, Anchor Books Doubleday, 1994.

Teaching as a Subversive Activity, by Neil Postman and Charles Weingarter, Delta, 1969.

Teaching for Diversity and Social Justice: A Sourcebook, ed. by Maurienne Adams, Lee Anne Bell, and Pat Griffin, Routledge, 1997.

Teaching/Learning Anti-Racism: A Developmental Approach by Louise Derman-Sparks and Carol Brunson Phillips, Teachers College Press, 1997.

Teaching Stories, by Judy Logan. Kodansha America, 1997.

Teaching Tolerance: Raising Open Minded, Empathic Children, by Sara Bullard, Doubleday, 1996.

The Gay Teen: Educational Practice and Theory for Lesbian, Gay, and Bisexual Adolescents, edited by Gerald Unks, Routledge, New York, 1995.

The Girl With the Brown Crayon, by Vivian Gussin Paley, Harvard University Press, 1997.

Too Much Schooling, Too Little Education: A Paradox of Black life in White Societies, by M. J. Shujaa, Africa World Press, Inc., 1994.

Waging Peace in Our Schools, by Linda Lantieri and Janet Patti, foreword by Marian Wright Edelman, Beacon Press, 1996.

Classroom Resources

Anti-Bias Curriculum: Tools for Empowering Young Children, by Louise Derman-Sparks and the A.B.C. Task Force, National Association for Education of Young Children, 1989.

Beyond Heroes and Holidays: A Practical Guide to K-12 Anti-Racist, Multicultural Education and Staff Development, eds. Enid Lee, Debra Menkart, and Margo Okazawa-Rey. Network of Educators on the Americas, 1998.

Early Violence Prevention: Tools for Teachers of Young Children, by Ronald G. Slaby, Wendy C. Roedell, Diana Arezzo, and Kate Hendrix, National Association for the Education of Young Children, 1995.

Freedom Fighters: Affective Teaching of the Language Arts, 2 E.,by Nancy Lee Cecil, Sheffield Publishing Company, 1994.

Freedom's Unfinished Revolution: An Inquiry into the Civil War and Reconstruction, foreword by Eric Foner. The New Press, 1996.

Integrating Socially: Planning Integrated Units of Work for Social Education, by Julie Hamston and Kath Murdoch, Heinemann, 1996.

Kids Explore America's Heritage, series written by Westridge Young Writer's Workshop, John Muir Publications, Santa Fe, New Mexico—Books in this series include Hispanic Heritage, Japanese American Heritage, Western Native Americans, and African Americans.

Making the Peace: A 15-Session Violence Prevention Curriculum for Young People, by Paul Kival and Allan Creighton. Hunter House. 1997.

Multicultural Resources for Young Readers, by Daphne Muse. The New Press, 1997.

Starting Small: Teaching Tolerance in Preschool and the Early Grades, by the Teaching Tolerance Project. Southern Poverty Law Center, 1997.

The People's Multicultural Almanac: America from the 1400's to Present, The People's Publishing Group, Inc., 1994.

Teaching for Success: Strengthening Child-Centered Classrooms, by Jim Grant, Bob Johnson, and Irv Richardson, Crystal Springs Books, 1995.

Teaching Young Children in Violent Times: Building A Peaceable Classroom, by Diane Levin, Educators for Social Responsibility, 1994.

When I Was Young I Loved School: Dropping Out and Hanging In, by Children's Express, eds. Anne Sheffield and Bruce Frankel, Children's Express Foundation, 1989.

Words Can Hurt You: Beginning a Program of Anti-Bias Education, by Barbara J. Thomson, Addison-Wesley, 1993.

Organizations

COLAGE
Children of Lesbians and Gays Everywhere
2300 Market St., #165
San Francisco, CA 94114 USA
Phone (415) 861-5437

Fax (415) 255-8345
email: colage@colage.org
website: http://www.colage.org

Since 1990, COLAGE has worked for the daughters and sons of lesbian, gay, bisexual, and transgendered parents of all racial, ethnic, and class backrounds. The organization produces a resource-filled newsletter and maintains a website and email discussion lists for youth of various ages.

P-FLAG
Federation of Parents and Friends of
Lesbians and Gays, National Office
1101 14th Street NW, Suite 1030
Washington, DC 20005
Phone (202) 638-4200
Fax (202) 638-4200
email: info@pflag.org
website: www.pflag.org

P-FLAG promotes the health and well-being of lesbian, gay, and bisexual persons, their families and friends through support, education, and advocacy.

Institute for Democracy in Education
Ohio University
McCracken Hall Rm. 313
Athens, OH 45701-2979
Phone (614) 593-4531

IDE is a partnership of all participants in the educational process—teachers, administrators, parents and students—who believe that democratic school change must come from the heart of education. *Democracy & Education* is the main editorial outlet of IDE which also sponsors conferences and workshops.

Educators for Social Responsibility (ESR)
23 Garden Street
Cambridge, MA 02138
Phone (617) 492-1764
Fax (617) 864-5164
email: esrmain@igc.apc.org

ESR's primary mission is to help young people develop the convictions and skills to shape a safe, sustainable, and just world.

The Society for Developmental Education (SDE)
Ten Sharon Rd.
PO Box 577
Peterborough, NH 03458
Phone (800) 924-9621
Fax (603) 924-6688

SDE's main objective is to support K-6 educators in creating child-centered classrooms where all children can learn and all children can succeed.

Anti-Racism Institute of Clergy Laity Concerned
77 W. Washington, Suite 1124
Chicago, IL 60602
Phone (312) 630-1960
Fax (312) 357-0991

ARI is currently embarking on a multiyear program for antiracist, multicultural educational development in schools. The goal of the initiative is to provide resources and supports to education and schools seeking to develop strategies for eliminating racism.

Northwestern University
Institute for Policy Research
2040 Sheridan Rd.
Evanston, IL 60208
Phone (847) 491-3518
Fax (847) 491-9916

The Institute for Policy Research links neighborhood organizations; community economic development groups; and public, private, and parochial educators to develop meaningful ways for schools to participate in the development of their local communities.

Chicago Metro History Education Center
60 W. Walson
Chicago, IL 60610
Phone (312) 255-3661
Fax (312) 266-8223

This organization serves as a research and action center focusing on "doing History" and transforming schools through history curriculum.

Children's Defense Fund
25 'E' Street NW
Washington, DC 20001
Phone (202) 628-8787
Fax (202) 662-3510
website: www.childrensdefense.org

Coalition for Quality Education (CQE)
1702 Upton Ave.
Toledo, OH 43607
Phone (419) 537-9246
Fax (419) 537-7102

Since 1978, CQE, whose members include parents/citizens, clergy, and educators from the Toledo area, has been a grassroots advocate for quality, equitable education; parent training and empowerment; and the development of home-school collaborations.

The Hesperian Foundation
1919 Addison Street, #304
Berkeley, CA 94704
Phone (510) 845-4507
Fax (510) 845-0539
email: hesperianfdn@igc.apc.org

The Hesperian Foundation is a nonprofit organization committed to improving the health of people in less-developed countries by providing tools and resources for informed self-care. They believe that people can and should take the lead in their own health care.

The National Association of Multicultural Education (NAME)
200 W. Baltimore St.
Baltimore, MD 21201

NAME is a grassroots organization started by educators whose aim is to create antibias classrooms for all students (pre-kindergarten through college).

National Coalition of Education Activists (NCEA)
P.O. Box 679
Rhinebeck, NY 12572
Phone (914) 876-4580
email: rfbs@aol.com

NCEA brings together parents and teachers to strengthen school reform efforts.

Network of Educators on the Americas (NECA)
PO Box 73038
Washington, DC 20056-3038
Phone (202) 238-2379
Fax (202) 238-2378
website:http://www.cldc.howard.edu/~neca/
email: necadc@aol.com

NECA is a national organization of K-12 teachers, parents, and community members which works with school communities to develop and promote teaching methods and resources for social and economic justice in the Americas.

Oxfam America
26 West St.
Boston, MA 02111
Phone (617) 482-1211
Fax (617) 728-2594
email: oxfamusa@igc.apc.org

Oxfam America is an advocate for the world's impoverished people. Its triple mandate is to create awareness of their plight, educate people about the underlying and social and political reasons for it, and take action to change it.

Southern Poverty Law Center
PO Box 548
Montgomery, AL 36101
Phone (334) 264-0268

A nonprofit legal and education foundation. Southern Poverty Law Center is a nonprofit legal and education foundation a small civil rights law firm in 1971. It is internationally known for its *Teaching Tolerance* magazine and education program, its legal victories against white supremacist groups, and its sponsorship of the Civil Rights Memorial.

The Gay, Lesbian and Straight Education Network (GLSEN)
121 W. 27th St., Suite 804
New York, NY 10001
Phone (212) 727-0135
Fax (212) 727-0254
email: glstn@glstn.org
website: http://www.glstn.org

GLSEN is a national federation of local groups working to address issues of homophobia and heterosexism in K-12 public, private, and parochial schools. GLSEN brings together gay, lesbian, bisexual, and straight teachers, parents, and concerned community members to work to create schools where all are respected.

Barrios Unidos
313 Front Street
Santa Cruz, CA 95060
Phone (408) 457-8208
Fax (408) 457-0389
email: barrios@cruzio.com

Barrios Unidos has twenty-seven chapters nationwide, convenes national peace summits for gang and nongang members, and sponsors youth programs in schools and communities.

Community Renewal Society
332 South Michigan Avenue
Suite 500
Chicago, IL 60604
Phone (312) 427-4830
Fax (312) 427-6130

CRS creates a sanctuary for young people and their elders, and works with churches to open their doors to abandoned youth.

Global Kids
561 Broadway, 6th Floor
New York, NY 10012
Phone (212) 226-0130
Fax (212) 226-0137
email: globalkids@igc.org

Global Kids prepares urban youth to become community leaders and global citizens. Academic and leadership programs help young people become aware of world issues and cultures, develop critical thinking and communicaiton and leadership skills.

Guild Complex
c/o Arts Bridge
4753 North Broadway
Suite 918
Chicago, IL 60647
Phone (773) 278-2210
Fax (773) 278-6855
email: guild@charlie.acc.iit.edu
http://www.iit.edu/~guild

An arts organization that empowers youth and addresses issues of violence prevention through literature and art.

Jobs for Future and Homeboy Industries
1848 East First Street
Los Angeles, CA 90033
Phone (213) 526-1254
Fax (213) 526-1257

An employment referral center for at-risk youths, Homeboy Industries employs former gang members, both men and women, in its three businesses: baking bread, printing designs on apparel, and selling gear featuring the Homeboy logo.

Mosaic Multicultural Foundation
PO Box 364
Vashon, WA 98070
Phone (206) 463-9387
Fax (206) 463-9235
email: mosaic@wolfenet.com

The project focuses on mentoring, rites of passage, and ways communities can use expressive arts to embrace cultural discord without resorting to violence.

National Campaign for Freedom of Expression
Western Regional Office
1402 3rd Avenue, #421
Seattle, WA 98101
Phone (206) 340-9301
Fax (206)340-4303
email: ncfe@nwlink.com

The organization defending freedom of expression nationally.

Periodicals

Bread Loaf News
A publication of The Bread Loaf School of English
Bread Loaf Office
Middlebury College
Middlebury, VT 05753
Phone (802) 443-5418

Children's Express Quarterly
30 Cooper Square, 4th floor
New York, NY 10003
Phone (212) 741-4700
Fax (212) 741-3555

A journal of writing and art by children and youth.

Choices
A publication of the Choices for the 21st Century Project.
Watson Institute for International Studies
Brown University, Box 1948
Providence, RI 02912
Phone (401) 863-2809
e-mail: www.Brown.Edu/Research.Choices

The Choices for the 21st Century Project develops curricula for high schools and colleges on current foreign-policy issues and offers workshops, institutes, and in-service programs for high school teachers. Course materials place special emphasis on the importance of educating students in their participatory role as citizens.

Closer Look
A publication of Designs for Change
220 South State St.
Suite 1900
Chicago, IL 60604

A publication working on issues surrounding Chicago school reform.

Connect
12 Brooke St.
Northcote 3070
Victoria
Australia

A journal dedicated to student participation.

Connections
A publication of the Center for Collaborative Education
1573 Madison Ave., Room 201
Phone (212) 348-7821

Connections is a journal of teacher's writing for teachers, exploring themes pertinent to their daily lives in the classroom.

Country Teacher
A publication of the National Rural Education Association (NREA)
PO Box 59
Weott, CA 95571

A journal of ideas and resources for rural teachers.

The Defense Monitor
A publication of the Center for Defense Information (CDI)
1500 Massachusetts Ave. NW
Washington, DC 20005
Phone (202) 862-0700
email cdi@igc.apc.org

CDI believes that strong social, economic, political, and military components and a healthy environment contribute equally to the nation's security. It opposes excessive expenditure for weapons and policies that increase the danger of war.

Democracy & Education
Institute for Democracy in Education
Ohio University
Athens, OH 45701

Democracy & Education is a magazine for classroom teachers published by the Institute for Democracy in Education. IDE promotes educational practices that provide students with experiences through which they can develop democratic attitudes and values.

Doing Democracy
A publication of the Center for Living Democracy
RR # 1
Fox Farm Rd.
Brattleboro, VT 05301
Phone (802) 254-1234
email: HTTP://www.Americannews.com

The Center for Living Democracy believes that "doing democracy" is a learned skill and one best carried out at the grassroots level. The center believes that ordinary citizens have a vital role in solving public problems, and that in so doing they are creating a growing "democratic revolution" in our country. The mission of the Center for Living Democracy is to encourage that everyday revolution they call Living Democracy.

Equity and Excellence in Education
The University of Massachusetts School of Education
Greenwood Publishing Group, Inc.
88 Post Road West
PO Box 5007
Westport, CT 06881-5007

Foxfire News
PO Box 541
Mountain City, GA 30562
Phone (706) 746-5828

Teachers share ideas on project-centered learning through this newsletter.

Highlander Reports
A publication of the Highlander Research and Education Center
1959 Highlander Way
New Market, TN 37820

The Holistic Education Review
39 Pearl St.
Brandon, VT 05733-1007

The Holistic Education Review aims to stimulate discussion and application of all people-centered educational ideas and methods. It is based
on the premise that human fulfillment, global cooperation, and eco-
logical responsibility should be the primary goals of education.

Horace
A publication of the Coalition of Essential Schools (CES)
Box 1969, Brown University
Providence, RI 02912

CES is a national network of schools committed to meaningful and
lasting school reform.

Journal of Ordinary Thought
Neighborhood Writing Alliance
1313 E. 59th Street
Chicago, IL 60637
Phone (773) 684-2742

JOT publishes reflections that "ordinary" people make on their personal histories and everyday experiences. JOT strives to be a vehicle
for reflection, communication, and change.

M.C.S. Sampler
Manhattan Country School
7 East 96th St.
New York, NY 10128

An occasional publication of Manhattan Country School's Public
School Outreach & Gender Equity Projects.

National Coalition News
A publication of the National Coalition of Alternative Community
    Schools
58 Schoolhouse Rd.
Summertown, TN 38483
Phone (615) 964-3670

Network
A publication of the Constitutional Rights Foundation (CRF)
601 Kingsly Dr.
Los Angeles, CA 90005
Phone (213) 487-5590

Since 1962, CRF has used education to address some of America's
most serious youth-related problems. Through a variety of civic education programs developed by CRF staff, young people prepare for
effective citizenship and learn the vital role they can play in our
society.

Pathways
Center for Teaching and Learning
Box 8158
University Station
Grand Forks, ND 58202

Pathways is a forum for progressive educators. Its purpose is to encourage teachers and administrators to write from their own experience; to speculate about teaching, curriculum, and learning; to
describe their classrooms and reflect on their schools; and to explore
the historical continuities which inform current practice.

Peace Education News (PEN)
A publication of the Canadian Peace Educator's Network
PO Box 839
Drayton Valley, Alberta T0E 0M0
Canada

PEN supports and promotes balanced and responsible formal education about peace and security issues.

Rethinking Schools
1001 East Keefe Ave.
Milwaukee, WI 53212
Phone (414) 964-9646

Rethinking Schools is an independent educational journal published by Milwaukee-based classroom teachers and educators who are dedicated to helping parents, teachers, and students solve the many problems that exist in our schools. Recognizing that discussion of educational issues is often dominated by administrators and educational consultants, Rethinking Schools gives teachers, parents, and students an effective voice in determining the future of our schools.

Two special editions of *Rethinking Schools*, both available from the above address, deserve mention:

Rethinking Columbus is a ninety-six-page collection of essays and resources for teaching about Columbus's arrival in the Americas. It provides a critical perspective on the Columbus quincentenary, introducing the perspective of the indigenous people whose lives were irrevocably changed by the "discovery" of the new world.

Rethinking Our Classrooms, a 208-page edition, "begins from the premise that schools and classrooms should be laboratories for a more just society than the one we now live in." It includes creative teaching ideas, compelling classroom narratives, and hands-on examples of ways teachers can promote values of community, justice, and equality, and build academic skills.

Teaching for Change
NECA
P.O. Box 73038
Washington, DC 20056
email: necadc@aol.com, www.teachingforchange.org

A catalog of thought-provoking resources for antiracist, multicultural education for K-12 teachers.

Teaching Tolerance
400 Washington Ave.
Montgomery, AL 36104
An outstanding journal whose name perfectly describes its purpose.
Written for K-12 educators.

Popular Education Institutes

Dr. Pedro Albizu Campos Puerto Rican High School
1671 Claremont Ave.
Chicago, IL 60647
Phone (312) 342-8023

A bilingual, bicultural alternative high school for hispanic students.

The Doris Marshall Institute for Education and Action (DMI)
64 Charles St. East
Toronto, Ontario M4Y1T1
Canada
Phone (416) 964-8500

DMI is an organization of social change educators working to strengthen the knowledge and skills required to organize and act for social change.

Highlander Research and Education Center
1959 Highlander Way
New Market, TN 37821

For nearly fifty years, the Highlander Center has been a leader in teaching for social change throughout the southern U.S.

Jesuit Centre for Social Faith and Justice
947 Queen St. East
Toronto, Ontario M4M 1J9
Canada

Lindeman Center
4945 South Dorchester
Chicago, IL 60615
Phone (773) 268-5774

The Lindeman Center houses a group of popular educators from around the Chicago area. They are committed to nurturing grass-roots educational initiatives and facilitating access to resources which promote and strengthen local struggles to solve community problems, and to linking educators and community activists locally, regionally, nationally, and internationally.

Websites

Resources for Activist Networks

Social Justice Connections:
http://www.shentel.net/sjc/home.html

COMMUNICATIONS

Association for Progressive Communications:
http://www.apc.org/about.html

Fairness and Accuracy in Reporting:
http://www.peacenet.apc.org/fair/

The Political Participation Project:
http://www.ai.mit.edu/projects/ppp/home/html

GAY AND LESBIANS

Yahoo! Society and Culture: Lesbians, Gays and Bisexual: Legal
Resource
http://www.grd.org/www/usa/illinois/oaw/
For more information, please call (312) 794-0359 or
write to P.O. Box 359, Chicago, IL 60690-0359
email=Oawon@aol.com

YOUTH

Plugged In:
http://www.pluggedin.org/

L.E.A.P.:
http://ww.leap.yale.edu/lclc/

GENERAL

Sojourners Online:
http://www.sojourners.com/sojourners/home.html

National Coalition for the Homeless:
http://nch.ari.net./

The Progressive Director at IGC:
http://www.igc.apc.org/

Institute for Global Communications
http://www.igc.apc.org/index.html

The institute is the nation's only unionized Internet Service Provider and features access to five online communities of activists and organizations: *PeaceNet, EcoNet, LaborNet, ConflictNet* and *WomensNet.*

—About the Authors

Hal Adams is President of the Neighborhood Writing Alliance, a nonprofit organization in Chicago, where he edits and publishes the *Journal of Ordinary Thought.* He has been a teacher and counselor in the Royal Oak, Michigan and Seattle, Washington public schools, and taught for twenty years at the College of Education at the University of Iowa.

Elizabeth Alexander is poet in residence at Smith College. She is the author of two books of poetry, *The Venus Hottentot* (University Press of Virginia, 1990), and *Body of Life* (Tia Chucha Press, 1996), and a forthcoming book of essays, *On Black Masculinity* (Oxford University Press).

Michael W. Apple is the John Bascom Professor of Education at the University of Wisconsin, Madison. He is author of several books including *Cultural Politics and Education,* (Teachers College Press, 1996).

William Ayers is professor of education and University Scholar at the University of Illinois at Chicago. His most recent book is *A Kind and Just Parent: The Children of Juvenile Court* (Beacon Press, 1997).

Rick Ayers is the father of four children, and teaches English at Berkeley High School in California.

Bill Bigelow teaches at Franklin High School in Portland, Oregon. He coedits the journal *Rethinking Schools.*

Barbara T. Bowman is a founder and current president of the Erikson Institute in Chicago. She is an authority on early education and a nationally recognized advocate for improved and expanded education for practitioners working with children and families.

Haywood Burns was University Law Professor and Dean at the City University of New York, School of Law. He was Founder and Chair Emeritus of the National Conference of Black Lawyers and a partner in the law firm of Van Lierop, Burns and Schaap at the time of his sudden death in South Africa in 1996.

Chris Carger is an assistant professor of education at Northern Illinois University. She is the author of *Of Borders and Dreams* (1996, Teachers College Press).

Jim Carnes is director of the Teaching Tolerance project of the Southern Poverty Law Center. He is the author of *Us and Them: A History of Intolerance in America* (Oxford University Press, 1996).

Linda Christensen has taught English for 20 years at Jefferson High School in Portland, Oregon. She is director of the Portland Writing Project, editor of *Rethinking Schools,* and a founding member of the National Coalition of Educational Activists. She has published numerous articles and poetry in *Rethinking Schools, Language Arts, The English Journal* and other education magazines. She is currently working on her book titled *Critical Literacy: Reading, Writing and Outrage.*

Lisa D. Delpit is the director of the Center for Urban Educational Excellence and the Benjamin E. Mays Chair for Urban Educational Leadership at Georgia State University in Atlanta. Winner of a MacArthur Fellowship, she is the author of *Other People's Children* (The New Press, 1995).

Jennifer Dorhn teaches midwifery at Columbia University and is the Director of the Morris Heights Birthing Center in New York City.

Michele Foster is professor of education at the Claremont Graduate School in California. She is the author of *Black Teachers on Teaching* (The New Press, 1997).

Henry A. Giroux is the Waterbury Chair Professor of Secondary Education at Pennsylvania State University. His recent books include *Border Crossing, Disturbing Pleasures,* and *Fugitive Cultures: Race, Youth and Violence.*

Maxine Greene is professor emerita at Teachers College, Columbia University and founder of the Center for Social Imagination. She is the author of *The Dialectic of Freedom* (Teachers College Press, 1988) and *Releasing the Imagination* (Jossey-Bass, 1996).

Caroline Heller is Assistant Professor in the College of Education, University of Illinois at Chicago. She is the author of *Until We Are Strong Together: Women Writing in the Tenderloin* (Teacher's College Press, 1997).

Diane Horwitz teaches sociology at Moraine Valley Community College in Illinois where she has worked with adult women students for over 20 years.

Susan Huddleston-Egerton is an assistant professor of education at Western Michigan University in Kalamazoo. She is the author of *Translating the Curriculum: Multiculturalism into Cultural Studies* published by Routledge Press in 1996.

Jean Ann Hunt is coordinator for the Institute for Democracy in Education and editor of *Democracy & Education.* She teaches in the College of Education at Ohio University.

Jaylynne N. Hutchinson is an assistant professor in the College of Education at Ohio University.

Noel Ignatiev is the author of *How The Irish Became White* and coeditor of *Race Traitor.* He has worked in steel mills, farm equipment plants, machine-tool factories, and universities.

Joseph Kahne is assistant professor in the College of Education at the University of Illinois at Chicago. His book, *Reframing Educational Policy: Democracy, Community, and the Individual,* was published by Teachers College Press (1996).

Jamie Kalven is a community activist, public citizen, and author of *Working with Available Light* (W. W. Norton, forthcoming).

Rashid Khalidi is a professor of History at the University of Chicago. His most recent book is *Palestinian Identity: The Construction of Modern National Consciousness* (Columbia University Press, 1997).

Rachel Koch is teaching 8th grade at Orozco School in Chicago and loving it, after a year's sabbatical and a session at the Walloon Institute, also known as Teacher Camp. She is also working on a collection of short stories.

Herbert Kohl is author of *36 Children, I Won't Learn From You* (The New Press), and *The Discipline of Hope* (forthcoming). He is a teacher and an activist who lives in Point Arena, California.

Jonathan Kozol is a noted author (*Savage Inequalities, Death at an Early Age*) whose most recent book is *Amazing Grace: The Lives of Children and the Conscience of a Nation* (Crown, 1995).

Gloria Ladson-Billings is professor of education at the University of Wisconsin, Madison. She is author of *The Dreamkeepers: Successful Teachers of African-American Children* (Jossey-Bass, 1994).

Patrick McMahon left classroom teaching not long after writing this essay. He is now a freelance writer publishing essays about families, location and Buddhism as well as writing short stories.

Kim Murray is now a student at DeVry Institute of Technologies majoring in Telecommunications Management at the Addison Campus.

Nelson Peery is the son of a postal worker, worked for many years as a brick layer and as a revolutionary. Meridel LeSueur taught him how to write in evening classes in Minneapolis. His memoir *Black Fire: The Making of an American Revolutionary* was published by The New Press.

Mark Perry, Ph.D. is a teacher educator and alternative high school teacher and principal. His book *Trying to Make It Real Compared to What: Evolving Identities of White Educators Working With Students, Teachers and Administrators of Color* will be published in 1998 by Teachers College Press. His work is guided by the question—What is worthwhile to know and experience? He currently resides in Seattle, Washington.

Kate Power has taught reading and writing in alternative high schools and adult literacy programs. Currently a doctoral student at the University of Illinois at Chicago, her research interests include translating critical, feminist, and multicultural theories into practical teaching models.

Therese Quinn is a museum educator and activist, exhibit developer, and a doctoral student in curriculum studies at the University of Illinois at Chicago. Her interests include democratizing public cultural spaces, and stomping on master narratives.

Maureen T. Reddy's most recent book is *Everyday Acts Against Racism* (Seal Press 1997), a collection of essays. She is currently working on a book on race and popular fiction. Reddy is a professor of English and Director of the Women's Studies Program at Rhode Island College.

Jay Rehak teaches English at Whitney Young High School in Chicago. He is the father of two beautiful daughters, Hope and Hannah, the author of two comedic plays, *Bedtime, a Comedy of Sorts,* and *Oh, No, Not Me!,* as well as a children's musical, *Noah's Ark,* coauthored with his wife Susan Salidor.

Luis J. Rodriguez is the author of the award-winning memoir, *Always Running: La Vida Loca, Gang Days in L.A.* (Curbstone Press,

1993; Touchstone Books/Simon & Schuster, 1994). He is a noted poet, journalist and critic, founder/publisher of Tia Chucha Press in Chicago, a cross-cultural, socially-engaged poetry press, and facilitator of Youth Struggling for Survival, which helps educate and empower poor urban youth.

Rosalie Romano is a visiting professor of teacher education at Antioch University in Seattle, WA. A classroom teacher for over 20 years, Romano now teaches teachers about ways of forging connections and community within their schools and classrooms.

Mike Rose is the author of *Lives on the Boundary* and, most recently, *Possible Lives* (Houghton Mifflin, 1995), and is on the faculty at the University of California at Los Angeles.

Jonathan Silin is a member of the Graduate Faculty at Bank Street College of Education in New York city. He is the author of *Sex, Death and the Education of Children: Our Passion for Ignorance in The Age of AIDS* (Teachers College Press, 1995).

Anna Deavere Smith teaches at Stanford University, where she is Ann O'Day Maples Professor of the Arts. Ms. Smith was awarded a MacArthur "genius" Fellowship in 1996, and heads Harvard's Institute on the Arts and Civic Dialogue.

Deborah Stern is a long-time high school teacher and social activist, and author of *Teaching English So It Matters* (Corwin Press, 1995).

William "Bill" Watkins is an associate professor of education at the University of Illinois at Chicago. Bill, a lifelong radical political activist and scholar supporting the causes of racial, economic, and political justice, explores the ideological, sociological, and historical foundations of black education and curriculum in his many writings.

Joel Westheimer is assistant professor in the Department of Teaching and Learning at New York University. His book *Among Schoolteachers: Community, Autonomy, and Ideology in Teachers' Work* is forthcoming from Teachers College Press.

George Wood, author of *Schools That Work* (Dutton, 1992), is currently principal at Federal Hocking High School in Stewart, Ohio.

—Index

Abernathy, Ralph, 150
Abraham Lincoln Brigade, 160
academic skills
    challenge to develop, 12–13
    grammar lessons, 120–21
    politics of "standards," 52
acting, 124–25
Acts of Meaning (Bruner), 257
Ad and the Ego, The (video), 34
Addams, Jane, 152
adult education
    parent writing program, 81–97
    women reentering school,
        68–80
affirmative action, 184–85
African Americans. *See also* racial is-
        sues; specific names
    black teachers, voices of, 133–
        34, 288–89
    education, great importance of,
        288–89, 292
    land reclamation on the South
        Side, 200–210
    white teacher of black women,
        108–23
AIDS unit, 282–83
Aid to Families With Dependent
        Children (AFDC), 69, 77, 79
"Ain't That Bad?" (Angelou),
        116–17
Ali, Muhammad, 201
Allende, Salvador, 46
Allison, Dorothy, 135
Altgeld Gardens (Chicago), 139–45
Angelou, Maya, 112–14, 116–17,
        120, 121, 122, 159
anger, 135–36
anti-Semitism, 212
Anzaldúa, Gloria, 165, 167
aptitude and achievement tests,
        41–45
Arendt, Hannah, xlii

Baldwin, James, 50, 288
Baskin, Roberta, 28

Bates, Douglas, 179–80
Baumol, William, 26
Bellah, Robert, 218
Benhabib, Seyla, xxxvi
Black Women for Beginners (Sharp),
        114–16, 121
Blake, William, xxvii
Bluest Eye, The (Morrison), 219
Bobbit, Franklin, 5
Bode, Boyd, 5
Bond, Julian, 150
books and periodicals, 295–96,
        303–8
Brecher, Jeremy, 26
Brecht, Bertolt, 22, 30
Brigham, Carl, 43–45
Bruner, Jerome, 257
business, 293
Butler, Morris, 207

Cahn, Edmond, xliv–xlv
Camus, Albert, xl–xli
Carmichael, Stokely, 150
CBS, 28
Chan, Anita, 29
Chavez, Cesar, 242
Cheney, Goodman and Schwerner
        Academy proposal, 211–14
childbearing center, 189–90
Christensen, Linda, 39–47, 216
Cisneros, Sandra, 215–16, 223–25
Clark, Septima, 150, 156
Clearwater Project, 242
Clinton, Bill, 32
Coffee Will Make You Black (Sinclair),
        228, 236
Collins, Leonard, 288
community development projects,
        249–53
Congress of Industrial Organiza-
        tions (CIO), 150
conservative reaction, 294
core curriculum, 3
Costello, Tim, 26
Counts, George, 4–5, 17–18, 152

Crown Heights (Brooklyn, NY), 211–12
cummings, e.e., 280
curricular approaches
    academic skills challenge, 12–13
    AIDS unit, 282–83
    black women/white teacher, 108–23
    chaos and hope (teacher's journal), 228–36
    Cheney, Goodman and Schwerner Academy proposal, 211–14
    children's input, fear of, 246–47
    co-created student-centered curriculum, 277–84
    community development projects, 249–53
    core curriculum idea, 3
    global sweatshop unit, 24–38
    indoctrination vs. education, 13–18
    life choice analysis, 280–82
    Mills school, 7–12
    NECA study guide, excerpts from, 215–27
    negativity and despair, overcoming, 34–35, 46
    "Rainbow Curriculum" (New York City), 14
    reading, teaching of. See literacy instruction
    social realities, awareness of differing, 255–69, 278–80
    social studies and project-based goals, 7–12
    storyline approach, 255–69
    teaching each other, 282–84
    value neutrality, 17–18
    writing classes and programs. See writing
C. Wright Mills Middle School, 1, 2, 6–18

Dare the School Build a New Social Order? (Counts), 4
Davis, Angela, 167
Delpit, Lisa, 51, 108, 235

Dewey, John, xliii, xxx, 5, 12, 13, 18, 144, 152, 230, 254, 290
Diary of Anne Frank, The, 212
Dr. Pedro Albizu Campos High School (Chicago), 145–48
Douglass, Frederick, xxii, xxvii–xxviii, 48
Du Bois, W.E.B., 288–89
Duckworth, Eleanore, 234
Duke, David, 159

Eddy, Sherwood, 152
Educational Testing Service (ETS), 43–45
"Eleven" (Cisneros), 215–16, 223–25
Ellison, Ralph, 168, 202
environmental issues
    land and place reclamation (Chicago), 200–210
    pledge of allegiance to the world, 241–44
    race and, 137–43
ethnocentrism, 53
Evans, Patricia, 204
"Everyday Use" (Walker), 219

Faludi, Susan, 165, 167
Farges, Bernard, 8
Fine, Michelle, xlii, xxxi
48 Hours (TV show), 28
Foundations of the Metaphysics of Morals (Kant), xxxv
Four Tops, the, 203
Foxx, Red, 203
Freedom Schools, xviii
Freire, Paulo, xl, xxx, 82, 95, 106, 122–23, 144, 145, 290
fun, 287

Gaines, Ernest, xviii–xxiii
Gandall, Bill, 157–60
gangbanger, analysis of, 280–81
Garcia, Marvin, 147–48
gay and lesbian issues
    openly gay teacher's story, 128–30
    pride day and division, 126–27

gay and lesbian issues (*continued*)
    student's high school story,
        131–32
    website, 310
Gaye, Marvin, 203
GED test, 103, 104–5, 108, 120, 270
Genocide (video), 212
Gibbs, Donna, 24
Ginsberg, Allen, 135
Global Exchange, 29
Gramsci, Antonio, 82, 95
Grassroots Think Tank, 91–97
Graubard, Stephen, xliii, xxxii
greed, 293
Greenberg, Jack, 135
Greene, Maxine, xxvii–xlvi, 257,
    267
group poem, 217–18
Gunz, Joel, 30
Guthrie, Woody, 153
Gutiérrez, Ana Sol, 215

Habermas, Jurgen, xlii, xxxiv,
    xxxvii–xxxviii
Hacker, Andrew, 180–81, 182
Hamer, Fannie Lou, 153
Hanna, Paul, 4–5
Harper's, 280
Haydon, Ted, 203
Heidegger, Martin, xxiv–xxv
Herbert, Bob, 28
Highlander Folk School, 150–56
Hitler, Adolph, 43
Hoffman, Eva, 262
homelessness, 8
    storyline curriculum approach
        to, 255–56, 259–68
homosexuality. *See* gay and lesbian
    issues
hooks, bell, 102, 184, 247
Hopson, Darlene and Derek,
    177–78
Horace's School (Sizer), xxxiii
Horton, Myles, 150–56
House of the Spirits (Allende), 46
Hughes, Langston, xxix, xxviii

Hurston, Zora Neale, 162–63, 167
Hyde Park-Kenwood (Chicago),
    201–6

Ignatieff, Michael, xxxii–xxxiii
imagination, 267
indoctrination question, 13–18
Indonesia: Islands on Fire (video), 29
inhibition and empathy, 124–25
I Still Love You (Windy City), 207

Jahmal, Amhal, 201
James, C.L.R., 82, 91, 95
Jenkins, Esau, 156
Johnson, Hazel, 137–45
Jones, Edward P., 220
Jones, Jim, 136
Jordan, Michael, 31, 32
Journal of Ordinary Thought, 81, 86–
    88, 306
"Justice. Do it NIKE!" coalition, 24,
    29, 32

Kant, Immanuel, xxxiv, xxxv, xxxvii
Kilpatrick, William, 3
King, Martin Luther, Jr., 150, 153,
    155
King, Rodney, 169, 171
Knight, Phil, 30, 31, 32, 33, 35
Kohl, Herbert, 150–51, 247,
    285–87
Kohl, Judith, 150–51
Kohlberg, Lawrence, xxxiv–xxxv
Kozol, Jonathan, xxxii, 279, 293

labor issues
    child labor, 24, 33
    downward leveling, 25–27
    global sweatshop unit, 24–38
    soccer ball, makers of, 22–24, 33
Ladson-Billings, Gloria, 235, 247,
    292
Lafayette, Bernard, 155
Lance, Major, 203
land reclamation, 200–210
Lao Tze, 55
Last Train North, The (Taulbert), 218

Latino-Americans, 194–95
    Cisneros story, study of, 215–16
    first-year teaching in dual-language program, 241–44
Léon, Tania, 215
lesbian issues. *See* gay and lesbian issues
Lesson Before Dying, A (Gaines), xviii–xxiii
life choice analysis, 280–82
Life magazine, 24
Liston, Sonny, 201
literacy instruction
    black slaves, for, 288
    black women/white teacher, 108–23
    business and justice, 293
    grammar lessons, 120–21
    METRO Literacy Initiative, 107–23
    power-sharing and confrontation in, 104–7
    round-robin reading, 102–4, 105
    welfare workbook, 270–76
Long Haul, The (Horton, Kohl, and Kohl), 150–51, 154
Lorde, Audre, 57, 136, 167
Los Angeles Times, 33
Lost in the City (Jones), 220
Louisiana, 138–39
Lovelace, Leroy, 288
Lugo, Lourdes, 147–48

Mabley, Moms, 203
McClintock, Barbara, 213
McFarland, Dennis, xliv
Malcolm X, 201
Markham, Pigmeat, 203
Marx, Karl, xxix, xxvii
Meier, Deborah, xxxvi, 13
Menchú, Rigoberta, 167
METRO Literacy Initiative, 107–23
Mickey Mouse Goes to Haiti (video), 28
midwifery, 189
Miracles, the, 203
Mishima, Yukio, 280

Moos, Elizabeth, 5
Moraine Valley Community College, 69
moral craft, 286–87
Morrison, Toni, 77, 219, 220
Mother Teresa, 145
Muhammad, Elijah, 201–2
Music Room, The (McFarland), xliv
My Name is Zami (Lorde), 167

name exercise, 216–17, 226–27
Native American culture, 255
negativity, overcoming
    activist forum, 48–53
    curricular critiques, 34–35, 46
Neil, A.S., 229
New York Times, 28
Nicaragua, 157–60
Niebuhr, Reinhold, 152
Nike Corp., 24, 28, 29, 30–31, 32–34, 35, 36
None of the Above (Owens), 43–44
Nussbaum, Martha, xxxvi

O'Connor, R. Olomenji, 209
Ogonu, Pamela, 288
Ortega, Daniel, 160
Owens, David, 43–44

Palestinian history, 186–87
Paley, Vivian, 258
parents' writing program, 81–97
Park, Robert, 152
Parker, Jonathan, 32–33
Parks, Rosa, 150, 153, 155, 156
participatory democracy, 2
    censorship in high school, fight against, 157–60
    children's input, fear of, 246–47
    C. Wright Mills Middle School, at, 2, 6–18
    indoctrination vs. education, 13–18
    political insignificance, 191–93
    project-based curriculum, 10–13
    youth focus, 290–91
Pendleton Co., 26

People for Community Recovery (PCR), 140–45
Pickett, Wilson, 203
Piercy, Marge, xxviii
Plague, The (Camus), xl–xli
play mothers, 144
pledge of allegiance to the world, 241–44
Plummer, Edourard, 288
political insignificance, 191–93
popular culture, 291
prayer in schools, 245
prison teaching, 165–67
Progressive Education Association (PEA), 3–6
Progressive Education at the Crossroads (Bode), 5
projects for community development, 249–53
Project 2061, 7–8
Prologue Alternative High School (Chicago), 277–84
Public and Its Problems, The (Dewey), xliii
Puerto Rico, 146

Question of Silence, A (film), 167
"Questions From a Worker Who Reads" (Brecht), 22, 30

Race Traitor: Journal of the New Abolitionism, 191
racial issues
    black teacher of white women, 133–34
    Cisneros story, study of, 215–16
    classroom exploration of, 211–12
    environmental racism, 137–43
    name calling in school, 169–73
    racism in society and school, 169–85
    school days (1940's), 59–67
    voices of black teachers, 288–89
    white teacher of black women, 108–23
    white woman in black family, 136–37

Raspberry, William, 218
Rawls, John, xxxiv, xxxv–xxxvi, xxxvii
reconstructionism, 188
Redding, Otis, 203
Regal Theater (Chicago), 203, 209
religion, 245
Renwick, Lucille, 33
resources
    books, 295–96
    classroom resources, 297
    organizations, 297–303
    periodicals, 303–8
    popular education institutes, 309
    websites, 309–10
Rich, Adrienne, xliii–xliv
Robert Taylor Homes (Chicago), 200–201, 205, 206, 208, 210
Robeson, Paul, 61
Robinson, Bernice, 156
Robinson, Cameron, 31, 33, 34
Robinson, Smokey, 203
Rodriguez, Luis, 194–95, 280
Rodríguez-Trias, Antonia, 215
Roemer, Buddy, 158
Roosevelt, Eleanor, 153
Rorty, Amelie, xxxvi
Rorty, Richard, xli–xlii
round-robin reading, 102–4, 105
Rugg, Harold, 2–3, 18

sabbaticals, 167–68
sacrifice, 280, 284
Sagan, Carl, 254
Said, Edward, xxxi
Savage Inequalities (Kozol), 279
Schanberg, Sydney, 24, 33, 34
Scheinberg, Cynthia, 229
Seeger, Pete, 153, 242
sex education
    AIDS unit, 282–83
    "subversive" teacher's story, 163–65
Shakespeare, William, 61–63
Shreveport Times, 158, 160
Shunryu, Suzuki, 100
Sinclair, April, 228, 236

Sizer, Theodore, xxxiii
Snyder, Gary, 200, 210
social efficiency movement, 5
social reconstructionists, 2–3, 10,
    17–18, 19
social studies-based curriculum,
    11–12
Spellmeyer, Kurth, 229
Stateway Gardens (Chicago), 200,
    205, 208
Stein, Gertrude, 137
storytelling. *See also* writing
    classroom community of stories,
        128–30
    storyline curriculum approach,
        255–69
    subversive imperative, 161–68
successes and failures (teachers' sto-
    ries). *See also* curricular ap-
    proaches
    advice for teaching and survival,
        285–87
    black teacher of white women,
        133–34
    chaos and hope, 228–36
    children's input, fear of, 246–47
    first-year teaching in dual-
        language program,
        241–44
    improvising in the first year,
        241–44
    leaving and returning to teach-
        ing, 237–40
    "subversive" teaching, 161–68
    white teacher of black women,
        108–23
Sula (Morrison), 220
Supremes, the, 203
suspensions, 98–101
Szymborska, Wislawa, xxiii–xxiv

Taulbert, Clifton, 218
Temptations, the, 203
theatrical techniques, 124–25
Their Eyes Were Watching God (Hur-
    ston), 162–63
Thelma and Louise (film), 166

Theory of Justice, A (Rawls), xxxv–
    xxxvi
Thomas, Norman, 152
Through the Eyes of a Villain, 90–91
Tomorrow We Will Finish (video), 29
tribalism, 53
Trudell, John, 136
Turn-A-Lot-Around program, 200,
    206–10
Tyson, Laura, 26

UNICEF, 29
Urey, Harold, 201

value neutrality, 17–18
video interviews, 278–80
violence
    gangbanger, analysis of, 280–81
    interdisciplinary curriculum ad-
        dressing, 8–10

Walker, Alice, 39, 182
Waller, Maxine, 154–55
Walt Disney Co., 28, 32
Warwick, Dionne, 203
Washburne, Carlton, 5–6
Washington Post, 28–29, 218
websites, 309–10
welfare workbook, 270–76
Wells, Mary, 203
White, Max, 24, 32
white supremacy, 184–85
Whitman, Walt, 135
Williams, Raymond, 290
Windy City, 207
Wollstonecraft, Mary, 167
Wood, George, 13, 248
writing. *See also* literacy instruction
    author's chair, 118–20
    chaos and hope, 228–36
    community organization based
        on, 91–97
    experience-based adult stories,
        84–86
    "garret people," writing about,
        218–19
    global economics, confronting,
        21–24, 30–34, 36–38

writing (*continued*)
  group poem from featured texts,
    217–18
  healing and understanding in
    high school, 39–46
  men's writing group, 89–91
  mentorship in, 133
  name exercise, 216–17, 226–27
  parent writing program, 81–97
  publishing, 86–88
  short stories step-by-step,
    219–22
  storyline collaborative approach,
    255–69

Young, Andrew, 153
Young, Iris Marion, xxxvii
youth focus, 290–91

—Related Titles from The New Press

Black Fire: The Making of an American Revolutionary
Nelson Peery
PB, $11.95, 1-56584-159-X; 352 pp.
"A portrait of a fascinating life and a history of twentieth-century black radicalism." —*Kirkus Reviews*

Black Teachers on Teaching
Michele Foster, foreword by Lisa D. Delpit
HC, $23.00, 1-56584-320-7; PB, $14.95, 1-56584-453-X; 192 pp.
An oral history of black teachers that gives "valuable insight into a profession that for African Americans was second only to preaching" (*Booklist*).

City Kids, City Teachers: Reports from the Front Row
William Ayers and Patrica Ford, editors
HC, $25.00, (1-56584-328-3); PB, $16.00, 1-56584-051-8; 368 pp.
Classic writings on urban education from America's leading experts.

A City Year: On the Streets and in the Neighborhoods with Twelve Young Community Service Volunteers
Suzanne Goldsmith
HC, $22.95, 1-56584-093-3, 304 pp.
An honest account of the triumphs and setbacks faced by an idealistic and experimental social program in its infancy.

Coming of Age in America: A Multicultural Anthology
Mary Frosch, editor
HC, $22.95, 1-56584-146-8; PB, $12.95, 1-56584-147-6; 288 pp.
The acne and ecstasy of adolescence—a multicultural collection of short stories and fiction excerpts that *Library Journal* calls "wonderfully diverse from the standard fare."

Crossing the Tracks: How "Untracking" Can Save America's Schools
Anne E. Wheelock
HC, $22.95, 1-56584-013-5; PB, $12.95, 1-56584-038-0; 336 pp.
A highly praised study of ways in which schools have successfully experimented with heterogeneous grouping in the classroom.

Dismantling Desegregation: The Quiet Reversal of Brown v. Board of Education
Gary Orfield, Susan E. Eaton, and the Harvard Project on School Desegregation; foreword by Elaine R. Jones
HC, $30.00, 1-56584-305-3; PB, $17.95, 1-56584-401-7; 496 pp.
"A wise . . . authoritative book" (Jonathan Kozol) on America's return to segregation.

Ellis Island and the Peopling of America: The Official Guide
Virginia Yans-McLaughlin, Marjorie Lightman, and the Statue of Liberty-Ellis Island Foundation; foreword by Lee Iacocca
PB, $19.95, 1-56584-364-9, 224 pp.
A primary source reader and resource guide to Ellis Island and issues of immigration.

Going Public: Schooling for a Diverse Democracy
Judith Renyi
HC, $25.00, 1-56584-083-6, 304 pp.
An historically informed overview of the multicultural education debate from a leading advocate.

Growing Up Gay/Growing Up Lesbian: A Literary Anthology
Bennett L. Singer, editor
HC, $21.95, 156584-102-6; PB, $9.95, 1-56584-103-4; 336 pp.
An award-winning collection of over fifty gay and lesbian coming-of-age stories. Teaching guide available.

"I Won't Learn from You" and Other Thoughts on Creative Maladjustment
Herbert Kohl
PB, $10.00, 1-56584-096-8, 176 pp.
"One of the most important books on teaching published in many years." —Jonathan Kozol

Lies My Teacher Told Me: Everything Your American History Textbook Got Wrong
James W. Loewen
HC, $24.95, 1056584-100-X, 384 pp.
The best-selling, award-winning, iconoclastic look at the errors, misrepresentations, and omissions in the leading American history textbooks.

Made in America: Immigrant Students in Our Public Schools
Laurie Olsen, foreword by Herbert Kohl
HC, $25.00, 1-56584-400-9, PB, $14.95, 1-56584-471-9, 244 pp.
An up-to-the-minute look at immigrant students in American public
schools, through a portrait of one prototypical high school.

The New Press Guide to Multicultural Resources for Young Readers
Daphne Muse, editor
HC, $60.00, 1-56584-339-8, 704 pp.
A comprehensive guide to multicultural children's literature, featuring over 1,000 critical book reviews, essays, indexes cross-referenced
by author, ethnicity, illustrator, and title, and extensive resource list-
ings.

Other People's Children: Cultural Conflict in the Classroom
Lisa D. Delpit
HC, $21.00, 1-56584-179-4; PB, $14.95, 1-56584-180-8; 224 pp.
A MacArthur Fellow's revolutionary analysis of the role of race in the
classroom. Winner of *Choice* magazine's Outstanding Academic Book
Award, the American Education Studies Association Critics' Choice
Award, and one of *Teacher* magazine's Great Books of 1995.

A People's History of the United States: Abridged Teaching Edition
Howard Zinn
HC, $25.00, 1-56584-366-5; PB, $13.00, 1-56584-379-7; 496 pp.
An abridged edition of Howard Zinn's best-selling—over 425,000
copies—history of the United States with added classroom materials.

A People's History of the United States: The Wall Charts
Howard Zinn and George Kirschner
Portfolio, $25.00, 1-56584-171-9, 48-page booklet with two posters
Two oversized posters based on Zinn's best-selling social history.

Rethinking Schools: An Agenda for Change
David Levine, Robert Lowe, Robert Peterson, and Rita Tenorio,
editors
PB, $16.00, 1-56584-215-4, 304 pp.
The country's leading education reformers propose ways to change
our schools.

Should We Burn Babar?: Essays on Children's Literature and the Power of Stories
Herbert Kohl
HC, $18.95, 1-56584-258-8; PB, $11.00, 1-56584-259-6; 192 pp.
The prize-winning educator's thoughts on the politics of children's literature.

"A Totally Alien Life-Form": Teenagers
Sydney Lewis
HC, $25.00, 1-56584-282-0; PB; $15.95, 1-56584-283-9; 320 pp.
Teens nationwide talk to the "legitimate heir to [Studs] Terkel" (*Chicago Tribune*). Free teaching

Available at your local bookstore or call W.W. Norton at 1-800-233-4830.

Subscribe to
DEMOCRACY & EDUCATION

Democracy & Education is published quarterly by the Institute for Democracy in Education. Members of IDE automatically receive subscriptions to *Democracy & Education,* as well as other publications and reduced fees for IDE activities. If you wish to subscribe to *Democracy & Education* without becoming a member of IDE, individual and library subscriptions are available. Fees for memberships and subscriptions are listed below.

*Check **one** of the six categories:*

> **Memberships** include journal, reduced fees for activities, access to IDE's curriculum and resource library, occasional papers, and reduced conference fees.

> ____ Accociate Membership — $30 ____ Canadian Membership — $35

> ____ Family Membership — $35 ____ International Membership — $40

> ____ Student Membership (must be full-time student) — $20

> ____ School Membership — $35
> (includes two copies of all publications sent to one address)

Subscriptions include *Democracy & Education* journal only.

> ____ Individual Subscription — $25 ____ Canadian Subscription — $35

> ____ Library Subscription — $35 ____ International Subscription — $35

Name _____

Address _____

_____

Work Phone (____) _____ Home Phone (____) _____

Institutional Affiliation _____

E-mail Address _____

Make checks payable to Ohio University.

You may charge your membership to your MasterCard or VISA:

_____ MasterCard _____ VISA

Card Number _____   *Mail subscriptions & address changes to*

Institute for Democracy in Eudcation

Bank Number _____   College of Education

313 McCracken Hall

Expiration Date _____   Ohio University

Signature _____   Athens, Ohio 45701-2979

IDE Ordering Information

Past Issues of *Democracy & Education*

Vol. 4:1	Fall 1989	Alternatives to Tracking and Ability Grouping	$3.00
Vol. 4:3	Spring 1990	Democratic Classrooms — Democratic Lives	$3.00
Vol. 6:1	Fall 1991	Project-Centered Teaching	$5.00
Vol. 6:2	Winter 1991	Multicultural Books for Children	$5.00
Vol. 6:3	Spring 1992	Restructuring for Democratic Classrooms and Schools	$5.00
Vol. 7:1	Fall 1992	Diversity and Democracy	$5.00
Vol. 7:2	Winter 1992	Books for Educators	$5.00
Vol. 7:3	Spring 1993	Healthy School Communities	$5.00
Vol. 7:4	Summer 1993	Building School Communities	$5.00
Vol. 8:1	Fall 1993	Building a Community of Learners	$5.00
Vol. 8:2	Winter 1993	Annual Books Issue	$5.00
Vol. 8:3	Spring 1994	Sharing the Vision: Teachers and Students Together	$5.00
Vol. 8:4	Summer 1994	Reclaiming Our Traditions	$5.00
Vol. 9:1	Fall 1994	Community Service-Learning	$5.00
Vol. 9:2	Winter 1994	Annual Books Issue	$5.00
Vol 9:3	Spring 1995	Teachers and Writers: Arts in the Classroom	$5.00
Vol. 9:4	Summer 1995	Building on Our Traditions	$5.00
Vol. 10:2	Winter 1995	Popular Education: Teaching for Social Justice	$10.00
Vol. 10:3	Spring/Summer 1996	Democracy & School Governance	$8.00
Vol. 11:1	Fall 1996	Back to School Issue	$8.00
Vol. 11:2	Winter 1997	Knowing Democracy	$8.00
Vol. 11:3	Spring/Summer 1997	Democratic Pedagogy	$8.00

Other Resources Available from IDE

Occasional Paper #2
Students Writing About Community Affairs

$3.00 IDE Members
$5.00 Non-Members

Occasional Paper #3
Whole Language: A Democratic Approach to Reading and Writing

$5.00 IDE Members

$7.00 Non-Members

John Dewey's Pedagogic Creed T-shirts with IDE logo
(*100% cotton, adult Large and X-Large only*)

$12.00 IDE Members
$14.00 Non-Members

Send your order to

The Institute for Democracy in Education
313 McCracken Hall
Ohio University
Athens, Ohio 45701-2979

Make checks payable to Ohio University.

Other Books From TC Press

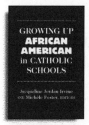

Growing Up African American in Catholic Schools

Edited by **Jacqueline Jordan Irvine** and **Michèle Foster**

1996/208 pp./Cl, $39/3530-2

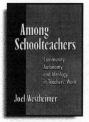

Among Schoolteachers

Community, Autonomy, and Ideology in Teachers' Work

Joel Westheimer

1998/192 pp./Pb, $17.95/3744-5
Cl, $38/3745-3

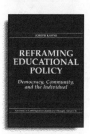

Reframing Educational Policy

Democracy, Community, and the Individual

Joseph Kahne

1996/208 pp./Pb, $22.95/3492-6
Cl, $48/3493-4

Teaching/Learning Anti-Racism

A Developmental Approach

Louise Derman-Sparks and **Carol Brunson Phillips**

1997/192 pp./Pb, $17.95/3637-6
Cl, $40/3638-4

The Long Haul

An Autobiography

Myles Horton, with **Judith Kohl** and **Herbert Kohl**

1998/256 pp./Pb, $17.95/3700-3

Schooling for "Good Rebels"

Also of Interest

Socialism, American Education, and the Search for Radical Curriculum

Kenneth Teitelbaum

1995/272 pp./Pb, $22.95/3486-1

Sex, Death, and the Education of Children

Our Passion for Ignorance in the Age of AIDS

Jonathan G. Silin

1995/264 pp./Pb, $18.95/3405-5
Cl, $39/3406-3

Looking Back and Thinking Forward

Reexaminations of Teaching and Schooling

Lillian Weber
Edited by **Beth Alberty**

1997/216 pp./Pb, $18.95/3673-2
Cl, $40/3674-0

TEACHERS COLLEGE PRESS

Available at your local bookstore or directly from TC Press:
P. O. Box 20 • Williston, VT 05495-0020

TO ORDER: 800/575-6566 • FAX: 802/864-7626
http://www.tc.columbia.edu/~tcpress

ISBN Prefix:
0-8077

Other Books From TC Press
by the contributors to
Teaching for Social Justice

Prices are subject to change without notice and are valid only in the U.S.A.

A Light In Dark Times

Maxine Greene and the Unfinished Conversation

Edited by **William Ayers** and **Janet L. Miller**

1998/288 pp./Pb, $21.95/3720-8
Cl, $48/3721-6

The Dialectic of Freedom

Maxine Greene

1988/168 pp./Pb, $13.95/2897-7
Cl, $18/2898-5

To Teach

The Journey of a Teacher

William Ayers

1993/160 pp./Pb, $14.95/3262-1

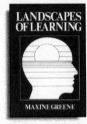

Landscapes of Learning

Maxine Greene

1978/255 pp./Pb, $18.95/2534-X

To Become a Teacher

Making a Difference in Children's Lives

Edited by **William Ayers**

1995/264 pp./Pb, $17.95/3455-1

Cultural Politics and Education

Michael W. Apple

1996/176 pp./Pb, $18.95/3503-5
Cl, $40/3504-3

The Good Preschool Teacher

Six Teachers Reflect on Their Lives

William Ayers

1989/176 pp./Pb, $17.95/2946-9

Until We Are Strong Together

Women Writers in the Tenderloin

Caroline E. Heller

1997/192 pp./Pb, $19.95/3646-5
Cl, $42/3647-3

TEACHERS COLLEGE PRESS

Available at your local bookstore or directly from TC Press:
P. O. Box 20 • Williston, VT 05495-0020

TO ORDER: 800/575-6566 • FAX: 802/864-7626
http://www.tc.columbia.edu/~tcpress

ISBN Prefix:
0-8077